CW01024738

# Tropical Medicine
# in the Twentieth Century

# TROPICAL MEDICINE
# IN THE TWENTIETH CENTURY

A HISTORY OF THE LIVERPOOL SCHOOL
OF TROPICAL MEDICINE
1898–1990

HELEN J. POWER

KEGAN PAUL INTERNATIONAL
LONDON AND NEW YORK

First published in 1999 by
Kegan Paul International
UK: P.O. Box 256, London WC1B 3SW, England
Tel: (0171) 580 5511  Fax: (0171) 436 0899
E-mail: books@keganpau.demon.co.uk
Internet: http://www.demon.co.uk/keganpaul/
USA: 562 West 113th Street, New York, NY, 10025, USA
Tel: (212) 666 1000  Fax: (212) 316 3100

Distributed by
John Wiley & Sons Ltd
Southern Cross Trading Estate
1 Oldlands Way, Bognor Regis
West Sussex, PO22 9SA, England
Tel: (01243) 779 777   Fax: (01243) 820 250

Columbia University Press
562 West 113th Street
New York, NY 10025. USA
Tel: (212) 666 1000   Fax: (212) 316 3100

ISBN 0-7103-0604-0

**British Library Cataloguing in Publication Data**
Power, Helen J.
Tropical medicine in the 20th century : a history of
the Liverpool School of Tropical Medicine
1. Liverpool School of Tropical Medicine - History - 20th century
2. Tropical medicine - History - 20th century
I. Title
616.9'883'0904
ISBN 0710306040

**Library of Congress Cataloging-in-Publication Data**
Power, Helen J., 1966–
Tropical medicine in the 20th century : a history of
the Liverpool school of Tropical Medicine / Helen J. Power.
Includes bibliographical references.
ISBN 0-7103-0604-0 (alk. paper)
1. Liverpool School of Tropical Medicine. 2. Tropical medicine--England-
-Liverpool--History--20th century.
I. Title.
RC962.G7P69   1998
616.9'883'0904--dc21          97-48878
CIP

For my parents,
Vera and David,
with love.

# CONTENTS

# LIST OF TABLES AND FIGURES

# ILLUSTRATIONS

# ACRONYMS

| | |
|---|---|
| AMD | Army Medical Department |
| AMRU | Army Malaria Research Unit (Oxford) |
| ARWP | Academic Review Working Party |
| *ATMP* | *Annals of Tropical Medicine and Parasitology* |
| *BHM* | *Bulletin of the History of Medicine* |
| BMA | British Medical Association |
| *BMJ* | *British Medical Journal* |
| CCB | Central Co-ordinating Board |
| CDA | Colonial Development Act |
| CDF | Colonial Development Fund |
| CDW | Colonial Development and Welfare Act |
| CMO | Colonial Medical Officer |
| CMRC | Colonial Medical Research Committee |
| CMRS | Colonial Medical Research Service |
| CMS | Colonial Medical Service |
| CO | Colonial Office |
| CTCMH | Certificate in Tropical Community Medicine and Health |
| DCH | Diploma of Child Health |
| DHSS | Department of Health and Social Security |
| DMSS | Director of Medical and Sanitary Services |
| DTC | Department of Technical Co-operation |
| DTCH | Diploma in Tropical Child Health |
| DTH | Diploma in Tropical Hygiene |
| DTM | Diploma in Tropical Medicine |
| DTMH | Diploma in Tropical Medicine and Hygiene |
| ECA | Economic Co-operation Administration |
| EMB | Empire Marketing Board |
| EMS | Emergency Medical Service |
| ETAP | Expanded Technical Assistance Programme |
| FAO | Food and Agriculture Organisation |
| FEPOW | Far Eastern Prisoners Of War |
| GMC | General Medical Council |
| GPI | General paralysis of the insane |
| ICI | Imperial Chemical Industries |
| IMS | Indian Medical Service |
| IO | India Office |
| ITMED | Institute of Tropical Medicine and Endemic Diseases (Ghana) |
| *JHMAS* | *Journal of History of Medicine and Allied Sciences* |
| LRI | Liverpool Royal Infirmary |
| LRO | Liverpool Record Office |
| LSHTM | London School of Hygiene and Tropical Medicine |

| | |
|---|---|
| LSTM | Liverpool School of Tropical Medicine |
| MCommH | Masters in Community Health |
| MO | Medical Officer |
| MOD | Ministry of Overseas Development |
| MOH | Medical Officer of Health |
| MRC | Medical Research Council |
| MTropMed | Masters of Tropical Medicine |
| NGO | Non-Government Organisation |
| NIMR | National Institute Medical Research |
| NRC | National Research Council (Ghana) |
| ODA | Overseas Development Administration |
| PHC | Primary Health Care |
| RAMC | Royal Army Medical Corps |
| RSH | Royal Southern Hospital |
| RSTMH | Royal Society of Tropical Medicine and Hygiene |
| SEAMEO | Southeast Asian Ministers of Education Organisation |
| TDR | Tropical Disease Research and Training (WHO) |
| TMRC | Tropical Medicine Research Committee |
| *TRSTMH* | *Transactions Royal Society Tropical Medicine and Hygiene* |
| UGC | University Grants Commission |
| UN | United Nations |
| UNESCO | United Nations Economic and Social Council |
| UNFPA | United Nations Family Planning Association |
| UNICEF | United Nations Children's Fund |
| WACMR | West African Council for Medical Research |
| WAMS | West African Medical Service |
| WHO | World Health Organisation |
| WO | War Office |

# ACKNOWLEDGEMENTS

It feels as if this book has been a long time coming. I would like to thank the Governors of the Wellcome Trust for their generous support in funding a post-doctoral fellowship and for providing an additional grant to travel to Thailand. As always librarians and archivists have made a significant contribution to various aspects of the research, this includes the staff of the LSTM library, the University of Liverpool library, the MRC and the Wellcome Institute for the History of Medicine.

I would like to thank my interviewees and correspondents who have provided me with factual information, access to personal papers and very many precious hours. In particular I would like to thank Mrs Joy Gordon, Mrs Lorna Maegraith, Professor Herbert Gilles, Professor Ralph Hendrickse, Dr Leo Gore, Brigadier White, the late Reginald Bark Griffiths, and the late James Williamson. I would also like to thank Professor Tan Chongsuphajaisddhi for his wonderful hospitality while I was in Bangkok. The staff and former staff of the Faculty of Tropical Medicine in Bangkok and others who studied in Liverpool made delightful interviewees and provided perceptive commentaries on the LSTM and tropical medicine as a discipline. Tan's secretary and Mr Sumjet of the SEAMEO organisation, and their friends provided me with excellent company and afforded me great respect. Dr Nicholas White gave me wonderful and unexpected interviews and showed a great enthusiasm for the value of history. At the LSTM, the Director David Molyneux, his secretary Mrs Joan Fahy, and Dick Ashford deserve my thanks. In the Department of Economic and Social History, I would like to thank Robert Lee (for initiating Wellcome support for this project in conjunction with David Molyneux and Sir Ian MacGregor of the LSTM), Andy Davies (for his encouragement and interest) and Di Ascott and Sharon Messenger (for the moaning).

There are many personal thanks. Bernard Brabin, Richard Hankins, Mark Harrison, Mike Service and Mick Worboys read early drafts for me. Lynne and Rick Forshaw made sure I did not go thirsty in the preparation of the book. Diana Newton stretched into twentieth century history on many occasions. Renate Hauser has provided wonderful hospitality, good company and practical support in my visits to Geneva. Lisa Wilkinson has swapped 'school' stories with me and generally shared the ups and downs of writing an institutional history. I have been lucky to have her company, it has made the whole experience less lonely and a great deal more fun.

There are three people who made the final stages of this book possible and to whom I owe considerable debts. Marisa Chambers has provided the most practical assistance at crucial moments, with grace and wonderful efficiency. Graeme Milne rose magnificently to the challenges of the CSD and the production of CRC. Bill Bynum has extended me his patience, interest and very dear friendship, besides his considerable skill. He made me believe it was possible to finish when I had forgotten how, by continuing to offer me the quiet confidence in my ability that I always felt from him. Despite all this help, any errors that remain are my own.

Marios Harris kept me going on the innumerable occasions when I was at best irascible, and often much worse. I recognise that his love was an important part of the writing of this book. He remains the best computer whiz on both the hard and software fronts. My parents are, as ever, the people to whom I devote my joy of and any margin of success in academic work, thank you for being so proud all these years.

# INTRODUCTION

Despite the upsurge of interest in the history of tropical medicine, international public health and the provision of health care in colonial and post-colonial tropical countries, no major text discusses the history of the academic discipline in the twentieth century.[1] Social historians of science and medicine have considered the formation of tropical medicine and its early history. [2] Its subsequent development and diversification still require analysis. Scholars who concentrate on particular regions of the world have examined the role of medicine in the processes of colonial rule.[3] The effects of decolonisation on medicine in the developing world have received much less attention. Historical sociologists concerned with development theory, third world debt and poverty discuss the status of health care delivery and the effects of continued dependence on the first world.[4]

In Britain, the two Schools of Tropical Medicine opened within six months of each other in the final year of the nineteenth century. They have played a pivotal role in developing tropical medicine, as an academic discipline in postgraduate medicine with an active research profile. The Schools also affected the development of health care in the tropical colonies. They trained the Medical Officers of the Colonial Medical Service and the indigenous doctors whose training failed to include infectious endemic diseases and lacked an emphasis on community health. The Schools also contributed to a body of knowledge applied by the colonial powers, international agencies and independent nation states as part of their health care programmes. Ultimately the Schools helped the developing world to establish its own priorities for health.

If the creation of schools of tropical medicine outside the tropics was counter-intuitive and relied upon an artificial system, such as colonialism and the economic necessities of global trade, their continuance, in the post-colonial era is perhaps even more surprising. In the case of the London School, the injection of Rockefeller money in the 1920s ensured its security by changing the emphasis from that originally envisaged. In Liverpool, the situation was different.

The LSTM remained for many years concerned with medicine and public health in the tropics and shared none of the concerns of its sister institution with public health in Britain and the development of epidemiology and medical statistics. These were much later additions to the recognisable expertise in Liverpool. This is not to imply that Liverpool lacked innovation. It took an alternative approach and in some cases tackled other problems. This was a function of the different structure of the two Schools, but it was also because of the size and the personnel. Liverpool was a smaller organisation. In the early years, it was spread over a number of sites including permanent laboratories overseas. It may well have retained such a structure had the financial and human resources been available. The smaller size meant that individual staff members could have a disproportionately large effect on determining the research and general direction of the School, if they chose to pursue a particular path. There was opposition and resistance from other members of staff and the governing body. The outcome was often that members of staff would move on because the disagreements were polarised and transparent within the small community making up the professional staff. Such disputes are part of the events of any institution's life, but they often bring into focus the differing priorities of the tropical medicine community and hence different facets of the discipline. The artificial way in which the discipline was created and the overriding importance of external social, political and economic factors shaping its development also permitted great potential diversity, providing resources were available. It was a discipline with few natural parameters.

As academic institutions, the concerns of the Schools of Tropical Medicine represent only one of the many possible histories of tropical medicine. The outlook from the Colonial Office, the views of Colonial Governments, nationalists and independent countries, international agencies are all obliquely served in this history of the LSTM, but await full accounts and ultimately synthesis. The history of the LSTM serves as an excellent vehicle to explore the development of the discipline in the context of colonialism, decolonisation and the rise of the Third World. It also demonstrates the dominance of the biomedical model and its application among people who may not subscribe to this system. It can begin to address central questions about the history of tropical medicine in the twentieth century. This history therefore asks what is understood as the discipline of tropical medicine, how has it changed over time and what have been the effects of applying this discipline overseas in a variety of contexts? The aim has been to begin to answer these questions by a series of chapters looking at the changing functions of the School. These guide the reader through the first hundred years of the School's history, but concentrate on certain specific aspects of the research, teaching and transfer of technology characterising the School. It has been necessary to be selective, for instance, details of School personnel and the support and administrative structures are restricted.

This history aims to inform on the development of the discipline of tropical medicine in the twentieth century as well as charting the successes and failures of a particular institution. To this end, this is a history of initiatives in tropical medicine at Liverpool. Many of the Liverpool 'firsts' are representative of 'firsts' for the academic discipline. It is not possible to trace these initiatives to the present day. The volume would be unmanageable. Consideration of further changes takes the place of the institutionalisation of familiar methods and directions of research. It is for someone else to consider in detail the development of the strands as I have tried to consider the development of the whole.

This is not to suggest that the history of tropical medicine at Liverpool is one of linear progress. It is not. A more appropriate model might be a maze with many lateral connections. This is also teleological for it implies that there is a natural end-point. What the LSTM has attempted to learn and to teach others is that this is not the case. The human race has been far more successful at making larger organisms extinct than it has in eradicating pathogens.[5] The spectre of new and re-emerging diseases poses new threats.[6] The elimination of poverty and the provision of the necessities of life are apparently equally difficult. The LSTM has realised that the process of trying to improve health in the developing world is not time-limited. Equally, it has suggested it is impossible for the First World to ignore the health of the developing world.

Chapter 1 discusses the foundation of the LSTM in the light of the existing historiography. It is apparent that the School lacked a clear policy. The managing committee allowed its staff, including Ronald Ross, to pursue their own research interests so long as the School could afford to continue as an institution. The succession of teaching laboratories in Liverpool and the establishment of research laboratories in Runcorn were a function of the overseas expeditions that characterised the first fourteen years. The research, particularly at Runcorn, is reviewed as the School established its reputation in isolating the aetiologies of tropical diseases in the optimistic 'discovery era'. This emphasis on research explores the importance of the parasite-vector model for tropical medicine at Liverpool. Fundamental research concentrated in the sub-disciplines of parasitology and entomology as it related to the vectors of disease. The School also showed an interest in understanding the effects of the parasite on the host. Parasitology replicated the studies of bacteriological infections. The effect of World War I and the contribution of the School conclude the first phase of tropical medicine in Liverpool.

The discovery era described in chapter 1 gave way to a less optimistic period during the inter-war years. In chapters 2 and 3, the consolidation of the School and potential new directions are discussed. Chapter 2 follows the School overseas with the foundation of a laboratory in Manáos, Brazil and the Alfred Lewis Jones Research Laboratory in Freetown, Sierra Leone. In particular the Freetown laboratory replaced the research expeditions, fulfilling many of the same functions. The establishment of a private laboratory in colonial territory highlights the difference between the aims of the School and the practice of tropical medicine in this colony. The laboratory reinforced the commitment of the School to working in the tropics. The financial difficulties affected the functioning of the laboratory and its relationship with the School in Liverpool. Out of choice staff concentrated on laboratory research, importing experimental animals to understand the interactions of parasite, vector and host. Out of necessity, they undertook pathology and survey work for the Colonial Government broadening the scope of their activities. The outbreak of World War II and the perpetual shortage of staff in West Africa forced the School to close the laboratory.

Chapter 3 discusses the progress of the School in Liverpool during the same period. The LSTM moved into its new purpose-built laboratories after the end of World War I and subsequently increased its establishment. Dedicated space allowed the School to plan its internal structure, and this reflected the development of the discipline in Liverpool. The renewed interest in tropical chemotherapy provided the means to understand the host/parasite relationship in terms of infection and immunity. The support of the MRC and pharmaceutical companies in the 1930s gave a new impetus to this research and provided the means to expand the School physically and intellectually. The outbreak of World War II focused the activities of the School, and staff contributed to the development of ICI's anti-malarial drug Paludrine.

The School emerged from the end of World War II to face new challenges. The LSTM was subject to change and reorientation. As the British Empire declined the obvious role of the School faded. The United Nations and its specialised agencies dominated the field of health, welfare and development without necessarily involving institutions like the School of Tropical Medicine. More parochially, the arrival of Brian Maegraith as the new professor of Tropical Medicine and Dean forced a different and determined direction on the School. Maegraith's forceful personality ensured that in the post-war era his ambitions and the development of the School were virtually synonymous. In the years after World War II there was a sense of intense optimism about the potential of science to improve the quality of life and remove freedom from want for the world's population. This Utopian future would apply basic science through a range of new technologies and would mobilise human resources. Chapter 4 reviews the arrival of Maegraith and discusses the formation of his pathophysiological research school exploring the processes of disease in the human body. This became the predominant activity, and Maegraith manipulated the School to realise his ambitions. For the first time, he provided clear objectives. This was crucial in a period of financial uncertainty when the LSTM needed to lose its colonial colours and join the vanguard of global health.

Besides these scientific initiatives, the LSTM styled itself as a model for education in tropical medicine. Chapter 5 discusses the emulation of this model in developing countries around the world. From the mid-1950s, building upon consultancies and policies to establish centres of excellence, various programmes were started to transfer overseas postgraduate medical education in tropical diseases. Three countries, Nigeria, Ghana and Thailand benefited from the expansive stance adopted by Maegraith. These initiatives were part of the formation of the unofficial School motto 'Our impact on the tropics must be in the tropics'. In his dealing with the Overseas Development Administration and colleagues alike, this sounded more like a battle cry. Fundamental research continued to expand the body of knowledge in this period. The sub-disciplines of parasitology and medical entomology employed increasingly sophisticated methods. Research in these areas could be located as easily in a university department as in an independent school of tropical medicine. In this way, a new identity for the School as an institute of higher education in Britain rather than a resource for the developing world emerged. This created a tension in the function of the School and the purpose of its component parts. This tension, a product of the definiteness of Maegraith's management style, remained with the School.

Chapters 6 and 8 discuss this tension with special reference to the expansion of the School from 1970 to 1990. Chapter 6 focuses on the Department of Tropical Paediatrics and Child Health, and chapter 8 on the Department of International Community Health. The commitment to the tropics was married to a desire to reorientate the School. This reflected changing priorities of health in the developing world no longer dictated by the needs of colonialism. In response to concern over the advisability of improving health in countries with high birth rates, the School promoted research and teaching in the field of tropical paediatrics and child health. The Department of Tropical Medicine and the Department of Child Health in the University launched a new diploma in Tropical Paediatrics and Child Health in 1970. This was the first postgraduate diploma in Europe educating paediatricians to work in the tropics. The course was a significant innovation for the LSTM. For the discipline of tropical medicine, it focused directly on many of the development problems of the Third World. It was a response by the School to changing conditions, particularly fears of increasing population. Chapter 6 reviews the plans to create a senior lectureship and the employment of Ralph Hendrickse, the formation of a separate Department of Tropical Paediatrics and Child Health, and its support by the ODA. The tropical paediatrics initiative indicated a new diversity within the School but reinforced its commitment to being an independent resource for the tropics.

The teaching programme affected the changing identity of the School discussed in the proceeding chapters. Chapter 7 traces the role of School as an educational resource from the first Certificate course for CMS officers to a range of recognised

University diplomas and degrees and short courses. Changes in teaching were indicative of the School's quick response to perceived needs in the tropics. This separate discussion of the teaching at Liverpool allows comparison of courses and their function for the School and the discipline. The School accepted non-British students from its inception, although its interest remained in teaching what was useful to the CO. After 1945, the School began to perceive its role to be in teaching foreign nationals at the diploma and higher degree level, rather than training British doctors to work for the CMS in the tropical empire. The overseas graduates returned home after their training to work on the endemic health problems of their own countries, many of which were preparing for independence or were newly independent. Theoretically, this offered opportunities to prioritise health care along different lines from the former colonial governments. The teaching became more responsive to short-term goals in tropical health. The aim was not to impart the results of recent fundamental research but to prepare a range of practitioners to work in primitive conditions. The expansion of the teaching programme to include non-medics and to focus specifically on teaching others to teach primary health care increased the virtual presence of the LSTM in the tropics. The teaching initiatives of the School represented more dynamic and immediate aspects of their practice of tropical medicine.

Where Tropical Paediatrics reinforced the commitment of the LSTM to tropical medicine by allowing a degree of reorientation, International Community Health challenged the definition and function of the School in Liverpool. The Department of International Community Health advocated that artificial geographical boundaries should be abandoned in favour of a socio-economic definition. Health care among the disadvantaged related less to climate than to poverty. A commitment to operational research in the 1980s strengthened the teaching programme reviewed in chapter 7. The School expanded physically and intellectually to accommodate this broadening of the discipline. The later 1970s and 1980s were periods of retrenchment in higher education and overseas aid. These were major sources of funding for the School. In this climate, the expansion of fundamental research in the scientific sub-disciplines competed with the innovations in the delivery of health care at Liverpool. The discipline threatened to become all encompassing and the core funding of the School dwindled. A rationalisation of activities followed an academic review in 1989. The report recognised the traditional strength of the School, its diversity, had become a weakness. For the first time, as a School, a policy of the future structure and function of the LSTM was established and with it, a new definition of the academic discipline of tropical medicine as practised from Liverpool.

NOTES

[1] H H Scott, *A history of tropical medicine*, 2 vols, London: Edward Arnold, 1939 and F E G Cox (ed), *Illustrated history of tropical diseases*, London: Wellcome Trust, 1996 are, as their titles suggest historical accounts of the diseases included in the discipline of tropical medicine at the date of publication. They do not discuss the socio-political context of the diseases. Important recent contributions are D Arnold (ed), *Imperial medicine and indigenous societies*, Manchester: MUP, 1988; R Macleod & M Lewis, (eds), *Disease medicine and empire*, London: Routledge, 1988; M Cueto (ed), *Missionaries of science: the Rockefeller Foundation and Latin America*, Bloomington: Indiana University Press, 1994; P Weindling (ed), *International health organisations and movements, 1918–1939*, Cambridge: CUP, 1995; J Siddiqi, *World health and world politics, the WHO and the UN system*, London: Hurst & Co, 1995; A Cunningham & B Andrews (eds), *Western medicine as contested knowledge*, Manchester: MUP, 1997.

[2] M Worboys, 'The emergence of tropical medicine: a study in the establishment of a scientific specialty', G Lemaine (ed), *Perspectives on the emergence of scientific disciplines*, The Hague: Moulton, 1976, pp. 76–98.

[3] M Vaughan, *Curing their ills: colonial power and African illness*, Cambridge: Polity Press, 1991; M Lyons, *The colonial disease: a social history of sleeping sickness in Northern Zaire, 1900–1940*, Cambridge: CUP, 1992; D Arnold, *Colonising the body: state medicine and epidemic disease in nineteenth-century India*, Berkeley: University of California Press, 1993; M Harrison, *Public Health in British India, Anglo-Indian preventative medicine 1859–1914*, Cambridge: CUP, 1994; R Macleod & D Kumar, *Technology and the Raj: Western technology and technical transfers to India, 1700–1947*, New Delhi: Sage, 1995; L Manderson, *Sickness and the state, health and illness in Colonial Malaya, 1870–1940*, Cambridge: CUP, 1996.

[4] T Allen & A Thomas (eds), *Poverty and development in the 1990s*, Oxford: OUP, 1992; D R Phillips & Y Verhasselt, *Health and development*, London: Routledge, 1994.

[5] The obvious exception is smallpox.

[6] L Garrett, *The coming plague: newly emerging diseases in a world out of balance*, London: Virago, 1995.

# 1

# TROPICAL MEDICINE ON
# TEMPERATE MERSEYSIDE

## INTRODUCTION

Liverpool's wealth began with the slave trade. After its prohibition in 1807, British ships looked for legitimate cargoes.[1] The tonnage of goods carried increased as the empire expanded. Liverpool became a centre of trade with the tropical world. Contact with the ports of the East and West coasts of Africa, Latin America and the West Indies was hazardous, but these countries supplied cheap food and many of the raw materials for industry. They also provided expanding markets for British manufactures. The ill-fated expedition up the Niger River in 1832, when the majority of the crew died from fever, was a sharp reminder of the potential risks. Even the systematic use of quinine could not sufficiently reduce the mortality rate on the coast to bring it into line with other parts of the tropical world.[2] Insurance companies charged higher premiums and Colonial Governments granted their staff longer periods of home leave.[3] Diseases such as malarial fever and beri beri often incapacitated those who worked on the ships for weeks at a time.

The growth of the city and port of Liverpool in the early part of the nineteenth century created immense public health problems. Unplanned urban expansion and the growth of slum housing encouraged the transmission of epidemic diseases such as typhus, typhoid and smallpox. The huge transient population exacerbated the incidence of disease.[4] Some stayed temporarily, earning enough for their onward passage; others remained to endure a life of perpetual under-employment in the dockyards.[5] The squalor of Liverpool's courts and cellar dwellings and their appalling mortality statistics earned the city a degree of notoriety in public health history. Amelioration of these conditions arose from a combination of progressiveness, civic pride and cameralism by the city council and business communities.

Additional risks came from the importation of foreign diseases later re-classified as 'tropical diseases'. Plague may not have returned to haunt the ports of Britain as in Africa and the East, but cholera struck in epidemics. The fear of these diseases promoted reactive and finally proactive action by the health authorities.[6] Concern over the economic cost of disease contracted overseas competed with the dread of imported diseases.

The health problems of a port city and the cost of tropical diseases on trading profits forced the city to respond. In the field of public health administration, Liverpool led the way by appointing the first Medical Officer of Health, William Henry Duncan, in 1847.[7] District nursing began in the early 1860s with the collaboration of Florence Nightingale and William Rathbone. In conjunction with Leeds and Manchester, Liverpool's Medical School became a leader of provincial medical education in 1884.[8] The foundation of the School of Tropical Diseases and Medical Parasitology in November 1898 ensured that in a particularly relevant field of postgraduate medicine Liverpool also became a centre of world renown. The Liverpool School was the first of its kind. Plans for a school in London had predated Liverpool's opportunistic enterprise, but London opened in October, some six months after Liverpool admitted its first student in May 1899.

The almost simultaneous provision of two schools of tropical medicine in Britain was not a chance occurrence. To tell the wider story of the foundation of one of the Schools is to tell the story of both.[9] The roles of Sir Patrick Manson, the 'father of tropical medicine', Joseph Chamberlain, Secretary of State for the Colonies, and Herbert Read, Parliamentary Private Secretary at the Colonial Office are well known.[10]

Michael Worboys has stressed the significance of commerce for Liverpool, and officialdom, through the CO, for London. He argues that these different contexts determined the style and content of tropical medicine practised by the two Schools.[11] June Jones has developed the theme of the special environment provided at the turn of the century by Liverpool's inter-linked commercial and scientific circles. This collaboration fostered the LSTM and other associated Schools of University College, creating a 'civic university' striving to provide direct benefits to Liverpool.[12] This chapter builds upon the existing historiography and concentrates on the development of the School and its role in shaping the new discipline of tropical medicine from 1898 to 1918.


TROPICAL MEDICINE


The foundation of the two Schools established tropical medicine as a postgraduate discipline in Britain. The practice of medicine in the tropics has a longer history, but the research and teaching activities of the Schools represented a new paradigm.[13]

Before the end of the century there was no formal teaching in tropical medicine for medical students. Recruits to the Indian Medical Service and Army Medical Department began their commissions at Netley undertaking courses in tropical medicine and hygiene, military medicine, and drill. Induction of new naval surgeons took place at Halsar. No dedicated laboratories conducted research. Manson urged Ross to return to India and work on the mosquito transmission of malaria in a place where this disease and its vector abounded.[14]

Ross's timing in determining the life cycle of the malaria parasite in the mosquito was fortuitous. 1898 was a pivotal year for the new discipline. The British Medical Association established a separate section for Tropical Medicine at its annual meetings. Specialists at home and abroad could now present and discuss their work in this prestigious forum.[15] The *Journal of Tropical Medicine*, the first dedicated British journal, issued its first number.[16] Patrick Manson published his *Tropical Diseases: A Manual of the Diseases of Warm Climates*. Compendia of tropical medicine had appeared throughout the nineteenth century. This new volume, designed for active service, guided practitioners in the accurate diagnosis of unfamiliar exotic diseases. It quickly became the premier text in the field.[17] In July 1898, the Royal Society's Malaria Committee, an advisory body chaired by the Society's President, Lord Lister, held its first meeting.[18] Edinburgh University established a Lectureship in Diseases of Tropical Climates for Andrew Davidson, an experienced tropical practitioner.[19] In Liverpool, businessmen, clinicians and medical scientists founded a school for teaching and research in tropical medicine. The School pasted together protozoology, helminthology, entomology and some bacteriology. Infusing this knowledge was a sense of urgency to maximise its application overseas. Together these elements formed the new discipline of tropical medicine.

Tropical medicine was an anachronistic title. Manson acknowledged the problems associated with this name in the introduction to his *Manual*.[20] Much of the later history of the School is involved with understanding its relevance. Today, current practitioners still do not share a common understanding of the precise constituents of their field. These difficulties highlight the importance of the social, economic and political as well as scientific and medical construction of this increasingly artificial discipline.

The teaching function of the discipline was initially easier to define. Syllabi for tropical medicine emphasised what the usual medical undergraduate curriculum ignored. Manson's motivation for a school in London was the need for dedicated training in tropical medicine. The aim was to prevent other practitioners meeting unfamiliar diseases only when they began their overseas careers, as he had done in his early years in Amoy.[21] The teaching functioned reasonably well in the first few years when the aim was to produce doctors for the Colonial Medical Service. However, the passive definition fails to explain the more amorphous research activity conducted under the title of tropical medicine.

Of the various exotic diseases, malaria was perceived as a tax on the health of those in the tropics. This disease provided a distinct model to differentiate the activities of tropical medicine from bacteriology and public health. The discoveries in malariology from 1880 onwards exemplified the new tropical medicine. The work of Charles L A Laveran, Camillo Golgi, Ross and his Italian rivals Giovanni Battista Grassi and Amico Bignami, established an etiological model for the discipline of tropical medicine and hygiene in Britain.[22] The natural history of single celled parasites and larger multi-celled helminths initially dominated tropical medicine, whether it was laboratory research conducted on the bench or public health measures applied in the tropics. Equally crucial to the new discipline was the role of arthropod vectors. These were not merely mechanical transmitters, but acted as a secondary host in which the parasite grew and developed. The involvement of man as a further host, albeit one sickened by the continued development of the parasite, was the final part of the life cycle.

The neat scientific model did not function in isolation. Simple single celled animals threatened man's dominance of the natural world. For the white colonialists, scientific discoveries indicating potential weaknesses occurred when the desire to rule the tropics was at its highest. If the new knowledge was initially a racial leveller, claims of native laziness, lack of hygiene and inherent stupidity reasserted white racial dominance and strengthened the purported validity of the colonial system.[23] Science would modify the disease-ridden tropics. The transfer of medical knowledge and sanitary practice reinforced the civilising mission of empire.[24] The LSTM, established for 'scientific, humanitarian and commercial reasons', developed this parasite-vector model conscious of the implications of their activities.[25]

## TROPICAL MEDICINE IN LIVERPOOL

Worboys and Jones have analysed the initial work of the two Schools. Worboys suggests that London, with its closer ties to the CO, followed policies of 'deferred development'. This prioritised the health of white Europeans who ran the colonies and postponed consideration of wider issues of native health. London's reliance upon personal prophylaxis and segregation, particularly residential segregation along racial lines, attested to this policy. The focus on the individual was characteristic of trends in British public health, controlling personal behaviour rather than emphasising sanitary infrastructures. In contrast, Liverpool is described as promoting public health measures that created improved living conditions from which coloniser and colonised would benefit. This represented the older environmental view of public health. The London model protected the governing classes, while that of Liverpool hoped to increase profitable trade, the direct concern of those financing the LSTM. A healthy labour force would be more productive, and a healthier population, living above the subsistence level, would be better able to buy British exports.

Worboys suggests these different approaches reflected opposing agendas driven by the funding and administration of the two Schools. Jones believes this dichotomy is over emphasised. She considers the LSTM initially followed a sanitary policy but changed to 'deferred development' after attempts at sanitary control proved too expensive and gave acceptable results only in very specific circumstances.

The authors concentrate on the role of Ronald Ross in the very early years of the School. Worboys contrasts Ross with Manson. Jones describes Ross's work in more detail using a model of entrepreneurial science in a civic setting. The reliance upon Ross, as epitomising Liverpool's definition of tropical medicine, introduces a distortion. Ross was indisputably a central figure in tropical medicine after discovering the mosquito vector of malaria in 1898 for which he won the Nobel Prize for Medicine in 1902. At Liverpool, he followed a changing personal agenda that did not necessarily follow any policy formulated by the LSTM or accurately represent the concerns of the other staff. Beginning in 1909, the CO funded various laboratory-based projects for Ross. These were quite different from his sanitary work of ten years before.

In addition, the roles of the Royal Southern Hospital and its staff have received little attention. This is an important omission, as the staff of the RSH constituted a powerful force on the governing body of the LSTM. Although outnumbered by the commercial representatives, they controlled the clinical side of the School. Unresolved tensions between the hospital and the laboratory side of the LSTM indicate the diversity of approaches to the subject and lack of a cohesive agenda for the development of the discipline.

This chapter supports Jones' thesis that the two Schools were not so different. Publicly the LSTM professed a general desire to make the tropics healthier. The way to realise this goal was a matter of individual concern. Staff independently pursued a range of techniques and methods. Personal ambition and romantic notions of exploration in the tropics or within the minute world of parasites flourished at Liverpool.

Over time, it is not clear that the School wished to champion public health over laboratory research. Moreover, there was no policy of prioritising the health of the native population.[26] In the early years of the LSTM the problems of keeping the institution afloat and mediating between competing demands on insufficient funds dominated the running of the School. The business men who donated funds and sat on the General Committee bought relatively little control of the scientific work: 'Financial assistance can have, and has had, inestimable value in promoting research work, but it cannot always command it.'[27] The Liverpool School lacked the resources to pursue a dedicated policy: a diversity of approach dominated the early years.


## FOUNDATION, EARLY ADMINISTRATION AND STAFFING

The Medical School in Liverpool, founded in 1834, became a part of University College in 1884, two years after the latter opened in 1882. In November 1884, University College joined Leeds as a constituent member of the Victoria University in Manchester: an institution whose medical degrees had been recognised by the General Medical Council in 1883.[28] The new status brought with it requirements for improved teaching facilities. Capital to endow chairs and build new laboratories for the basic medical sciences came from the ship owners who had previously endowed the arts in the same way. As Jones has shown, enthusiasm for a school of tropical medicine was an extension of the existing promotion of utilitarian science and medicine in a port city enjoying a vast trade with the tropics.[29] Liverpool's parochial interests coincided with a revitalised imperial spirit at the turn of the century. This was due to the Secretary of State for the Colonies, Joseph Chamberlain, with his ideas of constructive imperialism and the popular jingoism following the Boer War.[30]

The view of Manson and Read, that medical expertise was essential for economic development of the empire, led the CO to issue a circular: 'Proposals for the training of Colonial Medical Officers' on 11 March 1898. The circular addressed to the GMC and the leading medical schools called for the inclusion of tropical medicine in undergraduate curricula. In its reply the GMC endorsed the need for special instruction, but declined to incorporate this in their recommendations for ordinary curricula. A further circular, issued on 28 May 1898 and sent to the Governors of the colonies, repeated the need for special education for CMS officers and for research into malaria. These manoeuvres helped Manson's proposals for a school of tropical medicine, meeting with strong opposition from the consulting elite.[31] The 'unlooked for result' of CO propaganda was the 'formation of the Liverpool School'.[32]

On the night of 12 November 1898, at the Medical Students Society dinner, Dr William Carter, Physician to the RSH, spoke of the idea of developing the study of tropical medicine. In response the shipping entrepreneur and head of Elder Dempster, Alfred Lewis Jones, offered three hundred and fifty pounds for three years to foster this initiative.

16

Jones hosted a first meeting at his offices on 23 November to discuss the foundation of a 'School of Tropical Diseases and Medical Parasitology'.[33] William Adamson, President RSH; Richard T Glazebrook, Principal, University College; William Alexander, Senior Surgeon RSH; William Carter, Physician RSH and Professor of Therapeutics; and Rubert Boyce, Holt Professor of Pathology, Pathologist to the Liverpool Royal Infirmary and Consulting Pathologist, RSH, were present. These men agreed to 'form into a committee for promoting the study of tropical disease and...consider the best way to carry forward Jones' munificent offer'. Jones and Adamson were elected Chairman and Vice-chairman respectively.

Glazebrook had corresponded with Michael Foster, Secretary of the Royal Society. Foster's letter of 18 November to Glazebrook provided a framework for establishing the LSTM. He stressed the importance of the clinical-pathological method that 'worked with great success in America' and its appropriateness for the study of tropical diseases. Adamson, Carter and Alexander, appointed as the RSH's representatives, were unlikely to disagree with his recommendations.[34] The hospital had also suggested that Jones serve as a further RSH representative, as he was a member of their Governing Committee and gave generously to Hospital funds. Whether he officially accepted this position is unclear. Jones acted as a free agent without loyalty to the RSH. The Hospital staff saw the initiatives in tropical medicine centring on the RSH. The proposed laboratory at University College would assist their emphasis on clinical and pathological medicine.[35] It was a bitter disappointment in the coming years when they realised that they were an adjunct to the laboratories in Liverpool and Runcorn.

The second meeting of the Tropical Diseases Committee, in December 1898, decided to establish a permanent joint committee to manage the School. This was a similar arrangement to the other associated Schools of Art, Law and Hygiene in University College.[36] The Committee, the main governing body of the School, represented an association of commerce, education and clinical care in the city. This was embodied in its structure with representatives nominated from the Liverpool Chamber of Commerce (2); the Steamship Owners Association (2); the Sailing Ship Owners Association (2); Council of University College (2); Senate of University College (2); the Management Committee of the RSH (2) and the Staff of RSH (2). The scientific and medical staff formed a committee managing the intellectual side of the School. The Professional Committee reported to the General Committee but was largely free from lay intervention.[37] Within four months, these two committees had organised the finance, laboratory arrangements and admission of students. When Lord Lister opened the new Tropical Ward at the RSH on 22 April 1899 this also marked the official opening of the School.[38]

Jones has dominated accounts of the early history of the LSTM because of his initial and sustained generosity, and his role as the lay Chairman of the General Committee. Table 1 lists his financial contributions to general funds of the School and special donations. A self-made man, his shipping interests and involvement with the Chamber of Commerce, particularly the West African Section, has received considerable attention.[39] Jones emerges as a man aware of his worth who sought to reward a particular brand of independent action. He was tremendously energetic: 'we want to be daily at work with this School'; many of his ideas lacked consideration and caused embarrassment for the staff of the School and RSH.[40] Jones' galvanising influence was crucial, but many other members of the commercial community quickly joined him in funding the activities of the LSTM.[41] Indeed the commercial community was not the only supporter of the School. The first job of the Finance Sub-committee, appointed in 1904, was to make a formal application to the University requesting a grant towards recurrent laboratory expenses. From 1 October 1905, they received £200 per annum. In January of the same year, the Government began a five-year grant of £500 per annum.

The scientific environment in which the LSTM functioned was as important as the commercial funding. The Thompson Yates building of University College housed the first laboratory of the School. The Reverend Samuel Thompson Yates funded the construction of these new basic science laboratories. Lord Lister presided at the opening in October 1898, a month before the founding of the School. As Worboys indicates, the School was 'established outside existing medical education institutions', but, as part of the Thompson Yates Laboratories, there were many opportunities for integration with other medical sciences. Benjamin Moore, Charles Sherrington, Rubert Boyce and Henry Edward Annett led work in biochemical, neurophysiological, pathological and anatomical research. Several joint research projects attested to the potential for interchange of ideas and methodologies.[42] The *Thompson Yates Laboratory Reports* published research papers from all the disciplines.

This can be contrasted with the London School, established in purpose-built laboratories, adjoining the Seaman's Hospital Society Branch Hospital at the Albert Dock.[43] The close association with clinical material was an advantage. The clinical facilities in Liverpool comprised one dedicated ward in a general hospital with recognised teaching facilities. The distance between the RSH in the dock area of Liverpool and the laboratories in the University was a considerable disadvantage.

*Table 1* Alfred Lewis Jones' financial contributions, 1899–1910

| Year | Total donations (£) | Special donations (£) | Jones' donations (£) | Jones' donations as % of total |
|------|------|------|------|------|
| 1899 | 2,867 | | 350 | 12 |
| 1900 | 1,695 | | 350 | 21 |
| 1901 | 2,343 | 5,000 | 350 | 15 |
| 1902 | 1,237 | | | |
| 1903 | 1,279 | | | |
| 1904 | 2,367 | | 100 | 4 |
| 1905 | 1,300 | | | |
| 1906 | 2,917 | 1,260 | | |
| 1907 | 2,394 | 25 | | |
| 1908 | 1,814 | 200 | | |
| 1909 | 1,629 | | | |
| 1910 | 3,125 | | | |
| Total | 24,967 | 6,485 | 1,150 | |

Rubert Boyce provided the driving force behind the School. Ross's appointment as lecturer in Tropical Diseases brought international publicity; behind the headlines, the early character of the LSTM owes more to the efforts of Boyce. A graduate of London University, Boyce had also studied in Heidelberg and Paris before acting as Victor Horsley's assistant at University College London. In 1894, he became the new George Holt Professor of Pathology. He played an important role in developing the medical sciences in Liverpool, and was instrumental in establishing the School of Hygiene. His work was not restricted to University appointments. In May 1898, he began serving as City Bacteriologist. A lack of tropical experience appeared to present no limit to his enthusiasm for establishing a school of tropical medicine in Liverpool.[44] The contrast could not have been greater with Manson, his alter ego, in London.

Manson had the cumulative experience of working in difficult conditions with diseases unfamiliar to most British-based practitioners. Boyce brought a different portfolio of skills based on current pathological knowledge and techniques. He already enjoyed the status of a chair in University College and acted as a consultant to two hospitals. His interest in hygiene and public health bacteriology brought him into contact with others interested in scientific medicine and municipal health. He lacked any direct involvement with diseases associated with the tropics. Manson had no academic position. He was Physician and Medical Adviser to the CO. This generally mundane post required the patronage of Chamberlain to give its holder any power.[45] Boyce's trump card in

Liverpool was his connection with the commercial community. In 1901, he married Miss Kate Ethel Johnston, daughter of William Johnston. Following her death in childbirth, Johnston endowed new laboratories in the University in 1903 in her honour. Manson's equivalent was Chamberlain. The London School enjoyed the continued support of the CO long after Chamberlain ceased to be Secretary of State for the Colonies. Liverpool took second place. Not until 1900 did the CO agree to recognise the Certificate of the LSTM as acceptable for CMS officers. Financial assistance had to wait until 1904 when the newly constituted Tropical Diseases Research Fund provided a limited amount of funding for specific research. The CO had declined to give any financial support when first asked in February 1899.

The eclecticism of the School in the early years was due to Boyce's lack of specialist skills in tropical medicine. It may also have been responsible for the diverse policies of the School. It did not appear to diminish his self-promotion as the leader of the LSTM. During his period as Dean, from 1899 to his death in 1911, he established a reputation in the field and published actively.[46]

Staff appointments illustrate the diversity of the School under his direction. In the early years, he recruited innovative researchers who, like himself, did not necessarily have any experience in the tropics. Not surprisingly several members of the School staff were pathologists who either worked in the University department or were his personal associates. This provided a different research ethos to that evident among the staff who later worked for the LSTM. The obvious exception was Ronald Ross, the first lecturer in Tropical Diseases. There was no doubt about his knowledge of scientific research in the periphery, the diseases commonly found there and the social and economic difficulties attached to a career in tropical medicine.[47]

In December 1898, the Tropical Diseases Committee decided the administrative structure and discussed the appointment of professional staff. They considered it 'important that...the School should be in a position to contemplate the possibility of a gentlemen being appointed to this post who is not a member of the staff of the Royal Southern Hospital'. The intention was to appoint the new lecturer a consulting physician at the RSH, ensuring easy access to clinical cases. Boyce was keen to attract men of intellectual quality, with proven status who would complement his talents. Jones wanted to draw attention to Liverpool. Ronald Ross, the hero of the hour, recommended by Manson, must surely have been at the top of the list.

The clinical staff of the RSH did not share the same enthusiasm for an outside appointment. Following Ross's appointment, friction continued between the Hospital and LSTM. This may have been due to Ross's difficult personality and a lack of expertise in clinical medicine. The staff of the RSH, with established reputations in this field, regarded his appointment as an insult.

For his part, Ross was keen to leave India, and unable to get a position in London. The offer of a Lectureship, at £250 per annum and a share of the students' fees appealed to him. In addition to the income, there was also the possibility that someone else would pay Ross to develop the application of his previous painstaking microscopy.

Ross was always unhappy about his rewards from the School. Twice he resigned and then returned. On 21 April 1902, he left to take up a post at the Jenner Institute in London. He returned after a few months as Walter Myers Lecturer at £500 per annum and the promise of a chair in Tropical Medicine. In 1903, he became the Alfred Jones Professor of Tropical Medicine. In 1912 he resigned and went to London to develop his consulting practice. He became increasingly involved with committee work in London and resented the personal cost of travelling. He attributed his decision to leave Liverpool to a lack of recognition in financial and professional terms:

> Since I was appointed professor here in 1902 I have done not only the work for which I was engaged, but practically that of Director of the whole Institution, though I was not appointed as such officially (which I think ought to have been done).[48]

During his time at Liverpool, and after he left, he complained about remuneration levels at the School and made comparisons with the London School.[49] As professor of Tropical Sanitation, he returned each summer to give a series of lectures until 1917. Unlike the chair in Tropical Medicine, this was an honorary position and he received payment as a visiting lecturer.

For all their supposed unity of purpose, Ross and Jones shared an uneasy relationship. After Jones' death in 1909, and his replacement by William Lever (later first Lord Leverhulme) as Chairman of the Committee, Ross's fortunes within the School improved. He and Lever quickly established a good relationship, although the sanitary work overseas was replaced by clinical and laboratory investigations in Liverpool:

> I am convinced that the period has now come when research work on tropical diseases can be carried out in many respects even more effectually with the facilities of a great laboratory at home than under the rougher conditions in the tropics.[50]

Lever supported Ross's constant demands for national recognition and reward. He took this support to extremes. He tried to withdraw his covenanted support for the LSTM after the School declined to renew Ross's visiting lectureship in

1917 and confer an extra pension on him. When Ross resigned his chair in 1912, he also cashed in his University pension entitlements.

Although a prominent figure, Ross was not the first member of staff appointed. Dr Henry Edward Annett, the Demonstrator in Tropical Pathology, joined the School at a salary of £200 per annum. He combined this post with that of Demonstrator in Bacteriology at the RSH. Annett was a graduate of the Victoria University and a specialist in comparative anatomy and pathology. In 1896, in receipt of an 1851 Exhibition Scholarship, he studied the relationship of animal diseases to public health. He spent six months at the Royal Veterinary College in London and six months at Robert Koch's Institute for Hygiene and Infectious Diseases in Berlin. He maintained a correspondence with his German mentor. Boyce used this to good effect when promoting the School.

In 1903, Annett established the Liverpool Institute of Comparative Pathology. The object was the study of animal parasites, particularly those that hindered livestock husbandry in the tropics. Like the LSTM, the Institute occupied a floor in the Johnston Laboratories. Crofton Lodge, a row of cottages in Runcorn, thirteen miles inland along the river Mersey, provided additional premises for maintaining large animals. Boyce and Sherrington were Directors and Annett appointed lecturer in Comparative Pathology and Superintendent of the Serum Department. Evans Sons Lesher & Webb, producers of biological products, funded the Serum Department. Their interest was in developing commercially viable veterinary products. Annett resigned from the LSTM to take up his new position in Runcorn, but retained a close association with the School. With former colleagues he investigated basic problems in parasitology and published the findings as joint papers.[51] The similarities of human and animal parasitology and the need for basic research into parasite immunology made the neighbouring laboratories in Crofton Lodge common ground.[52] This association was characteristic of the eclecticism of the initial cohort of staff recruited by Boyce.

Ross's replacement in the Walter Myers Lectureship was John William Watson Stephens. He also took over the pathological work at the Tropical Ward, succeeding Annett as the Demonstrator. In Ross's absence, Stephens performed his teaching duties at the hospital. Before joining the LSTM, Stephens, had been a member of the Royal Society's Malaria Commission. His work from this period does not fit into the mould of public health associated with Liverpool. He appears instead as a proponent of 'deferred development'. His work with Samuel Rickard Christophers in West Africa associated malaria in Europeans with native children. His suggestion of the means to prevent this was to segregate the Europeans: a stance associated with the CO and London School.[53]

The LSTM was thus well equipped to embark upon its early work. Separate research took place on the expeditions, in the laboratories and at the RSH

Tropical Ward. The interrelation of these various projects provides a summary of the ways in which the LSTM developed the parasite-vector model of tropical medicine. This would apply not only to the development of the science but also to its socio-economic and political impact overseas.


## EXPEDITIONS AND LABORATORIES

From 1899 until the outbreak of World War I, the LSTM sent thirty-two expeditions abroad. Members of staff also took part in six other expeditions on behalf of the Royal Society, Government of the Belgian Congo, Suez Canal Company, Panama Canal Commission, CO, and British South Africa Company. The expeditions prompted much of the work of the School in this period.

A table of the expeditions appears as an appendix. The number of papers that appeared in LSTM publications: *Memoirs*, *Thompson Yates Laboratory Reports*, *Annals of Tropical Medicine and Parasitology*, and *Yellow Fever Bureau Bulletin* measures the outcome of these trips.[54] The *Annals* (the in-house quarterly journal) replaced the *Memoirs* in 1907. The editors accepted papers from elsewhere, but the majority of the papers related to the expeditions and subsequent laboratory research. From 1910, the *Annual Report* included summaries of research. This indicated the School's intellectual independence from its commercial sponsors and increasing maturity.

Overseas work gave the School a high profile. It also cost the lives of two members of staff. Walter Myers died of yellow fever on 20 January 1901 in Pará, Brazil and John Everett Dutton died of relapsing fever in the Belgian Congo on 27 February 1905.[55] Yet, John Todd and Dutton had written to Ross (before Dutton's death) explaining that 'they did not want to leave the Congo until they "had something good" or were "fagged out" and if the School could not afford to continue paying them they were prepared to finance themselves'.[56] Such men saw themselves embodying Chamberlain's development of the 'great estate' of the tropics. They regarded their work as part of a civilising mission that relied upon assumptions of white racial superiority legitimated by contemporary science and Christianity.

The expeditions also offered chances for personal glory. This was a period of optimism, innovation and excitement. Within six months of his appointment, after completion of his teaching duties, Ross led the first expedition to Sierra Leone. He hoped to identify the species of anopheline mosquitoes responsible for transmitting malaria on the West Coast. He also wished to demonstrate that effective campaigns against the vector would prevent malaria.[57]

Official bodies such as the India Office, the CO and Colonial Governments would not fund this work. His new employers were sympathetic but acted only after a large private donation gave Ross his chance. Early in 1901, he returned to West Africa with Matthew Logan Taylor, a pathologist. Aware of the nuisance value of bites as well as the more specific role of disease transmission, Ross launched his campaign to rid Freetown of mosquitoes. He organised gangs of local labourers into 'Mosquito Brigades'. They removed litter where mosquitoes might breed and repaired footpaths, streets and drainage facilities, to make these unsuitable for mosquito breeding. Ross saw this as the launch of his career as an advocate of public health measures:

> It may be stated that the experimental work at Sierra Leone and Bathurst has furnished useful information as to the lines on which Malarial Fever can be successfully combated in large towns, and the example is already being followed in many different parts of the world.[58]

The Royal Society's Anti-malaria Commission in India conducted further trials of his ideas as part of the controversial Mian Mir experiment.[59]

Ross's anti-mosquito measures endowed the term sanitation with a specific meaning and have been identified as the preferred policy of the LSTM. At times the role of the School did appear to be that of a sanitary hit squad who would respond to reported outbreaks of disease and rush to various locations to offer their advice:

> As somewhat alarming accounts had been received in the Autumn of 1902, of the unsatisfactory state of health of Europeans in the Gold Coast Colony, an expedition...was despatched...to make further investigations there and assist in carrying out [Dr Logan Taylor's] previous suggestions for sanitary reforms in that Colony.[60]

The sixteenth and twenty-second expeditions were also responses to requests for assistance. Those requesting help did not necessarily contribute to the cost of the trips. Ross refused to go to New Orleans in 1905, believing that the authorities should pay for the expert knowledge the School offered. Boyce went instead, not sharing Ross's objections. There was no intention of subsuming the responsibilities of the local public health authorities and taking over routine public health work. Requests for advice on disease prevention generated reports in response.[61] These activities resulted in the association of the School with public health rather than other aspects of the discipline such as laboratory research. In reality, it represented opportunism rather than a clear policy.

The sanitary model was only a part of the expeditions. The School released Ross to go to West Africa in 1901, and published his results in the *Memoirs*, but they would not fund the work. Basic biological discoveries from the expeditions and laboratories generated the same attention in the *Annual Reports* and other School publications. Announcements of new discoveries in parasitology or entomology apparently charmed the scientific community at Liverpool as much the sanitary work and made the local headlines.[62]

Some expeditions had specific predetermined agendas while others were less organised. All provided opportunities not available in Liverpool. On the spot microscopic examination of parasites and vectors reinforced the importance of the parasite-vector model to the discipline of tropical medicine. The clinical examination of large groups of people with the same condition was possible. The assessment of blood smears and other pathological specimens accounted for much of the investigators' time.

The expeditions served various functions. They acted as a vehicle for fund raising. It appears that there was some cost to the School in all the expeditions despatched, but, in six cases, separate public subscriptions provided the additional funds. This was particularly useful when it also increased donations to general funds. Several companies offered contributions in kind.[63] The expeditions were an advertisement. A lunch or dinner party sponsored by one of the patrons, demonstrating his individual philanthropy and commitment to the imperial cause, accompanied the departures and safe returns. These events warranted several inches of newsprint each time. This may well have soured Ross, paraded by the LSTM, without his ideas necessarily receiving specific recognition.

The expeditions extended the School beyond the confines of the University. The results of the work determined the direction for much of the laboratory research conducted at home. As Michael Foster suggested, 'The experts abroad can work with the men at home.'[64] The trypanosomiasis work in the laboratories, clinical cases brought from overseas and lodged in the RSH, and the activities of staff overseas in the Belgian Congo represented different facets of the same research programme.[65] In 1908, during the eighteenth and nineteenth expeditions, research from Runcorn continued overseas and recommenced after staff returned home.[66] Similarly, the third and fourth commissioned expeditions to Nyasaland and Rhodesia filled six notebooks with experimental data that accompanied the material brought home.[67] The experimental work continued at Runcorn. The Yellow Fever Bureau established at the LSTM in 1911, under the Directorship of Dr Harald Seidelin, facilitated research between the metropolitan laboratory and overseas for a specific disease. No other medical discipline conducted research in this way during this period. The London School sent out expeditions to a lesser extent, but the special circumstances in Liverpool created innovative methods in the pursuit of the parasite-vector model. The metropolitan laboratory was an expansive unit in early twentieth-century tropical medicine.

The expeditions provided a source of raw material for research and teaching in the School essential for such an institution located outside of the tropics. A network for exchanging specimens between other tropical medicine workers in Britain and Europe did not obviate the constant need to bring home new material. A motivation for starting the laboratory in Runcorn was the need to house large animals for experimental purposes. Maintenance of parasite strains in a greater variety of animals was then possible.[68] Regular consignments of prepared specimens and infected small animals arrived at the laboratories in Liverpool from the stock in Runcorn. This ensured that students received current information in a rapidly expanding discipline.

The growth of knowledge in the field of medical entomology was equally important for the development of tropical medicine.[69] It also brought non-medically qualified workers into the LSTM for the first time. The appointment of Richard Newstead in 1905, as lecturer in Economic Entomology and Parasitology, made the LSTM independent of the British Museum in the identification of entomological specimens on expeditions or brought back from overseas. Newstead's contribution to the identification and differentiation of a range of insects and arthropods of medical and economic importance was a considerable advantage. Liverpool became a clearing-house for tropical specimens and Newstead's opinion was sought by outside bodies. His background was not that of a tropical specialist, or even an academic, yet his work was of great significance. He too illustrates well the diversity of the initial staff.[70]

The Runcorn laboratories provided excellent opportunities for studying the relationship between parasites and their mammalian hosts. An active research programme was developed aimed at improving knowledge in the field of anti-parasitic chemotherapy. Harold Wolferstan Thomas, appointed as a research assistant in September 1903, became Director of the laboratory at Runcorn a year later. At Runcorn, he continued his research from Canada, investigating anti-trypanosome drugs. The successive Directors at Runcorn, John Todd, Anton Breinl and Warrington Yorke, continued chemotherapy research on a range of human and animal parasites. In some cases, the research aimed at producing immediate results. A cure for sleeping sickness using arsenical compounds was a priority and Breinl successfully developed the organic arsenical, atoxyl. In other cases the object was fundamental research: understanding the relationship between parasites and hosts, the immune reaction and pharmacological properties of various experimental compounds. An active network of correspondence, specimen and reprint exchanges involving key European scientists such as David Bruce, Charles Nicolle, Laveran, Charles W Daniels, William Leishman, Charles Wenyon, Manson, Robert Koch, Paul Ehrlich and Felix Mesnil, maintained contact with others at the forefront of such work.[71]

Evidence of the fabled visit by Ehrlich, the 'father of chemotherapy', is proven by the most mundane but essential of markers: a request for the reimbursement of his train fare.[72] Ehrlich's interest was due to his research on the use of arsenic to treat syphilis. His visit is significant because it indicates that contemporaries held the laboratory in high regard.

Much of the working day at Runcorn involved continuing parasite lines by inoculating fresh host animals. The hosts ranged from guinea pigs and mice to primates, goats and donkeys. It was a donkey infected with trypanosomiasis that embroiled the School in unwanted publicity and litigation after an anti-vivisectionist incorrectly accused Yorke of cruelty. Animals were consecutively numbered. It was possible to trace the history of a parasite strain in its successive passages through different host animals. Inoculation was either by transfer of blood or by biting insects depending upon the experiment.[73] Various professional and non-professional staff assisted the Director. The other laboratories in the Johnston building offered potential recruits. Maximilian Nierenstein, Research Assistant from February 1908 to April 1909, had previously worked with Benjamin Moore in the Biochemistry Department. Moore agreed to let Nierenstein transfer to the LSTM where he worked on the treatment and immunology of sleeping sickness.[74]

The identification of parasites and their morphological differentiation was a crucial part of the work undertaken in Runcorn. The numerous sheets of trypanosome drawings made by Anne Maud Brookfield, laboratory secretary and illustrator from 1906 to 1913, carefully recorded the observations made daily during prolonged research periods. The best of these appeared as coloured illustrations in papers announcing the identity of new strains.[75]

At the Johnston Laboratories and the RSH, research also flourished. With grants from the Tropical Diseases Research Fund, Ross supervised clinical, protozoological, cytological, and chemical research on Blackwater fever, malaria, trypanosomiasis and beri beri. Private donations funded tests on cryotherapy (the effects of cold) on these diseases in animals and man. Harold Benjamin Fantham and Stephens worked on amoebic dysentery and trypanosomiasis. The amount of work generated also demanded support staff. Mr Walter Stott of the Royal Insurance Company worked as an Honorary Statistician assisting members of staff in analysis of their work. Mr Walter W Drawz became the Malaria Bibliographer. He began by 'card-indexing the immense literature on Malaria'.[76] When this was complete, he made abstracts and translations from the growing scientific periodical literature concerned with tropical medicine, issuing a monthly list of references: an in-house forerunner of the *Tropical Diseases Bulletin*.

World War I brought an end to the expeditions and the Runcorn Research Laboratory. Warrington Yorke and Donald Blacklock left on the last expedition in November 1914. Their destination was the same as the first expedition: Sierra Leone. They sought a suitable site for a permanent laboratory provided for in the will of the late Alfred Lewis Jones. When it became apparent that the war would not be over by Christmas 1914, the expedition returned and the plans for the laboratory were postponed. Blacklock had been Director of Runcorn until his departure for Sierra Leone. Upon his return, he joined the navy. There was no one to replace him at Runcorn. Evans Medical took the accommodation at Crofton Lodge.

## CLINICAL TROPICAL MEDICINE

There were three general voluntary hospitals in nineteenth-century Liverpool: the Royal Infirmary, Northern and Southern. The Southern, the last of the three, opened in 1842 as the Southern and Toxteth Hospital. Located in the expanding dock area in the south of the city, its foundation was a response to an increasing number of accidents and rising incidence of disease. Prince Arthur opened a new larger building called the Royal Southern Hospital in 1872.

The RSH cared for many of the tropical disease cases entering the port either as in-patients in the general wards or as outpatients. In 1861, an Egyptian frigate arrived with a crew suffering from 'fever', probably typhus or typhoid. The RSH admitted sailors from the ship and subsequently several members of staff became ill. The Port Sanitary Authority established an isolation hospital at New Ferry for emergencies of this kind after the 1872 Public Health Act. Typhoid and typhus were not necessarily tropical in origin, but malaria was. From 1857 to 1898, when the Tropical Ward opened, there was an average of forty-eight ague or malarial fever cases each year (in and outpatients).[77] The foundation of the LSTM in association with the RSH threatened to concentrate all cases of tropical disease there. This did not meet with approval from the staff at the LRI who feared losing teaching material from their wards.[78]

*Figure 1* Malaria admissions by month, 1899–1910

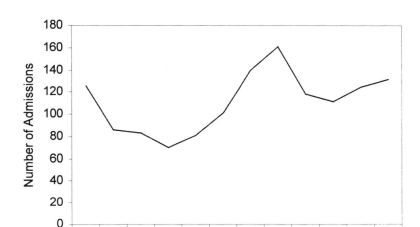

The RSH set aside a landing for the tropical cases with a laboratory and nurses' room. The Samuel Henry Thompson Ward, with fourteen beds, collected these cases together rather than scattering them through the general wards.[79] This regularised the existing situation rather than initiating anything new.[80] Additional accommodation was available in the neighbouring Nightingale ward and some private beds in a side ward were available if necessary.[81] Sister Nightingale and two nurses cared for the patients.

Plans for a plot of land opposite the RSH, recently purchased with money donated by Jones, included facilities for tropical medicine. After the death of Mary Kingsley, the West African travel writer, in 1900, Jones pushed for the erection of the 'Mary Kingsley Tropical School' on this land.[82] The RSH Committee postponed immediate discussion of this matter and later abandoned the scheme for lack of funds.[83] This did not please Jones. He maintained a strained relationship with the RSH and allied his interests with the University side of the LSTM.[84]

Outpatient facilities at the RSH opened at the end of 1901. Ross and Annett attended at 3.00pm on Mondays and Thursdays.[85] The scheme failed because they were frequently absent. The hospital committee were extremely angry and rejected later plans for outpatients.[86] Although the hospital consented to appoint the lecturer in Tropical Diseases a member of the honorary consulting staff, this position carried with it no admission rights or control over the beds.[87] The RSH

*Table 2* RSH In-patients, 1899–1912

| Occupation | Number | % of 1801 |
|---|---|---|
| Government | 44 | 2.4 |
| Trade | 61 | 3.4 |
| Medical | 9 | 0.5 |
| Missionary | 9 | 0.5 |
| Seamen/Sailors | 863 | 47.9 |
| Steward | 240 | 13.3 |
| Fireman | 195 | 10.8 |
| Engineer | 50 | 2.8 |
| Others | 330 | 18.3 |
| Total | 1,801 | 100.0 |

General Committee rejected Ross's request to issue special admission cards.[88] In isolated circumstances, the hospital admitted patients at the request of the School. In 1905, they accepted five cases of sleeping sickness from the Congo Free State. They allowed a notice on board steamers returning from the tropics informing passengers about the Tropical Ward.[89] On occasion, the Hospital issued circulars to local practitioners encouraging referrals.

The Tropical Ward at the RSH was usually full. Except for four women admitted in the 1899, the remainder of the 1,801 admissions from 1899 to 1912 were male. On average, the hospital admitted 129 in-patients each year. In August admissions peaked and remained at a high until the following January. This was due to increases in the incidence of malaria, see figure 1.

The majority of the in-patients worked in the shipping trade. Others worked in some form of official or government service and in trade (see table 2 for details). Seventy-five per cent of admissions were of English, Irish, Scottish and Welsh origin. Thirty different nationalities made up the remaining twenty-five per cent. From the correlation between nationality, disease and date of admission, many ships brought in several cases of disease at one time. This is particularly apparent in cases of beri beri, more common among sailors of Asian origin.

Inpatients had a range of tropical and non-tropical complaints.[90] In the case of non-tropical admissions sometimes a secondary diagnosis was tropical in origin. At other times, patients came merely because they were sailors.[91] It might also represent efficient use of empty beds by the RSH. The overwhelming reason for admission was malaria, 'when malarial disease is prevalent the ward is full to overflowing'.[92] Also described as malarial fever and ague, seventy-four per cent of admissions from 1899 to 1912 were for malaria. After 1910, when School staff had a greater involvement in pathology at the Tropical Ward, increasingly precise diagnoses related to the species of parasite causing the infection and replaced the term malaria or malarial fever. This implied routine identification by microscope and indicated a more scientific approach. The clinical facilities, despite the limitations at the RSH, provided School staff with parasites in one of their natural hosts.

Over the period 1899 to 1912 there were seventy-six deaths, 4.22 per cent of the admissions. Some cases died on the day of admission, obviously arriving in a critical condition. Malaria required the longest periods of hospitalisation. One case remained in hospital for 176 days. Cases of schistosomiasis and beri beri warranted stays of 156 and 123 days respectively. Tropical disease compromised the health of those working the shipping routes between Europe and the tropics. Conditions such as malaria and beri beri were occupational health hazards for sailors in the same way tuberculosis or silicosis were for mine and slate workers (See figure 2 for details of the duration as an in-patient for 1899 to 1903). Private patients paid a weekly fee of two to three guineas depending upon the amount of nursing required. At this rate, the American Missionary who stayed for 176 days with malaria could have been charged seventy-five guineas. Residence on the West Coast of Africa was recognised as injurious to health but the morbidity attached to working on the ships requires further analysis. There was clearly a need to provide skilled medical care in a city such as Liverpool in the early years of the century. The foundation of the School rationalised this provision.

The first prospectus of the LSTM listed teaching and research as the twin aims. Students' fees were a vital contribution to the financial viability of the new School. A satisfied alumnus was a good advertisement, and students were potential recruits to the expeditions and staff of the School. Recognised qualifications were a crucial marker for a new discipline. They indicated expertise. Holders of these qualifications could advertise their status, patients were able to identify specialists and fund providers were sure of a recognised level of competence. Chapter 7 discusses the development of the range and type of teaching within the School and the changing profile of the students. Here the emphasis is on clinical teaching at the RSH and its relationship with clinical care and research. It highlights the difficulties associated with teaching tropical medicine outside the tropics.

Manson's original ethos of preparing new medical graduates for service overseas by exposing them to unfamiliar conditions beforehand included experience at the bedside as well as the laboratory bench. In Liverpool, teaching took place in the laboratories and museum at the University and the Tropical Ward at the RSH. The RSH had an established role in clinical medical

*Figure 2* Duration as in-patient: Patients with malaria, 1899–1903

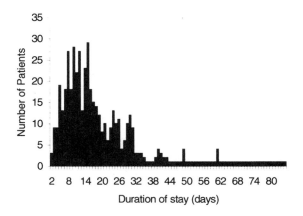

education. In 1858, the Hospital had become a Chartered Institution for the admission of surgical pupils and in 1870 for physicians and apothecaries. The Medical School granted recognition as a teaching hospital with the same status as the LRI in 1892. This tradition partially explains the resistance of the honorary Hospital staff to the appointment of less experienced outsiders as teachers and practitioners in the Tropical Ward. Staff at the RSH considered they had expertise in the field before the foundation of the LSTM. They enjoyed a lucrative private practice among the wealthier classes that periodically ventured overseas for business.[93]

In the face of Ross's appointment as lecturer at the LSTM, the Medical Board made him an Honorary Consulting Physician for Tropical Diseases.[94] Ross disliked not being able to teach at the RSH. Students attended his lectures at the University and experienced a further set of unrelated lectures on the Tropical Ward from RSH staff.[95] An uneasy few years followed. In 1905, problems with the arrangements for teaching at the RSH emerged again. This time the students complained that they lacked access to sufficient clinical material during their studies. The School used the disputes over teaching to enhance facilities for research.

Without involvement in admissions to the Tropical Ward the School could not select clinical material for the students. Despite its popularity with the merchant seaman, the hospital did not present a sufficient variety of tropical cases for the students. Cases were often in an advanced stage before patients sought admission. Opportunities for observing the early symptoms of disease, important in differential diagnosis, were infrequent. Michael Foster had stressed the importance of 'a pathologist working with the physician or surgeon in clinical charge of the sick'.[96] This was possible in principle, but continuity between the laboratory and the clinic was not realised in practice.

Jones planned to enhance teaching and research at the RSH, 'It occurs to me that it would a good thing for Liverpool to organise a staff of malaria experts to deal with cases arriving at this port.'[97] He offered additional funds if the ward came directly under the control of 'teachers in the Tropical School, who should have experience, not only of tropical diseases but also an intimate practical knowledge of the conditions obtaining in the tropics'.[98] In this scenario, the School staff had an appreciable advantage over their clinical colleagues at the RSH who had not served overseas. The RSH reacted strongly to Jones' proposals. They refuted the implication that the consultants were not experts, particularly 'to the great end of *curing* diseases'.[99] They also argued that Ross could not be a Medical Officer at the RSH. As a member of the School staff, he would not be responsible to the Trustees: an untenable position for a charitable enterprise such as a voluntary hospital.[100]

The General Committee also declined an offer made by Jones the following year in 1906 to have Drs William T Prout and Arthur J N O Evans appointed to the RSH to carry out clinical and pathological work in the Tropical Ward.[101] In annoyance Jones wrote: 'I think you have missed the greatest chance that the world has ever known certainly that the RSH has ever known. Of course I cannot sit still and as I cannot get what I want I must get it elsewhere.'[102] Much to the consternation of the RSH, Jones floated ideas for a rival scheme for a private nursing home for tropical diseases in Liverpool in 1907. This was something of an embarrassment for the LSTM. Jones' interests were not consistent with those of the LSTM Committee on all occasions.

In January 1908, the RSH board invited Ross to apply for the post of Honorary Medical Officer to the Tropical Ward. He cabled from Mauritius where was working that he would be happy to accept the appointment.[103] Six months later Stephens became Honorary Pathologist in Tropical Medicine to the RSH.[104] These appointments belatedly strengthened the position of School staff within the hospital. In return, the physicians to the Tropical Ward joined the Professional Sub-committee of the LSTM. Ross made the most of this position for his new laboratory investigations on malaria. In 1911, he became Clinical Pathological Assistant to the Tropical Ward.[105] These appointments improved the facilities for students. Ross was now able to teach in the ward, but, more importantly, this enabled 'a large amount of material to be made use of which was formerly going to waste'.[106]

In the longer term, this was too little too late. In October 1911, Lever informed the RSH that the School was transferring the clinical work to a new site.[107] Despite their protestations the School went ahead with plans to build a ward and attached laboratory at the LRI using the money left in Jones' will. In drawing up a formal notice of the arrangement with the LRI the School took care not to replicate the problems associated with the RSH.[108] In 1916, the School withdrew its grant of £200 per annum for the upkeep of the Tropical Ward but invited the RSH General Committee to continue nominating two representatives to the LSTM Committee.[109] Effectively the association between the Hospital and School was at an end.

## WORLD WAR I

On the eve of World War I, the School was about to enjoy a face-lift. In July 1914, the Countess of Derby opened the newly constructed Sir Alfred Lewis Jones Tropical Ward and Clinical Laboratory at the LRI. Instead of the cramped conditions in the Johnston Laboratories, the School would have a new four-storey building, 300 metres from the University. The outbreak of war ensured that the LSTM did not benefit from such improvements until the 1920s. The staff who did not join the combatant forces curtailed their research activities and suspended teaching of the DTM.

When war began, the LSTM offered the new tropical ward for the treatment of non-tropical emergency cases.[110] Early in 1915 when the new laboratories were nearing completion the War Office announced the establishment of temporary military hospitals in Liverpool for casualties arriving at the Port. Francis C Danson, Chairman of the Committee, offered the building to the military for this purpose.[111] The military authorities accepted this offer on 22 March 1915 and the School of Tropical Medicine Auxiliary Medical Hospital opened on 8 December 1915 with two hundred beds.

Wards on the second and third floors admitted dysentery and other tropical cases under Professor Stephens.[112] Captain Llwewllyn Morgan RAMC (T) assisted. As the number of tropical cases rose, the LSTM suggested that the wards on the other floors be set aside for tropical cases.[113] Poor hygiene in the Mediterranean brought numerous dysentery cases into Liverpool from Gallipoli, Salonika, Egypt and Mesopotamia. Three other hospitals in Liverpool, besides the School, admitted tropical casualties.[114] Woolton took convalescent cases and two camps in Birkenhead and Litherland housed those treated and passed fit for service. The School functioned as a central site for stool examinations for parasitic cases. Other laboratories in the University conducted bacteriological examinations.[115] The concentration of dysentery cases in the hospitals in Liverpool offered excellent opportunities for research, which began in January 1916.

Stephens led the work. Under him was a team of existing School staff (Fantham and Henry Francis Carter) and others seconded by the WO (Doris L Mackinnon, DSc) and recommended by the Royal Society (J R Matthews and A Malins Smith). The LSTM paid the salaries of the additional staff. Fantham's wife, A Porter Fantham, DSc, offered her assistance. The nursing staff performed the daily collection of stool specimens. The research was broad ranging: diagnostic procedures,[116] epidemiology,[117] treatment,[118] basic biological science[119] and clinical observations.[120] This work complemented other research conducted for the WO with the aid of the MRC by Ross, Clifford Dobell and Margaret Jepps. The WO facilitated research in Liverpool by concentrating cases, but the LSTM dictated the research.

A project on the treatment of malaria followed the work on dysentery. From August 1916, the number of malaria casualties arriving in Liverpool under the Western Command increased significantly. In September, the School offered to examine malaria cases before their discharge from hospitals in the Liverpool district and issue individual directions for treatment to prevent relapse. In January 1917, the DGMS asked Stephens to develop ongoing research on the treatment of malaria.[121] Ross organised the concentration of malarious casualties under special consultants in February 1917. Ross and Stephens became Special Consultants in Malaria. Stephens had responsibility for the Western, Northern and Scottish Commands with a temporary commission in the RAMC at the rank and allowances of a Lt-Col. Ross took control of the Southern and Eastern Commands.[122] He claimed responsibility for Liverpool's selection as a research centre and expressed his annoyance at receiving no acknowledgement.[123]

The research group at the LSTM systematically investigated the relative benefits of oral, intravenous and intramuscular administration of the alkaloid and various salts of quinine on three species of malaria parasites. They also evaluated the effects of single, interrupted, prolonged and massive doses of quinine. After the work in Liverpool, the recommended treatment for benign tertian malaria no longer used prolonged and heroic doses of quinine.

Liverpool was an obvious choice for this research. The WO facilitated the concentration of cases as they had with the dysentery patients, but again School staff directed the research and monitored its progress. They were well aware of the opportunity that the malarious casualties and pensioners presented for research into malaria. The work appeared as a series of thirty-two papers in the *ATMP*, 'Studies in the Treatment of Malaria'.[124]

Work on the chemotherapy of tropical diseases had begun at the Runcorn laboratories with Thomas and Breinl. Yorke and Blacklock continued the research until the outbreak of war. In 1916, released from active duty, Yorke returned to LSTM and with Stephens formed a team to exploit the situation provided by wartime needs and raise the profile of the School.

As a major port, Liverpool had a tradition of providing care for military casualties. In the nineteenth century, during the Ashanti wars, the RSH admitted tropical and other casualties at the request of the WO. Liverpool also provided hospital beds during the South African war. However, the city played a significant role during World War I in research as well as care because of the LSTM. The appointment of Stephens as the WO malaria consultant reinforced this new status. The war work acknowledged the LSTM as a centre of expertise in a discrete discipline: tropical medicine.

## CONCLUSION

From its hurried foundation on the back of the idea for the London School the LSTM had developed considerably in the first twenty years. The demands for laboratory space increased until a dedicated building moved the School to the edge of the University Campus. The provision of clinical facilities, a point of tension in the first ten years, improved after the move to the LRI. In 1898, Foster outlined useful methods the School might use to pursue tropical medicine as a discipline. The difficulties of pursuing tropical medicine in a temperate country served to flesh out these general plans. Although equipped with useful ways of doing tropical medicine, a clear direction for the School remained elusive.

The School gathered the raw materials necessary for teaching and research in Liverpool in a series of high-profile expeditions. These visits reinforced the diversity of approaches taken by the School. Attempts at discovering the cause and means of transmission of existing clinical conditions and the application of this knowledge in the prevention of disease reinforced the parasite-vector model. This model distinguished tropical medicine from other related disciplines such as bacteriology. It dominated the definition of tropical medicine at Liverpool. There was no mention of poverty and the negative effects of colonial policies. The School reinforced the concept of empire based on white racial superiority and the exploitation of the natural world to support this hierarchy.

The laboratory research refined the biomedical model for future application, but also indicated that staff wished to pursue fundamental research on the relationship between the host and parasite. They applied the contemporary methods of bacteriology and immunology to the study of parasitic diseases. Drugs for use in the treatment of trypanosomiasis were an immediate result. Some members of staff, including Ross, accepted that there would be long-term objectives in the control of disease in the tropics. The School effectively closed for the duration of the World War I. Tropical casualties provided unexpected opportunities for research that served to raise the profile of the School. Based on the accumulated experience of the past twenty years, the School was ready to begin anew when the war ended.

## NOTES

[1] S Marriner, *The economic and social development of Merseyside*, London: Croom Helm, 1982.

[2] P Curtin, *Death by migration: Europe's encounter with the tropical world in the nineteenth century*, New York: CUP, 1989.

[3] *Idem*, 'Medical knowledge and urban planning in tropical Africa', *American Historical Review*, 90, 1985, 594–613; R S Dumett, 'The campaign against malaria and the expansion of scientific medical and sanitary services in British West Africa, 1898–1910', *African Historical Studies*, 1, 1968, 153–197.

[4] T Lane, *Liverpool: gateway of empire*, London: Lawrence & Wishart, 1987.

[5] E Taplin, *Liverpool dockers and seamen 1870–1890*, University of Hull: Hull, 1974.

[6] A Hardy, 'Cholera, quarantine and the English preventative hospital system, 1850–1895', *Medical History*, 37, 1993, 250–269.

[7] W M Frazer, *Duncan of Liverpool: being the work of Dr W H Duncan, Medical Officer of Health, 1847–63*, Preston: Carnegie, 1997.

[8] S V F Butler, 'A transformation in training: the formation of University medical faculties in Manchester, Leeds and Liverpool, 1870-84', *Medical History*, 30, 1986, 115–132.

[9] The history of the London School has been told several times but for a definitive history see L Wilkinson & A Hardy, *The London School of Hygiene and Public Health: a twentieth century quest for global public health*, London: Kegan Paul, 1998.

[10] I McGregor, 'Patrick Manson, 1844-1922: the birth of the science of tropical medicine', *TRSTMH*, 89, 1995, 1–8; D M Haynes, 'From the periphery to the centre: Patrick Manson and the development of tropical medicine in Great Britain, 1870-1900', PhD thesis, University of California, 1992.

[11] M Worboys, 'Science and British colonial imperialism, 1895-1940', DPhil thesis, University of Sussex, 1979; *idem*, 'Manson, Ross and colonial medical policy: tropical medicine in London and Liverpool, 1899-1914', R Macleod & M Lewis (eds), *Disease, medicine and empire*, London: Routledge, 1988, pp. 21–37.

[12] In addition to the work of Worboys and Jones, the *Historical Record 1898–1920*, Liverpool: LUP, 1920, provides a detailed and fairly accurate factual history from the LSTM's inception to the move into purpose-built laboratories in Pembroke Place. The initials at the end of the text indicate it was prepared by Stephens, Yorke and Blacklock. The foundation has also been described by the former Dean, B G Maegraith, 'History of the Liverpool School of Tropical Medicine', *Medical History*, 16, 1972, 354–368. See also D Allmand, 'LSTM scientific record', *ATMP*, 15, 1921, 1–48.

[13] M Harrison, 'Tropical medicine in nineteenth century India', *British Journal History of Science*, 25, 1992, 299–318. See also D Arnold (ed), *Warm climates and western medicine: the emergence of tropical medicine 1500–1900*, Amsterdam: Rudopi, 1996.

[14] E Nye & M Gibson, *Ronald Ross: malariologist and polymath*, Basingstoke: Macmillan, 1997.

[15] H Power, ' "Bringing the horse to water": Leonard Rogers' research on amoebic dysentery and its reception in Britain, 1902 to 1908', W F Bynum (ed), *Gastroenterology in Britain: Historical essays*, London: WIHM, 1997, pp. 81–95.

[16] E Chernin, 'The early British and American journals of tropical medicine and hygiene: an informal survey', *Medical History*, 36, 1992, 70–83.

[17] P Manson, *Tropical diseases: a manual of the diseases of warm climates*, London: Cassell, 1898. This book passed through its sixth edition before Manson's death in 1922. It was continued by his son-in-law Philip Manson-Bahr. It is now in its 20th edition: G C Cook (ed), *Manson's Tropical Diseases*, London: W B Saunders, 1996.

[18] W F Bynum, 'An experiment that failed: malaria control at Mian Mir', W F Bynum & B Fantini (eds), *Malaria and ecosystems: historical aspects*, *Parassitologia*, 36, 1994, 107–120.

[19] F J Wright, Letter, *Proceedings of the Royal College of Physicians of Edinburgh*, 25, 1995, 709–710.

[20] P Manson, *Tropical Diseases*, 4th edition, p. xiii.

[21] P Manson, 'The need for special training in tropical diseases', *Journal of Tropical Medicine*, 2, 1899, 57–62; *idem*, 'The necessity of special education in tropical medicine', *Lancet*, ii, 1897, 842–845.

[22] On the history of the malaria discoveries see G Harrison, *Mosquitoes, malaria and man: a history of hostilities since 1880*, London: John Murrary, 1978.

[23] W Anderson, 'Immunities of empire: race, disease and the new tropical medicine 1900–1920', *BHM*, 70, 1996, 94–118.

[24] D M Schreuder, 'The cultural factor in Victorian imperialism: a case study of the British "civilizing mission" ', *Journal Imperial Commonwealth History*, 4, 1976, 283–317.

[25] Liverpool Daily Post, 13 February 1901.

[26] The Professional Sub-committee minutes (TM/4) where one might expect to find directions for research and specific agendas does not contain this kind of discussion. The General Committee minutes (TM/3), dominated by the lay staff, also lack any formal discussion of the direction of the LSTM.

[27] *Annual Report of the MRC, 1925–1926*, London: HMSO, 1926, p. 12.

[28] S V Butler, 'A transformation in training'; Lord Cohen of Birkenhead, 'The Liverpool Medical School and its physicians 1642–1934', *Medical History*, 16, 1972, 310–320.

[29] J Jones, 'Science utility and the second city of empire: the sciences and especially the medical sciences at Liverpool University 1881–1925', PhD thesis, UMIST, Manchester, 1989.

[30] J M Mackenzie, *Propaganda and empire: the manipulation of British public opinion 1880–1960*, Manchester: MUP, 1984.

[31] G C Cook, 'Dr Patrick Manson's leading opposition in the establishment of the LSTM: Curnow, Anderson and Turner', *Journal of Medical Biography*, 3, 1995, 170–177.

[32] Historical Record, p. 5.

[33] This name appeared on the first prospectus and the first *Annual Report* of 30 December 1899. Thereafter it is referred to as the Liverpool School of Tropical Medicine.

[34] LRO 614 SOU 1/2, RSH Committee Minute Book 1892–1904, General Committee, 5 December 1898.

[35] LRO 614 SOU 1/2, RSH Committee Minute Book 1892–1904: Memorandum from Adamson to Jones, 14 November 1898: "Your liberal offer to contribute £350.00/annum for the study of Tropical Diseases in connection with the Royal Southern Hospital was received with considerable enthusiasm on Saturday evening, and on behalf of the committee of that institution I thank you...The laboratory part of the work could well be handled at the University College, but, the proximity of the Southern Hospital to the docks, especially your steamers, points to this institution as being the one where the clinical part must be done if the safety of the patients is to be considered".

[36] TM/15/1.2, Report of the Tropical Diseases Committee (Liverpool) in connection with University College and the RSH, 12 December 1898. Membership of the Tropical Diseases Committee: Alfred Lewis Jones, William Adamson (President, RSH), William Alexander (Senior Surgeon, RSH), William Carter (Physician, RSH & Professor of Therapeutics), Rubert Boyce.

[37] These two groups were initially responsible for running the School. On 30 January 1905, the School was incorporated under the Companies Act with a Memorandum and Articles of Association. In 1904, a Finance Sub-committee was appointed. In 1934, the General Committee was re-styled as School Council after a new Memorandum and Articles of Association were signed. The Professional Sub-committee became the Professional Committee. In 1965, this became the Management Committee and in 1969, the Executive Management Committee.

[38] Lister's support for the School did not end with these public duties and it was he who petitioned Chamberlain to review his requirement that future CMOs should all attend the London School.

[39] P N Davies, *Sir Alfred Jones, shipping entrepreneur par excellence*, London: Europa, 1978, *idem*, *Trading in West Africa 1840–1920*, London: Croom Helm, 1976.

[40] TM/8/A.1, Jones to Ross, 26 October 1906.

[41] The role of John Holt in supporting the idea for a school of tropical medicine and for financial contributions is under-appreciated. Personal communication, Mr Noel Holt, 26 April 1993.

[42] For examples of joint work see R Boyce, R Ross & C Sherrington, 'The history of the discovery of trypanosomes in man', *Lancet*, i, 1903, 509–513; B

Moore, M Nierenstein & J L Todd, 'A note on the therapeutics of trypanosomiasis', *ATMP*, 1, 1907, 161–162; *idem*, 'Concerning the treatment of experimental trypanosomiasis', ibid., 273–284; *idem*, 'Notes on the effects of therapeutic agents on trypanosomes', *ATMP*, 2, 1908, 221–226.

[43] G C Cook, *From the Greenwich hulks to old St Pancras: a history of tropical disease in London*, London: Athlone, 1992.

[44] P Manson-Bahr & A Alcock, *The life of Sir Patrick Manson*, London: Cassell, 1927.

[45] E Chernin, 'Sir Patrick Manson: physician to the Colonial Office, 1897–1992', *Medical History*, 36, 1992, 320–331.

[46] In addition to three monographs, R Boyce, *Mosquito or man? The conquest of the tropical world*, London: Murray, 1909; *idem*, *Health progress and administration in the West Indies*, London: Murray, 1910; *idem*, *Yellow fever and its prevention: a manual for medical students and practitioners*, London: Murray, 1911, he made two (joint) contributions to the *Thompson Yates & Johnston Laboratory Reports*, three contributions to the School's *Memoir* series and published four papers in the *ATMP*.

[47] E Chernin, 'Sir Ronald Ross, malaria and the rewards of research', *Medical History*, 32, 1988, 119–141.

[48] TM/14/DaF/30b, Ross to Lever, 1 July 1912.

[49] TM/14/DaF/33, 38a, 38b, 38c.

[50] *12th Annual Report of the LSTM, 1910*.

[51] H E Annett & A Breinl, 'Short note on the mechanism of haemolysis in *Piroplasmosis canis*', *ATMP*, 2, 1909, 383–385.

[52] The association between the Veterinary School of the University and the LSTM was later formalised in the 1920s by a joint lectureship in Veterinary Parasitology.

[53] J W W Stephens & S R Christophers, 'The native as the prime agent in the malaria infection of Europeans', *Reports of the Malaria Commission of the Royal Society*, Series 2, 1900, 3–19; *idem*, 'The malarial infection of native children', ibid., Series 3, 1900, 2-13; *idem*, 'The segregation of Europeans', ibid., 21–24; *idem*, 'Proposed site for European residences in the Freetown Hills', ibid., Series 5, 1901, 1–4.

[54] Occasionally papers reporting on the expeditions appeared elsewhere, but as the ethos was to publish in-house they were generally duplicate accounts.

[55] Pará is now known as Belem. The Belgian Congo became Zaire following independence.

[56] M Lyons, *The colonial disease: a social history of sleeping sickness in Northern Zaire 1900–1940*, Cambridge: CUP, 1992, p. 81.

[57] R Ross, 'The possibility of extirpating malaria from certain localities by a new method' *BMJ*, ii, 1899, 1–4.

[58] *3rd Annual Report of the LSTM, 1901*, p. 8.

[59] W F Bynum, 'An experiment that failed: malaria control at Mian Mir'; M Harrison, *Public health in British India: Anglo-Indian preventive medicine 1859–1914*, Cambridge: CUP, 1994, pp. 158–160.

[60] *4th Annual Report of the LSTM, 1902*, p. 6.

[61] Appendix 1, Expeditions 9, 12, 16, 17, 20, *1, *2, *3, *4, *5, and *6.

[62] J E Dutton, 'Preliminary note upon a trypanosome occurring in the blood of man', *Thompson Yates Laboratory Reports*, 4, 1902, 455–469; *idem* & J L Todd, 'The nature of human tick fever in the eastern part of the Congo Free State', *Memoir*, 17, 1905, 1–18; S R Christophers & R Newstead, 'On a new pathogenic louse which acts as the intermediary host of a new haemogregarine in the blood of an Indian field-rat (*Jerbellus indicus*)', *Thompson Yates Laboratory Reports*, 7, 1906, 1–6; A Breinl & A Kinghorn, 'Note on a new *Spirochaeta* found in a mouse', *Memoir*, 21, 1906, 1–52; R Newstead, 'On a new *Dermanyssid acarid* found living in the lungs of monkeys (*Cercopithecus schmitdi*) from the Upper Congo', *Memoir* 18, 1906, 41–45; *idem*, 'On another new *Dermanyssid acarid* parasitic in the lungs of the Rhesus monkey', ibid., 47–50; J W W Stephens, 'Two new human cestodes and a new linguatulid', *ATMP*, 1, 1907–1908, 549–556; *idem*, 'A new human nematode, *Strongylus gibsoni*', ibid., 2, 1908–1909, 315–316; R Newstead, 'Descriptions of a new genus and three new species of Anopheline mosquitoes', ibid., 4, 1910, 377–383; *idem*, 'On an new genus of *Psyllidae* from Nyasaland', *Bulletin of Entomological Research*, 2, 1911, 85–104; *idem*, 'On some new species of African mosquitoes (*Culicidae*)', *ATMP*, 5, 1911, 233–244; *idem* & H F Carter, 'On a new genus of *Culicidae* from the Amazon region', ibid., 4, 1911, 553–556; *idem*, 'A new tsetse fly from British East Africa', ibid., 6, 1912, 129–130; J W W Stephens, 'A new malaria parasite of man', ibid., 8, 1914, 375–377.

[63] For the Jamaica Expedition of 1908 Alfred Lewis Jones defrayed the cost of local board and lodging; the Direct West African Mail Service Company provided free passages to and from the island, and Apollinaris Company gave 25 dozen bottles of mineral water.

[64] LRO 614 SOU 1/2, RSH Committee Minute Book 1892–1904, Foster to Glazebrook, 18 November 1898.

[65] H J Power, 'Keeping the Strains alive and more: Trypanosomiasis research at the LSTM's laboratory in Runcorn', paper given at the Oxford Wellcome Unit, 22 February 1996.

[66] TM/11/12.3, Notebook, Observations and experiments in Nyasaland, 17 March 1908 to 28 October 1908.

[67] TM/11/15, Six notebooks entitled 'Animal experiments'.

[68] These include various strains of human and veterinary parasites: *Piroplasma canis, T. gambiense, T. rhodesiense, T. percorum, T. brucei, T. dourine, T. vivax, T. equipendum, T. evansi, Spirocheates*. The parasites were maintained by repeated passage through laboratory animals.

[69] M W Service, 'A short history of early medical entomology', *Journal of Medical Entomology*, 14, 1978, 603–626.

[70] TM/14/NeR/15.1, Autobiographical notes supplied by Newstead to the Royal Society, together with a list of his publications; G Lloyd Morgan, The history of archaeology in Chester, Chapter 2, 'The Newstead Years (1886–1947)', monograph in preparation.

[71] TM/11/2.2, Circulation list for reprints.

[72] TM/14/ThW/12/2b; TM/11/2.1, Milne to Breinl, 22 November 1907.

[73] Three species of ticks were bred at Runcorn to carry the relapsing fever of mice, African tick fever of fowls and the piroplasms responsible for Redwater in cattle.

[74] TM/11/2.1, Breinl to Nierenstein, 3 December 1907.

[75] TM/11/16, Drawings of Trypanosomes.

[76] *12th Annual Report of the LSTM, 1910*, p. 16.

[77] LRO 614 SOU 12, Annual Reports of the Royal Southern Hospital, 1857–1897.

[78] LRO 614 INF 3/3, Minutes of the Medical Board of the LRI, 9 March 1899.

[79] LRO 614 SOU 12/16, 63rd Annual Report RSH for the year ending 31 December 1904. Edward Thompson gave £2,000 in memory of his father, £1,000 of which was used to furnish the Samuel Henry Thompson Ward. His brother had given the funds for the Thompson Yates Laboratories in the College.

[80] LRO 614 SOU 1/2, RSH Committee Minute Book 1892–1904, Adamson to Jones, 14 November 1898.

[81] LRO 614 SOU 1/2, RSH Committee Minute Book 1892–1904, General Committee, 9 July 1903.

[82] LRO 614 SOU 1/2, RSH Committee Minute Book 1892–1904, Adamson to Jones, 28 June 1900.

[83] LRO 614 SOU 1/2, RSH Committee Minute Book 1892–1904, General Committee, 2 February 1903.

[84] For examples of discord see LRO 614 SOU 1/2, RSH Committee Minute Book 1892–1904, General Committee, 5 February 1901.

[85] LRO 614 SOU 1/2, RSH Committee Minute Book 1892–1904, General Committee, 2 December 1912.

[86] LRO 614 SOU 1/3, RSH Committee Minute Book 1905–1916, General Committee/Medical Board, 10 April 1905.

[87] LRO 614 SOU 3/3, RSH Medical Board Minutes 1893–1899, 5 June 1899.

[88] LRO 614 SOU 1/2, RSH Committee Minute Book 1892–1904, General Committee, 4 March 1901.

[89] LRO 614 SOU 1/2, RSH Committee Minute Book 1892–1904, General Committee, 3 June 1901.

[90] This is defined by inclusion or omission of the diagnosis in Manson's *Tropical diseases*.

[91] LRO 614 SOU 1/3, RSH Committee Minute Book 1905–1916, Adamson to Jones, 13 July 1906.

[92] LRO 614 SOU 12/15, *60th Annual Report for the year ending 31 December 1901.*

[93] Dr James Milner Helme prepared his MD thesis on malaria using clinical material from the hospital.

[94] LRO 614 SOU 1/2, RSH Committee Minute Book 1892–1904, General Committee, 1 May 1899.

[95] LRO 614 SOU 1/2, RSH Committee Minute Book 1892–1904, Ross to Milne, 30 March 1900.

[96] LRO 614 SOU 1/2, RSH Committee Minute Book 1892–1904, Foster to Glazebrook, 18 November 1898.

[97] LRO 614 SOU 1/3, RSH LRO Committee Minute Book 1905–1916, Jones to Adamson, 20 March 1905.

[98] LRO 614 SOU 1/3, RSH Committee Minute Book 1905–1916, Jones to Carter, 29 March 1905.

[99] LRO 614 SOU 1/3, RSH Committee Minute Book 1905–1916, General Committee/Medical Board, 10 April 1905 (Emphasis in the original).

[100] Ibid.

[101] LRO 614 SOU 1/3, RSH Committee Minute Book 1905–16, General Committee, 2 July 1906.

[102] LRO 614 SOU 1/3, RSH Committee Minute Book 1905–1916, Jones to Adamson, 10 July 1906.

[103] LRO 614 SOU 1/3, RSH Committee Minute Book 1905–1916, General Committee, 6 January 1908.

[104] LRO 614 SOU 1/3, RSH Committee Minute Book 1905–1916, General Committee, 6 July 1908.

[105] LRO 614 SOU 1/3, RSH Committee Minute Book 1905–1916, General Committee, 3 July 1911.

[106] LRO 614 SOU 12/17, *68th Annual Report RSH for the year ending 31 December 1909.*

[107] LRO 614 SOU 1/3, RSH Committee Minute Book 1905–1916, General Committee, 3 October 1911.

[108] LRO 614 INF 2/14, Minute Book 1908–1917, 28 November 1912.

[109] LRO 614 SOU 1/3, RSH Committee Minute Book 1905–1916, General Committee, 4 February 1916.

[110] *17th Annual Report of the LSTM, 1915*, p. 3.

[111] Ibid.

[112] Stephens was elected to the chair of Tropical Medicine following Ross's resignation in 1912.

[113] *17th Annual Report of the LSTM, 1915*, p. 6.

[114] Mill Road Infirmary, 1st Western General (Fazakerley) and Highfield Military Hospitals.

[115] *17th Annual Report of the LSTM, 1915*, p. 6.

[116] H F Carter, D L Mackinnon, M A Matthews & A Malins Smith, 'The protozoal findings in 910 cases of dysentery examined at the LSTM from May to September 1916', *ATMP*, 10, 1916–1917, 411–426; *idem* & J W W Stephens, 'Protozoal investigation of cases of dysentery conducted at the LSTM, Second report', ibid., 11, 1917, 27–68; H F Carter & R J Matthews, 'The value of concentrating the cysts of protozoal parasites in examining the stools of dysenteric patients for pathogenic entamoebae', ibid., 195–204; J R Matthews & A Malins Smith, 'The intestinal protozoal infections among convalescent dysenterics examined at the LSTM, Third report', ibid., 13, 1919–1920, 83–90.

[117] W Yorke, H F Carter, D L Mackinnon, J R Matthews & A Malins Smith, 'Persons who have never been out of Great Britain as carriers of *E. histolytica*', *ATMP*, 11, 1917–1918, 87–90; J R Matthews & A Malins Smith, 'The spread and incidence of intestinal protozoal infections in the population of Great Britain. I Civilians in Liverpool Royal Infirmary. II Army Recruits', ibid., 12, 1918–1919, 349–360, *idem*, 'The spread and incidence of intestinal protozoal infections in the population of Great Britain. III Children', ibid., 361–370, *idem*, 'The spread and incidence of protozoal infections in the population of Great Britain. IV Asylum patients. V University & school cadets', ibid., 13, 1919–1920, 91–94.

[118] J W W Stephens & D L Mackinnon, 'A preliminary statement on the treatment of *E. histolytica* infections by Alcresta Ipecac', *ATMP*, 10, 1916–1917, 397–410.

[119] J R Matthews, 'Observations on the cysts of the common intestinal protozoa of man', *ATMP*, 12, 1918–1919, 17–26; *idem*, 'A mensurative study of the cysts of *E. coli*', ibid., 259–272; A Malins Smith, 'A contribution to the question of the number of races in the species *E. histolytica*', ibid., 13, 1919–1920, 1–16.

[120] A Malins Smith & J R Matthews, 'The intestinal protozoa of non-dysenteric cases', *ATMP*, 10, 1916–1917, 361–390; *idem*, 'Further records of the occurrence of intestinal protozoa in non-dysenteric cases', ibid., 11, 1917, 183–194; H F Carter, 'Remarks on the *spirocheates* occurring in the faeces of dysenteric patients', ibid., 10, 1916–1917, 391–396; J R Matthews, 'The course and duration of an infection with *E. coli*', ibid., 13, 1919–1920, 17–22.

[121] TM/14/DaF/81.3b.

[122] Ross was appointed Lt-Col in 1913 and Consulting Physician for tropical diseases to the Base Hospitals for Indian Troops in England in 1914.

[123] TM/14/DaF/81.1, Ross to Milne, 19 September 1917.

[124] See J W W Stephens et al., *ATMP*, 11, 1917–1918, to *ATMP*, 14, 1920–1921, & *idem*, 'Studies in the treatment of malaria XXXII: Summary of studies I – XXXI', ibid., 17, 1923, 303–316.

# 2

# SIERRA LEONE: THE PERMANENT RESEARCH EXPEDITION

## INTRODUCTION

The Treaty of Versailles ushered in a new era in which Britain no longer dominated the international economy. The older staple exports were not competitive and the new industries could not sufficiently replace the lost markets. Invisible earnings that had made the City of London the financial capital of the world also declined. In the 1920s, Britain still relied on trade for twenty-five per cent of its GNP. In an increasingly competitive and shrinking market freight rates fell. In the 1930s, following the depression, contraction in the world economy meant there was less desire to move goods around the world. The role of the colonial territories and their economic development remained important albeit contested issues throughout the years of the depression. In 1932, an empire-trading bloc with protective tariffs replaced free trade in an attempt to stimulate the British economy and enlarge the sterling area. Although this was focused on the white Dominions of Canada, Australia, New Zealand and South Africa, it included the tropical colonies. Any political decisions aimed at the promotion of international commerce and colonial development were of major consequence to Liverpool, the shipping firms that controlled the local economy, and the financial fortunes of the School of Tropical Medicine.

As part of the general spirit of optimism after the Armistice and the brief economic boom that lasted until May 1920, the School rejuvenated its overseas links.[1] The LSTM reopened in new purpose-built laboratories in Pembroke Place. Before the war the School had been counting the cost of continually sending research expeditions overseas and had planned to rationalise this by a new policy of supporting periods of extended research in permanent research stations in the tropics. As the expeditions characterised overseas work in the pre-war period, the overseas research laboratory characterised this work in the inter-war years.

Legislation aimed at managing the British economy and developing the colonial territories affected the School as did the changing perceptions of the discipline of tropical medicine in the inter-war period. The rate of accumulation of basic biological knowledge declined. There was a growing realisation that application of scientific facts offered neither cheap nor easy solutions to the health problems in the tropics created by poverty.[2] A range of other problems representing a potential increase in the scope of the discipline joined the parasite-vector model.[3] Malnutrition among the general population of a tropical colony was not the concern of the hard-pressed commercial community in Liverpool. As a member of staff commented,

> In the early days...there was a pressing need on the part of shipowners and trading firms to reduce, if possible, the high death rate of their employees in the tropics. For this purpose, funds were obtained without much difficulty. In a few years, however, the rapid discoveries of medical science had reduced this death rate to reasonable figures. There was not thereafter the same imperative necessity for providing funds for tropical medicine research.[4]

In the post-war era, the School needed to find new sources of funding if it was to survive. It was only partially successful in this goal. As a progressive institution with a reputation for original research, it also needed to stay abreast of developments in tropical medicine and in medical science more generally. The energy of Warrington Yorke and his interest in tropical chemotherapy is representative of this spirit and is considered in the next chapter. Here, the focus is the laboratory established in Sierra Leone which, while representing many of the traditional activities of the School, also experimented with fresh approaches to the discipline.

## OVERSEAS RESEARCH IN THE INTER-WAR PERIOD

Chapter 1 reviewed discussions about initial differences between the Schools in London and Liverpool. In the inter-war period, there are substantial differences in the intellectual direction of the two institutions. The involvement of Rockefeller money in expanding the public health activities of the London School and hence in changing its exclusive focus on the tropics was crucial. There was no equivalent for Liverpool either intellectually or financially. Where London expanded into public health work at home, Liverpool committed itself to the tropics though the establishment of two permanent laboratories in Manáos, Brazil and Freetown, Sierra Leone.

These laboratories replaced the succession of research expeditions in the pre-war years. They provided similar general benefits. First, they ensured a supply of parasitological and entomological specimens. Second, they gave staff experience in tropical conditions and enabled them to teach on this basis.[5] The General and Professional Committees at the School supported the laboratories because of their perceived prestige.[6] Nevertheless, the laboratories drained the financial resources of the LSTM as the expeditions had done. In the 1930s when recruitment into tropical medicine was difficult, keeping even a minimal staff in the Freetown laboratory threatened the quality of work at home. The 'fiasco' at Manáos determined the relationship between home and overseas laboratories.[7]

A prolonged connection with Latin America dates from 1905 when a temporary laboratory opened as part of the fifteenth expedition. Harold Wolferstan Thomas led the expedition and he remained in Manáos after the other members of the team returned home. Thomas came back to Liverpool briefly on two occasions in 1909 and 1914 but in effect from 1905, he became absorbed in his work in Latin America. In 1914, the Booth Steamship Company offered £750 for three years to pay for the salaries of three assistants. The outbreak of war postponed these plans. In 1919, the laboratory changed its title from the Yellow Fever Research Laboratory to the Manáos Research Laboratory and implemented Booth's offer.

A circular advertising the three posts invited applications from 'young medical graduates, unmarried, for appointment to the research staff of the Manáos Lab'.[8] The successful candidates obtained the DTM and undertook preliminary research in Liverpool before sailing for Brazil. The starting salary was £300 per annum rising to £400. In addition the School provided 'furnished quarters, mess and laundry...a first-class passage, £10 travelling expenses both ways' and £75.00 for the 'necessary tropical outfit'.[9] The advertisement did not specify the gender of the applicants, but the School appointed men. Dr C J Young worked there from July 1920 to July 1921, Dr Burnie from February 1920 to July 1920 and Rupert Montgomery Gordon (Tim) from December 1920 to March 1922. A Dr Hore also worked under the auspices of the laboratory during Gordon's tenure.

The Manáos Research Laboratory had a chequered existence. It served as the 'main research base' for 'the expeditions up the various rivers of the Amazon State'.[10] A wealthy American couple, Dr and Mrs Rice gave the Laboratory a motor launch, but it was not used because of intractable difficulties with the customs service.[11] This was a common problem and Thomas used the arrival of new members of staff to 'smuggle' equipment past the authorities.[12] The research positions were tenable for a period of three years, terminable by either party on three months notice after the first twelve months. Young and Gordon managed to last the twelve months, but Burnie left to join a private company after only six months. Obviously none of these individuals shared the commitment to Brazil that

Thomas did or perhaps they did not feel a commitment to him. He remained as the only European member of staff after 1922 when Gordon returned to Britain.

The School could not control the general running or the scientific programme in Manáos because Thomas failed to communicate with them and followed his own interests. He was particularly concerned with the health problems of the local people and trained the medical practitioners in the diagnosis and pathology of tropical diseases. An insistence that his European staff learn to speak Portuguese as soon as possible illustrated this commitment,

> I have fixed you [Gordon] up at the Pensão Senna...There is an English lady and her husband staying there, but all the rest are Brazilians so that you should be able to pick up the language. This is the most essential factor if you are going to get along in Brazil.[13]

Gordon quietly ignored Thomas' demands over the language and moved from the Pensão Senna to live with other Europeans as soon as he could. The headed notepaper from Thomas' lab carried the ship and eye of the LSTM but was otherwise in Portuguese. The local medical community appears to have revered Thomas, mourning his passing and the subsequent closure of the laboratory in 1931. A plaque marks the laboratory building and an elegant tombstone his grave.

In one of the frequent letters to his family in Ireland, Gordon described Thomas as 'a big fat man who drives his body round with an extraordinarily active mind. A very hard worker, he confines himself to his own work and lets us labour in what direction we like. Often the day passes without our speaking to him.'[14] Gordon apparently worked in isolation, 'I'm jogging along in the dark at mosquito work...one's hope is to keep piling together little scraps of information and then sit juggling them round in the hope that some day they may suddenly slide into the position'.[15] He published eight papers based on his thirteen months work in the Amazon, four of which were concerned with the *Stegomyia calopus* (*Aedes aegypti*) mosquito.[16] He also performed some pathological investigations on man and animals.[17] The *ATMP* published his papers. It was a contractual obligation that the research staff in Brazil submitted their work to the in-house journal. The papers indicated the broad direction of much of Gordon's later work and his particular interest in the host-parasite-vector complex.[18] By contrast, Thomas had not published anything since he left Liverpool in 1905.

Thomas successfully integrated himself with the local medical community. Relations were much more difficult for the staff in Freetown who had to deal with members of the West African Medical Service and the native doctors from Sierra Leone. There was no equivalent of the WAMS in Brazil and Thomas' relationship mirrored the informal empire in Latin America. He became the pathologist at the

Santa Casa Hospital, a private institution for employees of the European firms. He also offered a free pathology service for the state medical authorities.[19]

Thomas was deeply concerned with health of the indigenous people, particularly those impoverished by the fall in the price of rubber. This was not the concern of the LSTM and communication between the School and Thomas ceased. The School paid his salary but sent no further assistants. Thomas continued his work until he died. The situation in Sierra Leone was different.

## SIERRA LEONE

In 1787, a group of philanthropists established the Colony of Sierra Leone to provide a home for various groups of ex-slaves. The Crown assumed control of the Colony in 1808. After the abolition of the slave trade, significant numbers of liberated Africans increased the population of the major settlement at Freetown. Freetown offered the finest harbour on the West African coast. Ships traded directly with this part of the world or took on supplies before reaching India and Malaysia via the Cape of Good Hope, the Pacific via Cape Horn or the ports of Brazil and Argentina. The traders of Liverpool dominated these routes.[20] Palm oil and palm kernels replaced the cargoes of slaves from West Africa. The British gradually annexed the Coastal lands of Sierra Leone from 1861 to 1881 to protect this 'legitimate' trade. In 1896 annexation of the hinterland warded off aggressive French expansion, although Sierra Leone and The Gambia became isolated British enclaves in otherwise French territory.

The Colony was a peninsula of high-forested mountains some eight degrees north of the Equator and extending twenty-four miles long by ten miles wide into the Atlantic. It was connected to the mainland by a strip of land four miles wide along which ran the only road into the Protectorate: an area of 27,925 square miles. In 1895, work started on a railway that terminated near the border with Liberia in the east. This linked the peasant farmers with the harbour at Freetown and the international markets. However, the Colony and Protectorate were too small for 'optimum economic development'.[21]

The British viewed the inhabitants of the Colony in a special light. Through education and conversion to Christianity the Creole people of Sierra Leone and their descendants were to be 'beacons attracting indigenous Africans from the darkness of superstition and slavery'.[22] The Colony offered facilities for higher education, although additional university education in Britain still supplemented degrees from Fourah Bay College. Doctors, lawyers, churchmen, newspaper editors, and higher-ranking civil servants formed an upper class in Freetown society. In addition, the traders and commercial people encouraged their children to enter the professions. Local people copied the habits and dress of the ex-patriot community and read popular literature from Europe in a conscious emulation of European lifestyles.[23]

Ross's visit to Freetown to look for anopheline mosquitoes in July 1899 was the first contact between the Colony and the School. Ross returned two years later in June 1901 to promote his sanitary measures. He returned for a third time the following year in February 1902. Dr Matthew Logan Taylor continued his work in October after a visit to the Gold Coast. Some eight years passed before Sir Rubert Boyce visited again on behalf of the School.

Leo Spitzer argues Ross's hunt for the malaria carrying mosquito coincided with hardening racial attitudes across the empire and was used as justification for segregation of the 'susceptible' whites and the more 'robust' Creoles on health grounds.[24] The white community built Hill Station in 1904 at an initial cost of £46,000 for the bungalows and water supply. The advent of segregation and the creation of residential boundaries designated the Creoles as second-class citizens despite their acculturation. The construction of Hill Station turned the medicine they aspired to practice against the Creole people.

Discrimination also applied within Government Services such as the Colonial Civil and Medical Services.[25] A committee established to inquire into the formation of a single medical service for British West Africa recommended the exclusion of non-Europeans from this service. Hereafter they could gain employment only as Native Medical Officers on a lower scale of pay and subordinate to the most junior WAMS officer whatever their qualifications or experience.[26] In the inter-war years the Creole people, excluded from European society in Freetown and educated by watching Europe destroy itself in World War I, began to identify with the indigenous inhabitants of the Protectorate. They looked inwards to the continent of Africa instead of outwards to the removed and racist Europe that they had previously emulated. In response to political agitation, the Colonial Government took more interest in the 'up-country' inhabitants, their economic development and welfare.

## THE ALFRED LEWIS JONES RESEARCH LABORATORY

Jones' will contained three substantial bequests for the School. First, he financed the new laboratories in Pembroke Place. Second, he financed the new Tropical Ward at the LRI. Third, he gave £10,000 as capital to establish a laboratory in Sierra Leone. This bequest concentrated the overseas work in one location. The money allowed for the construction of a laboratory and housing for the staff. It did not provide an endowment for salaries, a library, material for research or publications. The home institution paid for these consumables. The laboratory in Freetown therefore affected strategic decisions at home as well as overseas, although it was some years before this was fully appreciated by those running the School in Liverpool.

Yorke and Blacklock had selected a site of one and a half acres near the military barracks on Tower Hill on their visit to Sierra Leone in 1914. The School leased the land from the WO at a peppercorn rent in June 1920 and appointed architects immediately afterwards. It was with a renewed vigour that Blacklock returned to Sierra Leone in 1921 to oversee the construction of the Alfred Lewis Jones Research Laboratory, by Messrs H E B Greene of Liverpool, Colonial Contractors and Constructional Engineers.[27] They completed the building work in October 1921. Blacklock's staff began work early in 1922.

The main laboratory, sixty feet in length, was north facing, and had the advantage of a projecting kiosk that admitted light from three sides. The laboratory fittings were recycled from the decommissioned clinical laboratory at the RSH. Behind the laboratory were two smaller rooms used for storage and as a dark-room. A walkway connected the two-storey kitchen and pantry with the main building. In the grounds, there was a separate animal house thirty feet by fifty feet. Above the laboratory were living quarters for the resident research staff. Designed in its own grounds and removed from contact with the native people of Freetown, the laboratory provided a self-contained enclave for laboratory research in the hills above Freetown. The building epitomised academic tropical medicine in this period.

The Professional Sub-committee decided that a complement of three fully qualified Europeans was the minimum required for efficient functioning of the laboratory and an acceptable cycle of overseas tours and home-leave. The School appointed Blacklock as the first Director. Before the war, he had led the research laboratories in Runcorn. The appointment in Sierra Leone represented a promotion as it carried with it a University chair in the Tropical Diseases of Africa. The advertisement for staff for Sierra Leone was similar to the advertisement for Manáos.[28] Female applicants were ineligible 'owing to the difficulty of accommodation in Freetown'.[29] However, there was no stipulation over the length of the appointment or notice periods and a contract of employment followed only after some difficulties with staff.[30] This indicates a lack of policy for the work of the laboratory.

Saul Adler and Edward J Clark joined Blacklock in West Africa. Following Clark's resignation in November 1922, Dr Philip A Maplestone became Assistant Director. In 1924, Maplestone and Adler resigned and George MacDonald and Gordon arrived as replacements. Gordon became Assistant Director. After his resignation from the Manáos laboratory and return to Britain, Gordon had served as House Physician at the Tropical Ward in the LRI and clinical pathologist for the School.

The team of Blacklock, Gordon and MacDonald remained together until 1929 when Blacklock returned to Liverpool to become the Walter Myers Professor of Parasitology. Gordon succeeded him as Director and professor of Tropical Diseases of Africa. MacDonald also left in 1929 to continue his career in malariology in India. His research in Sierra Leone earned him a University of Liverpool MD in 1932.[31] In his place came Thomas Herbert Davey, initially appointed as a research assistant, he became Assistant Director to Gordon in 1934. Gordon and Davey formed the backbone of the staff during the latter half of the 1930s. Davey became the third and final Director, succeeding Gordon in 1938, after he returned home to become professor of Entomology. By the time of Davey's appointment, the University was looking to curtail the number of chairs. Yorke managed to persuade the Standing Committee on Chairs that Davey was worthy of the title. Davey wrote to Yorke: 'I quite understand that the University may wish to sink the Professorship of Tropical Diseases of Africa and do not really mind about the title so long as I can go on working here.'[32] This stoic attitude characterised the permanent staff of laboratory.

Among the temporary staff, the same level of dedication was less evident. These men worked and lived together as part of a small European community in Freetown. Davey wrote to Yorke that Arthur Judson Walker or 'Johnnie' as he became affectionately known 'is a man of somewhat unbalanced temperament and a difficult man to work or live with'.[33] Walker remained on the staff of the laboratory until its closure. Joseph Fine was unable to redeem himself: 'the crux of the matter is his effect on our relations with the Government medical and other officials...Dr Fine is not an asset to the general working of the laboratory'.[34] His actions outside the laboratory caused consternation, crossing the boundaries of acceptable European behaviour. During a stay in hospital two Creole women visited Fine. Blacklock reported that his 'quarters were in such a condition that we were quite ashamed of them and the sterilisation of the mattress was only one of the necessities'.[35] He lasted only one tour.

The School found it difficult to find replacements. Service overseas in any form was unpopular in the inter-war period, and tropical medicine as a discipline found it difficult to recruit suitable candidates who were willing to live abroad and had a potential for research. Advertisements in the medical press for new assistants yielded a poor response. Among the limited number of applicants, the School found few they considered worth employing and tried direct methods. They poached Geoffrey Richard Walker, who held a DTM from the School, from a Booth's ship sailing to Pará. He became the first of two Leverhulme Research Fellows in 1934. Davey and Gordon spent part of their home-leave in Ireland visiting medical schools in hope of finding interested young researchers.

The weak financial position of the laboratory made it difficult to retain current staff,

As you know any one with an ounce of intelligence could do much better financially than he [Gordon] can do in this post and given the bad climate and conditions of life generally there is nothing to attract an experienced man except the title of professor and the prospect of getting home to a university life again.[36]

In 1929, in response to a letter from Blacklock arguing for an increase in the size of the laboratory, Yorke advocated the opposite, 'our policy at the present should be consolidation and not expansion...there are very urgent needs in connection with this place'.[37] The uncertainty of the early 1930s hardened Yorke's attitude. In his opinion, the West African governments must increase their support: 'conditions of service must be made to enable us to obtain the right sort of young men. If we cannot obtain the financial support necessary for this, then I think we had better close'.[38]

Initially, 'two illiterate creoles' aided the European staff who lamented the lack of white laboratory assistants and the standards of native staff.[39] By 1930, the number of native assistants had risen to four.[40] Davey expressed his concern that the amount of routine pathology made it essential that the current cadre of reliable assistants be offered an incentive in terms of pay and career prospects otherwise they would be lost.[41] He referred to an assistant named Cole, who after sixteen years of service was still on a salary of £7.00 per month. A salary review and contributory Provident Fund followed.

## AIMS OF THE LABORATORY

Despite the heavy additional burden created by the Freetown laboratory, the School initially planned on a grand scale after the war. A list of 'Suggestions for the development of medical research in West Africa' written in 1923 began with the ambitious statement: 'The Liverpool School of Tropical Medicine has adopted the policy of establishing branch laboratories in the tropical countries. In so far as West Africa is concerned the first branch has been established at Freetown in Sierra Leone.' The gap between rhetoric and reality became apparent lower down the page where item number seven called for 'The endowment on a satisfactory basis of the existing posts – one director, one assistant director and one assistant.'[42]

The period of time between Jones' death in 1907 and the completion of the laboratory in 1921, ensured that in real terms the money was worth much less than when originally given. In addition '...the School is very hard up at the present time and the Finance Committee is putting on the screw all round...it [is] absolutely impossible to raise money at the present time'.[43] The situation did not improve sufficiently to relieve the staff in Liverpool and Freetown of the burden of raising extra money to keep the laboratory open. The majority of the outside funding came from the Government of Sierra Leone in return for a pathology service, but other British colonies in West Africa were persuaded to make contributions at various times. Negotiations to find this money were time-consuming and often infuriating. They involved the Colonial Governments and the CO. Yorke demonstrated little patience with bureaucrats. Officials at the CO particularly tested his patience.

Financial stringency led to under staffing. This compromised the ideal of three European staff on a rota and contributed to several breakdowns in health.[44] Davey in particular seems to have suffered as a consequence of overwork. After suffering from typhus in 1936, he spent time convalescing at home in Ireland. Members of the LSTM staff who had not seen him for some years were shocked at his appearance.[45] The intransigence of the CO to find assistance for him following the outbreak of World War II and assumption of all pathology for the Colony led for a further breakdown in Davey's health. This prompted closure of the laboratory. Although unpleasant for the individuals, the financial difficulties bring sharply into focus many of the issues in inter-war colonial medicine.

There was no policy for the function of the Freetown laboratory. The title of Blacklock's chair provided a reasonable indication of the general interests of the laboratory. Two weeks after Blacklock sailed for Freetown, Yorke wrote to Ronald Miller of Miller Brothers of Liverpool, a member of the West African Trade Association and the General Committee.[46] Miller complained that Sierra Leone was a poor choice for a research laboratory. Unaware of the precise terms of Jones' bequest he considered Nigeria or the Gold Coast offered better facilities for research and pleasanter working conditions. The School considered it appropriate that it consolidate the relationship with Sierra Leone. The shipowners in Liverpool had carried goods from Freetown for many years. Mary Kingsley, in her travelogues, made frequent references to Freetown, the United Africa Company and Unilever had interests in various West African countries.[47]

Miller also asked what the goals of the laboratory were. This request and the nature of Yorke's answer make it quite clear that the Committee had not discussed these matters. He informed Miller, that the laboratory permitted 'continuous work over a period of years'. This was a contrast with expeditions of limited duration, and reinforces the argument that the laboratory institutionalised the functions of the expeditions. The potential areas of research read like an overview of tropical medicine at this time. The laboratory would concentrate on the prevalence and distribution of the parasitic diseases and biting or blood-sucking insects. Work on measures to reduce the prevalence of these diseases by the 'application of prophylactic measures' followed the basic science. These must be 'economically feasible' and included 'curative measures'. He mentioned possible work on the effects of the West African climate on Europeans and the nature of epidemics among domestic stock. Yorke also indicated there was some potential for involvement with the Medical Department through routine pathology and clinical examinations. Wherever the School went pathology skills appear to have been in demand, though members of staff were not unanimous in their desire to undertake such work.

## GOVERNMENT PATHOLOGY

The most constant source of additional income for the laboratory came from the pathology service offered to the Sierra Leone Government. When the laboratory opened in 1921 the Medical Department was without a full-time pathologist. A Native Medical Officer, Edward Awunor Renner, worked part-time as a pathologist in addition to his general duties as MO. Despite his holding the DTM and DTH from Liverpool in addition to the MB ChB of Edinburgh University, the Medical Department quickly accepted the assistance offered by the Freetown laboratory. The laboratory offered its services to earn money and to appear co-operative. In most colonial territories, the pathology service was poor and the staff from Liverpool therefore represented considerable expertise. Discussions at the CO and the Tropical Medical Research Committee in 1937 reiterated the need to have 'something better than clinicians'.[48]

Early in 1923 negotiations commenced with Dr W I Taylor, Principle MO, with a view to the laboratory providing some support for routine pathology and a specialist service. Previously the Colonial Government had paid £800.00 a year to the Yaba Laboratory in Nigeria.[49] Under an agreement made on 14 April 1923, the Government of Sierra Leone agreed to pay this sum to the Alfred Lewis Jones Research Laboratory from 1 January 1924.[50] In addition to easing the finances of the laboratory, this arrangement also gave access to clinical material. Blacklock requested ten beds.[51] As School staff could not engage in private practice this was important. The Medical Department 'granted permission to examine cases in the town' and offered help when travelling in the Protectorate.[52]

This agreement also curtailed Renner's opportunities to develop his skills as a pathologist. Now he was subordinate not only to the colour bar of the WAMS, but also the private laboratory of the LSTM. In 1928, the Colonial Government appointed a full-time pathologist in addition to Renner. This considerably reduced the amount of routine pathology the laboratory was required to undertake and came at an opportune moment. Gordon was preparing to develop the metazoan immunity project and Blacklock embarking on a survey of the diseases of the Protectorate.[53] Retrenchment soon followed this fleeting moment of expansion. In 1930, the Medical Department reduced its establishment, cutting the posts of the full-time pathologist and two other MOs. This triggered a fresh set of negotiations between the laboratory and the Colonial Government.

Gordon, as Director, proposed a scheme whereby the Government would pay for the refitting of the 'Main Hospital' on Mount Aureol. This proposal guaranteed more bench space and relieved the housing problems for laboratory staff, which was a further drain on its limited resources. This would become the new Sir Alfred Lewis Jones Research Laboratory. In return, Government would assume ownership of the existing building. The Colonial Government would increase their grant to £2,300 per annum. In return, the new laboratory would perform all the routine pathology of the Colony as well as the special investigations. The Director would have the title of Consulting Pathologist to the Sierra Leone Government. Employment of an extra fully qualified member of staff would assist with meeting the increased workload. The new title of Consulting Pathologist ensured Renner's continued subordination. As assistant he would continue to 'do all the pure routine examination of faeces and blood films etc', but although in Government employment he would work under a non-Government doctor who would perform 'all the work beyond his scope'.[54]

In principle, the School and the Medical Department of Sierra Leone accepted the scheme although neither could resource the transfer to Mount Aureol and the additional recurrent budget. The Sierra Leone Government applied on behalf of both parties to the Colonial Development Fund created under the Colonial Development Act of July 1929.[55] Progress was slow, with protracted communication between the laboratory, the School, the CO and the Colonial Government. Yorke reminded Gordon in a private letter of 20 January 1931 that 'the financial position of the country and of all our Colonies seems to be appalling'. He cautioned that the only possible course for the School and by default the laboratory was 'to endeavour to live as nearly as possible within our means'. He warned Gordon that it might prove 'foolish at the present moment to change the laboratory to Mount Aureol'.[56]

Yorke's pessimism was well founded. A letter from the CO dated 11 September 1931 informed the School that after due consideration the Colonial Development Advisory Committee considered the

> Laboratory has been carrying out useful work in the field of medical research and is under competent direction... [but]the assistance desired would appear to provide for no new service, but would be in the nature of a subsidy for maintaining an existing organisation. As development and not maintenance, is the main object of the Colonial Development Act, such assistance should, in the Committee's view be obtained from sources other than the Colonial Development Fund.[57]

Havinden and Meredith interpret the CDA of 1929 as a means of increasing Britain's industrial output though extra markets and not as a boost for welfare provision in the colonies.[58] In this context, an application to support the pathology service of Sierra Leone must have appeared an absurd anachronism.

The School had no option but to reduce the European staff to the Director and one assistant. The question of who would perform the Colony's pathology remained unsolved. Yorke wrote to Gordon and urged him to undertake the increase in routine, 'I feel that if the Sierra Leone Laboratory is to be continued, you will have to be prepared for the next few years to subordinate research to routine clinical pathology.'[59]

In Freetown, the Colonial Secretary, C E Cookson, expressed his views on Government's role in research:

> The craze for Research, as a purely Government undertaking is a modern contraption and a most expensive one. Vast sums could be saved by cutting it out of all colonial expenditure and subsidising private Research laboratories...there are always enthusiasts who would willingly give service for comparatively small remuneration, why not accept it, as Government cannot afford to pay everyone full value for everything done.[60]

While his polemic might appear repugnant, Cookson's views struck a chord with the laboratory, the Governor and the Medical Department. Discussion of various cheaper schemes continued.[61] A quick resolution to these deliberations became necessary after the opening of a new session of the Legislative Council on 14 November 1932. The Governor, Sir Arnold Hodson, read a statement drafted for him by Cookson, and which had not been agreed beforehand with McDouall, 'It is hoped in the near future such arrangements will be made that this well-equipped, up-to-date and efficient laboratory will undertake our Pathological work, thus ensuring a considerable saving to Government.'[62]

On 29 November 1932 the Governor, McDouall and Gordon discussed the situation. Rather than concede the rash nature of his statement Hodson offered an increase in the grant to the laboratory enabling an extra member of staff to be appointed. However, in a letter of 29 March 1933, Hodson informed Gordon that the Colony had decided to appoint Renner as pathologist after he completed a period of study in 1934. He continued that this would not affect the subsidy paid by Government to the laboratory. If there were no adverse financial implications in this, there were certainly some personal ones. It was a complicated situation whereby the official Government pathologist, who happened to be a native, was subordinate to unofficial Europeans in a private laboratory.[63] Davey was most uncomfortable about working with Renner and derogatory about his abilities.[64] His attitude created friction between himself and Renner, and between the laboratory and the Medical Department. Gordon and Yorke were concerned to stop this behaviour.[65] The existing grant from the Colony appeared to be the only possible means of keeping the laboratory open.

In a final attempt to secure a degree of security the School approached the CO and Sierra Leone Government and asked them to regard it as an official government institution. They were successful. In a letter of 19 July 1934 the Under Secretary of State for the Colonies indicated his intention to 'invite the Governor formally to recognise Professor Gordon as Consulting Pathologist to the Government of Sierra Leone' and approve an increase in their contribution from £800 to £1,200 per annum. This brought an additional grant of £750 for three years from the capital of the West African Yellow Fever Commission fund.

The financial situation improved but the laboratory had become more of an adjunct to the Medical Department than a research laboratory. A small grant from the Leverhulme Trust and Yorke's judicious deployment of staff funded by the MRC mitigated the increase in routine work but research dwindled. With the outbreak of World War II, research ended. The laboratory took over all pathological work for the Colony. Renner became a Senior Medical Officer, the first such post held by an African. The RAMC shared bench space while their laboratory was equipped. The needs of the national emergency overtook public and private interests. Davey's health broke down again in 1940 and the School took the only sensible course of action: the laboratory closed in September 1941. Davey returned to Liverpool and 'Johnnie' Walker took a job with the Firestone Company in Monrovia.


## DIVERSE RESEARCH ACTIVITIES

It is easy to trace the extent and direction of the pathology. Regular reports to Government list the range and quantity of work.[66] It is more difficult to impose order on the research output of the laboratory. With no clear objectives, evaluation of the success of the laboratory is problematic. The regular reports from Freetown to Liverpool divided the activities of the laboratory into two categories: routine and scientific.[67] 'Routine' referred to the pathology work and epidemiological studies requested by the Government.

Under the heading 'scientific' were the self-directed investigations of the staff and certain special requests from the Colonial Government. In 1923, they were concerned about the incidence of relapsing fever. WAMS officers sent blood slides to the laboratory for analysis. In the same year, also in response to a request from the Medical Department, Blacklock investigated schistosomiasis in Kaiyima, a village in the District of Konne in the South Eastern Territories. He received free railway passes and a travel grant for trekking expenses. Sanitary improvements over a number of years apparently led to a significant reduction in the incidence of this disease in Kaiyima and an interest from neighbouring villages in obtaining advice and assistance.[68] Fieldwork of this sort brought the laboratory staff into contact with 'up-country' members of the WAMS that would have been difficult otherwise.[69] Because of the initial survey, schistosomiasis became a subject to which various members of staff returned periodically, at the behest of Government or as the result of a personal interest. This was a pattern repeated with other investigations.

Besides the permanent staff, several groups of people contributed to the work of laboratory. There was a steady flow of visitors. Heading the list of mere observers was the Prince of Wales who came as part of his official tour in April 1925.[70] Governors of other West Coast Colonies were entertained on several occasions, as were officials from the CO. Members of the local branch of the BMA twice held their meeting at the laboratory in 1924 and 1926. Various international health bodies included the laboratory in their itinerary even if this was just on a social level. In May 1926, The League of Nations Health Commission for West Africa visited while on tour.[71] In May 1931 Drs James Y Brown and Marshall Albert Barber of the Rockefeller Yellow Fever Research Institute in Nigeria were guests at Freetown for several weeks and joined members of staff on a mosquito survey.[72] Staff of the London School used the laboratory for a few weeks.[73] Naturally, staff from Liverpool would stay at the laboratory when in West Africa for any reason.

Temporarily, experts worked with the permanent staff. In 1925 Alwen Myfanwy Evans, assistant lecturer in entomology since 1918, spent three months undertaking a survey of the mosquitoes in Freetown. In Liverpool, she identified insects beyond the scope of the staff in Sierra Leone. Dr Marion Watson joined the Metazoan Immunity Project because of her specialist bacteriological and serological knowledge. She arrived in Freetown in November 1928 with excellent references having just completed a course of study at the London School with W W C Topley. These were the only women employed by the laboratory, although Dr Mary Blacklock, Blacklock's wife, conducted research into the health of women and children in Freetown while her husband was Director of the laboratory.

D H Davis, introduced by G M Findlay of the Wellcome laboratories in Euston Road, worked at the laboratory on an external grant.[74] Davis, a zoologist, was keen to do fieldwork in Africa. He secured a grant from the Tropical Diseases Research Fund of the Royal Society with Yorke's help to undertake research into the bionomics of the rat population in Freetown.[75] The laboratory staff had to clear Davis's research with the DMSS in Freetown. While not actively obstructive the authorities regarded this as a waste of time. Freetown had not experienced outbreaks of plague and thus rats posed no specific threat. The laboratory was aware that Duncan, the acting DMSS, resented 'any incursion of "outsiders", including ourselves [Freetown laboratory staff] into health matters'.[76] Fortunately at this time Davey and Gordon reported their discovery of typhus (X190 and X20 types) in West Africa, citing the domestic rat, *Rattus rattus*, as the a reservoir for the X190 strain.[77] The insect vector remained to be found and this gave Davis's proposed research greater validity.[78] Gordon and Davey persuaded the relevant authorities to allow the survey to go ahead and they provided some assistance with local labour for trapping.[79] Although the School could offer him nothing after the Royal Society's two-year grant expired, Davis was fortunate to get a job in South Africa on the strength of his West African research.[80] Hankins has considered research at the laboratory under the chronological succession of Directors.[81] This is an accurate narrative and raises several interesting questions about the direction of research. Here the work of the laboratory is categorised under three headings: chance observations, surveys and projects. These are not mutually exclusive categories. In many cases, the surveys yielded results that became the basis for a specific project. Others reflect existing interests of the staff predating their work in Sierra Leone. With this framework, the effect of local conditions on the laboratory, how it functioned, and how it contributed to determining the parameters of tropical medicine in the inter-war period can be determined.


## CHANCE OBSERVATIONS

The earlier discussion on the aims of the laboratory highlighted the undirected nature of the research. If this is linked with the requirement to act as consultants for the government a situation is created where there is plenty of opportunity to 'discover' new knowledge, but not necessarily any intellectual framework or incentive to exploit the discovery.

As part of his initial work in setting up the laboratory, Blacklock stocked the animal houses with a range of laboratory animals. Guinea pigs, rats and mice came from England. Other larger animals, particularly primates, came from dealers in Africa. This was considerably cheaper than importing these animals into Liverpool. On treks into the interior it was possible to shoot wild game to ascertain additional hosts for various diseases.

One of the first cohort of chimpanzees had malaria parasites in its blood morphologically indistinguishable from those causing *falciparum* malaria in man.[82] Blacklock tried infection of human volunteers by direct blood transmission and by anopheline mosquitoes. These experiments were not successful and the sudden death of the animal delayed further work. A post-mortem revealed that the cause of death had been due to 'invasion of the lungs by larvae of a nematode worm of the genus *Strongyloides*'.[83] The damage caused by these larvae in the lungs was poorly understood and Blacklock thought it worth recording.

He ordered limited further investigations into the malaria question. Adler went up country to obtain animals to determine if the parasites could be differentiated from human ones. He concluded that the parasites were indistinguishable. He also found the older animals to be asymptomatic. This was similar to the human picture as found among natives in West Africa.[84] There was no further work. Adler left the laboratory in January 1924 to take up a post at the Hebrew University in Jerusalem.

The parasite-vector model in tropical medicine ensured that there was always an interest in species of biting insects. For two weeks in July of 1924, Blacklock worked in the Protectorate collecting specimens. In 1925, he spent two months in the Konno district evaluating recommendations made on his previous visit to combat schistosomiasis. During this tour, he became aware of the incidence of onchocerciasis among the villagers recognisable by characteristic nodules under the skin. His attention was also drawn to the complaints of biting insects that he identified as belonging to the genus *Simulium*. Perhaps stimulated by his survey from the previous year, he dissected a number of specimens and designed a series of feeding experiments to determine if *Simulium damnosum* was the vector of this disease. This work could not progress until a technique was developed to keep the flies alive long enough for complete development of the parasite to take place under laboratory conditions. However, he was confident enough to send in preliminary results for publication in the *ATMP*.[85] He went on to demonstrate the complete life cycle and made a presentation to the 1926 meeting of the local branch of the BMA.[86] Thereafter Blacklock appears to have done no further work on this subject. It was a theme to which the School returned after World War II, in Kumba in the Cameroons.

## SURVEYS

The number of Government requests for surveys indicated reliable statistics of disease in West Africa were poor. The Government surveys fall into the following categories summarising the work involved: general enquiries into disease or vector incidence; survey of settlements or areas for development; surveys connected with programmes of disease control. The testing of new drugs against schistosomiasis and sleeping sickness used the existing therapies as a control.[87]

Surveys of the health status of particular locations tended to be self-contained. Staff visited the site, recorded the incidence of existing diseases, advised on potential health hazards and submitted their report to the relevant authorities. Publication of the reports followed in some instances.[88] Others became the basis for further research such as the inspection of school children in 1924. Detection of an infection rate of one hundred per cent for malaria stimulated research on various aspects of clinical malaria in Freetown with particular reference to children and pregnant women. Such extended work reinforced the value of a constant presence in the tropics.

In 1924, Blacklock surveyed the military camp at Daru, the headquarters of the West African Frontier Force. He spent eleven days on tour in September. Comments in the *Annual Health and Sanitary Reports* had previously described the health problems of the camp, at least of the European officials, as malarial rather than dysenteric. Blacklock therefore concentrated on the 'discovery of *Anopheline* breeding places and secondarily to evolving methods by which the breeding places could be eradicated or controlled'.[89] He paid some attention to standards of general sanitation between the anti-malarial work.

In the absence of sufficient money to drain or fill in the swamps, Blacklock recommended a series of measures to reduce the breeding places. The native troops could act as labour force for improving the health status of the barracks and surrounding area. He commented 'A native soldier in the tropics should be as familiar with the bionomics of mosquitoes and other insects as are his Officers.'[90] A soldier who had received the relevant training could serve as a 'mosquito hunter' on a weekly rota. It would be his responsibility to find breeding places and mark them enabling appropriate action to be taken. Blacklock emphasised the value of the education and its primacy in this context:

> Each individual will become imbued with ideas which will render him an extremely useful ally in the campaign against insect-borne disease. The more clearly native troops in tropical countries grasp the essential elements of hygiene, the more efficient they will become as a fighting force...It is not a policy which could be carried out successfully in any casual community, but the community at Daru is not a casual one but a highly specialised one.[91]

His recommendations had an additional advantage: 'on leaving the service [these men would] act as a leaven among the mass of the population'.[92] Blacklock's advice on educating the native soldier indicates the laboratory staff were aware of wider implications of their work, but that the outlet for this was apparently extremely limited.

Surveys of a similar nature were carried out for the Government at the oil palm plantation at Mabang in 1928, for the United Africa Company in connection with a proposed mining camp at Marampa in 1930 and for the Sierra Leone Development Company at Sahrmarank and Pepel in 1931.[93] In February 1938, at the request of the DMS, a survey of the mosquitoes in the Protectorate began.[94] It continued during 1939 and was the only research to survive the outbreak of the war. This was indicative of a grudging awareness on the part of the Colonial Government that they could not ignore the welfare of the Protectorate people. With the closure of the laboratory, the School staff never capitalised on this demanding exercise and it is doubtful if the Medical Department made use of the unpublished data.

In 1935, Sir Arthur Richards, Governor of The Gambia, asked the CO for a loan to finance a land reclamation project at Bathurst. He asked the LSTM if their staff would be interested in contributing as advisers. Richards informed Yorke that he had 'the greatest respect for scientific investigators and the value of their work'. He cautioned that in order to achieve anything involving the CO 'One has to do good by stealth and to overlay the work for posterity with a little practical if sordid amelioration of the lot of the present generation.'[95] Yorke and Gordon visited The Gambia in 1936 and, with the engineers, restructured the project. This increased the cost considerably. In response, the CO transferred Richards to Fiji avoiding the increased costs of the scheme. The new Governor of The Gambia, Sir Thomas Southorn, did not share his predecessor's commitment to the project and shelved the plans.[96]

This survey is significant for two reasons. First, Yorke planned to close down the Freetown laboratory and transfer all activities to The Gambia.[97] The work at Bathurst would provide an excellent basis for the new Department of Tropical Hygiene.[98] The survey required the presence of a full-time research staff in the tropics. The potential of The Gambia, under Richards, for a field station for his interests in chemotherapy attracted Yorke. If the scheme had been successful, it would have focused the overseas work of the School in these directions.

Second, the request for the survey indicated a wider appreciation of the expertise of the School in colonial West Africa. Despite the failure of the Bathurst plans the reputation of the laboratory increased. The Yaba Medical Research Institute in Lagos, Nigeria hosted the West African Medical Conference in November 1938. On the agenda was the foundation of a West African Government Research Laboratory. William P H Lightbody, the DMSS for Sierra Leone, proposed that the laboratory of the School become the official centre for medical research in West Africa. Rather than being solely responsible to the School, a local committee would have direct reference to the Tropical Medicine Research Committee of the MRC. However, the link with the LSTM, a metropolitan institution, added kudos to the Freetown laboratory. The outbreak of war disrupted these proposals. Davey chaired the West African Research Committee consisting of the senior members of the laboratory services of Nigeria, the Gold Coast and the Director the of Freetown laboratory, but there were no other developments.[99] These initiatives indicated an awareness of a need to plan and co-ordinate, broadening the scope of tropical medicine. Such a formal and integrated policy would bring the School out of its private isolation and into direct involvement in government research projects.

## PROJECTS

In a number of instances, chance observations and the surveys stimulated research in the laboratory and the field. Why some results dictated the direction of the laboratory and not others is difficult to determine. Hankins raises the important issue of why the School's laboratory should have devoted so much time to the metazoan immunity project, a veterinary problem, in favour of human diseases acknowledged as immediate and pressing public health problems. The paucity of parasite immunology also makes this an interesting project. Early research at Runcorn had involved attempts to understand the immunology of the host-parasite relationship. After World War II, when immunology became increasingly important, the School ignored this approach until much later.

The metazoan immunity project investigated the reaction of the host animal to the larva of the 'Tumbu fly', *Cordylobia anthropophaga*.[100] Larvae penetrate the skin to continue development for approximately ten days. This produces lesions resembling boils. In humans, this was a painful and potentially disfiguring infection. In cattle it significantly reduced the value of cattle hides and diminished milk production because of their unrest and agitation. In West Africa, the export of hides was an important part of the economy.[101] This provided an obvious incentive and demonstrated an awareness of the need for economic development in the colonies. However, these issues only explain in part the interest of the laboratory in initiating the project and seeking additional outside funding to the virtual exclusion of other work.

The metazoan immunity project was preceded by a paper by Dr and Mrs Blacklock describing the life history of the Tumbu fly and by two jointly authored papers on the subject by Blacklock and Gordon.[102] These publications described the experimental immunisation of animals in Sierra Leone against the larvae of the Tumbu fly.[103] Further work indicated that the nature of the immunity was quite different from the process understood to occur in bacterial immunity, and this project therefore had the potential to contribute to understanding the basic science of infection and immunity.

Blacklock and Gordon defined metazoan immunity as an acquired immunity following a previous infection or vaccination and involving the death of the parasite in the host within a specified time. This was distinct from reports of metazoan tolerance. Here the host could harbour an increasing parasite load without a corresponding increase in, or even a diminution of, perceptible adverse effects. Immunity against the toxic effects of the parasites occurred without the host destroying the parasite.

At first, they assumed that the observed immunity affected the whole body of the animal. This was not borne out by further experimental work. Blacklock and Gordon reported a failure to obtain any evidence of the production of a general immunity. Injection of whole blood from immune to non-immune animals failed to transfer the passive immunity. A series of standard tests to demonstrate the presence of antibodies in immune serum also gave negative results.[104] Further experimental work corroborated the emerging evidence that antibodies in the general circulation were playing 'no easily recognisable part in this form of immunity'.[105] This involved the intraperitoneal and subcutaneous injection of an emulsion of third instar larvae (after the second moulting) without conferring any degree of immunity. Despite the apparent lack of involvement of antibodies in the circulating blood, immune animals did prevent the development of larvae. 'Out of fifty larvae put on an area of skin on an immune guinea pig, not a single larva developed. Of fifty similarly applied to an identical area of skin on a non-immune guinea-pig, thirty developed normally.'[106]

Blacklock and Gordon concluded that the immunity must be 'at first localised to the site of larval development'. The simple use of a different skin area for repeat experiments provided confirmation. The researchers had been in the habit of using the same area of shaved skin merely as a matter of convenience. Transferring the experimental site on the same animal allowed larvae to develop at least partially. Frequent movement of the experimental site tended to produce animals that were generally immune. This raised important questions about the mechanism of immunity, and its mode of development in the tissues as opposed to the blood. These issues had recently begun to attract the attention of some bacteriologists.[107]

Blacklock and Gordon considered there were two main lines for further investigation. Although expressed in general terms, they fall into the categories of basic and applied research. The metazoan immunity project was to tackle the 'general nature and laws governing metazoan immunity' in the tropics where a trained research staff could utilise the abundance of human and animal metazoan infections. The effects of metazoan parasites such as the larvae of the Tumbu fly were negligible, but other metazoa were more significant for human health: filariasis, schistosomiasis and ankylostomiasis were established areas of interest for the Freetown staff.[108] The project would also attempt to develop 'skin dressings, or inoculations, with larvae or larval extracts' as a commercial means of inducing artificial immunity for the cattle trade. Large cattle farms made this part of the work more feasible in Britain than Freetown.[109]

The link with the economy of the tanning industry was obvious. This work also represented a different intellectual direction for the staff of the laboratory and the discipline of tropical medicine. An immunological approach to infectious diseases had largely focused on viruses and bacteria. Only a few laboratories in Britain, with a focus on larger parasites, including the Horton hospital attached to the LSHTM, had adopted immunology as a research methodology.[110]

There were several advantages to using larvae of the Tumbu fly. As an experimental model, they were useful because they could be 'kept under observation for the entire period of their parasitic life, which is spent in the skin and subcutaneous tissue'.[111] Moreover, where funding for tropical medicine research had become increasingly scarce, money for development of the tropical economies via the Empire Marketing Board was an untapped source that the laboratory exploited. In 1926, the Imperial Economic Committee established the EMB to promote the consumption of raw materials and foodstuffs produced in the empire. The increased purchasing power of the colonies would stimulate British exports, improve manufacturing output and reduce unemployment at home. Contemporary research showed empire produce was of an 'inferior quality in relation to price'.[112] Hence, the EMB's interest in supporting work that promised to improve the quality of hides for the leather industry. Naturally the applied research was attractive to the EMB, but the laboratory staff drafted their application in such a way that the grant could be spent on basic research overseas.

On 4 April 1927, Gordon visited Sir William Clark, Comptroller of the Department of Overseas Trade in London following an introduction from Sir Ransford Slater, Governor of Sierra Leone. Clark stated that 'within the past fortnight there had been a delegation to the Department of Overseas Trade from various trades and firms interested in hides, asking that an effort should be made to deal with the warble pest'.[113] The warble fly caused the same kind of damage as the Tumbu fly. The recently formed 'Warble Committee' had so far not proven useful, and the work of Blacklock and Gordon appeared promising and opportune. The only difficulty appeared to be the view that money would be forthcoming for work in England rather than supporting overseas research. Although the United Tanners Federation and the British Leather Manufacturers Research Association were interested in sponsoring the project, their initial reaction was to spend money only within Britain. The academic support from Professor Carpenter, Keeper of the Manchester Museum, the acknowledged expert on Warble fly, and Walter Fletcher of the MRC seems to have convinced the EMB that the West African work was worthy of support.

The EMB informed the School that they were prepared to offer £9,000 over a three-year period on the understanding that the School would dedicate an equal sum to metazoan immunity research in Sierra Leone. This financial support would allow 'the opportunity for continuous work', which the laboratory staff had been increasingly denied by the burgeoning demands of the Sierra Leone Government.[114] This represented the first well-funded laboratory based research project the Freetown staff had undertaken. The EMB requested that the School provide details of proposed expenditure and their reply highlights the priorities for equipping the project.[115]

The largest sum provided for additional staff at a cost of £1,500 per annum. This included two qualified members of staff, one unqualified European assistant and two additional native assistants. Of the qualified Europeans, one was to be a biochemist. This was a new departure for the staff of the laboratory and the School. After a tour in West Africa, the biochemist would work in the superior laboratories at Liverpool for the remainder of the time.[116] Experimental animals such as chimpanzees, rabbits, guinea pigs and their maintenance would cost £200 per annum. Over the three years it was estimated that expenditure on animal houses, laboratory apparatus and library requirements would reach £1,200.

The staff intended to develop a research programme on metazoan immunity, but the request for support from the EMB was also part of the perennial problem of financing the future of the laboratory. In the interval between making the application to the EMB on 23 May and the letter informing the School of their success in August, Blacklock agreed to undertake a health survey of the Protectorate. The laboratory could not afford to lose the support of the Colonial Government. The survey would involve periods away from Freetown. Blacklock intended to shorten his trekking time and undertake general supervision of the project that would now be under the immediate control of Gordon. In return, Gordon would be the principal author of any publications. Blacklock considered that the EMB

> cannot expect more: after all the money is put up for extending and continuing research – and that will be done. They would never expect that all work in this laboratory should be set aside in order to concentrate on one object and it would be fatal to encourage the idea that we are prepared to do this.[117]

The use of the EMB money for 'continuing and extending' the existence of the laboratory stretched the point. After three years, the results of the research programme were mediocre and the School had defaulted on providing the counterpart funding. The EMB needed some persuasion to supply the final instalments of their grant.[118] It was not renewed.

Lack of funds was not entirely responsible for the poor results. A series of misfortunes delayed the research programme. Epidemics among the experimental animals repeatedly hampered progress, 'Another epidemic has broken out amongst our stock of guinea-pigs and resulted in about forty deaths during the past month. In consequence the Metazoan Immunity investigations which had just reached an interesting stage, [have] been very much hampered.'[119] The problem lay with the supplier in England. Destruction of the remaining stock of animals, disinfection of the animal houses and restocking after a period was the only solution.[120] Fresh supplies of imported animals came from the MRC laboratories.[121] These proved much healthier and permitted some continuity of research. By this time, the grant had nearly expired. Reluctantly the laboratory relinquished the expert services of Marion Watson. This left two European staff in Freetown. In 1927, on leave in Britain, Gordon had spent some time at the Lister Institute 'picking up some useful knowledge...or at any rate...acquiring some idea of what an appallingly vast subject immunology is'.[122] Without specialist help the programme of research into parasite immunology could not continue. The traditional research bias of the tropical expert, concerned with a natural history approach to life cycles and the application of such knowledge through sanitary measures, could not support the newer biomedical sciences. The final report of the project remained unpublished and the laboratory returned to an increased workload of routine pathology.[123]

## CONCLUSION

The Alfred Lewis Jones Laboratory in Sierra Leone continued the close relationship between the School and the West Coast of Africa. It was the final tribute to Jones, whose bequest had funded the construction of the laboratory. It confirmed the expanded model of laboratory research developed in the expedition era. This arrangement was more transparent than the research policy of the laboratory. The School was unclear about its precise function in 1921 while the laboratory was under construction. Financial difficulties constantly hampered the work of the laboratory. In these circumstances, it proved impossible to develop a coherent policy for research. Nevertheless, it reinforced the importance of sustained contact with the tropics and the value of this to the tropical medicine practised from Liverpool. The more obvious differences with the LSHTM in this period indicated a potential for divergence in the definition of the discipline.

The laboratory brings into focus the relationship between a private institution and a colonial government.[124] The weak financial position of the laboratory tended to give the Government the upper hand in negotiations over the amount and type of consultancy work undertaken. If it had been adequately endowed the staff would not have taken on routine pathology to the same extent. The same applies to some of the survey work. This was of more interest to the staff but was ill-timed in some instances. A greater interest in tropical hygiene and the development of programmes of public health may well have occupied Blacklock and Davey if circumstances had permitted. In comparison with Thomas in Manáos, the staff at Freetown remained at a distance from the general health conditions of the Colony and Protectorate, because this was quite clearly the provenance of the WAMS. The difficulties lay not only with the Colonial Government in Sierra Leone but also with the CO in Whitehall. It was a four-way relationship between local and metropolitan colonial authorities and local and metropolitan tropical science. By the late 1930s, the barriers had largely broken down.[125] The moves to involve the laboratory officially in Government medical policies in the late 1930s would have broadened the scope of the School. Where the commercial companies had once sought to influence research in Liverpool, in Freetown the Colonial Government increasingly gave an external focus to the work.

The immunological investigations are significant despite their failure to produce any tangible results. The laboratory was innovative in approaching parasitic infections from the immunological standpoint. The research promised to contribute to a fundamental level of understanding moving the discipline of tropical medicine beyond its tendency to concentrate on natural history. The use of immunology as a methodology is unusual for this period in tropical medicine. It is representative of tentative forays into mainstream twentieth-century medicine discussed in the following chapter. The employment of the biochemist in Freetown predated a similar appointment at home.

It was the only externally funded basic research project run at Freetown. On a practical level, the Warble fly continued to cost leather-producing countries considerable sums.[126] It was thus a failure for the EMB, and their policies to stimulate the British economy. The School had a strong commitment to veterinary parasitology and used this lateral connection to good effect. A successful research proposal for this kind of organisation shows the potential broad focus of the discipline of tropical medicine.

Thomas' disassociation from the LSTM and the failure of the metazoan immunity project highlighted the inherent difficulties in running overseas laboratories, they were far from home when things went wrong. Moreover, the provision of essential facilities such as a library duplicated resources. In human and financial terms, the overseas laboratory drained the home institution. In the pre-war era, the constraints on activities were evenly distributed because there were no clear priorities. While the Freetown laboratory continued without a clear direction, in Liverpool, Yorke imposed a clearer agenda on his own department and the public face of the School. The ramifications of this prioritising of activities affected the School and increasingly the fortunes of the overseas laboratory.

The plans connected with The Gambia illustrated Yorke's interests. He was prepared to break the historic links with Sierra Leone to further his work in chemotherapy. Blacklock and Gordon supported this move because of the potential for tropical hygiene, otherwise a weak department. For the principle of maintaining an overseas laboratory Yorke would not impoverish the LSTM, leave departments understaffed, and threaten the potential for his own research. The laboratory in Sierra Leone represented an older version of the School, relatively undirected and buffeted by fortune. The opportunities for School staff to develop the application of tropical medicine were too limited and research too difficult to maintain in the prevailing circumstances. Tropical medicine as practised from Liverpool in the inter-war period was concerned with finding a clear direction for the future. The overseas research laboratory was not part of that future.

## NOTES

[1] J Lawrence, 'The First World War and its aftermath', P Johnson (ed), *20th century Britain: economic, social and cultural change*, London: Longman, 1994, pp. 151–168.

[2] On the difficulties of applying the findings of tropical research see W F Bynum, 'An experiment that failed: malaria control at Mian Mir', W F Bynum & B Fantini (eds), *Malaria and ecosytems: historical aspects, Parassitologia*, 36, 1994, 107–120.

[3] On increasing the boundaries of the discipline see M Worboys, 'The discovery of colonial malnutrition between the wars', D Arnold (ed), *Imperial medicine and indigenous societies*, Manchester: MUP, 1988, pp. 208–225.

[4] TM/14/BlD/2, D B Blacklock, Laboratories of the Liverpool School in the Tropics.

[5] TM/13/60/5/1, Yorke to Blacklock, 28 June 1926; TM/13/61/5/2, Yorke to Blacklock, 27 February 1928; TM/13/61/18/2, Yorke to Blacklock, 26 November 1928; TM/13/76/27, Gordon to Davey, 24 November 1937.

[6] TM/14/GoR/124, Report of visit of John Burdon Sanderson to Brazil with comments on the work of the School's laboratory in Manáos.

[7] TM/13/59/17/2, Yorke to Blacklock, 2 February 1922.

[8] TM/14/GoR/6.1.

[9] Ibid.

[10] Ibid.

[11] TM/12/20.

[12] TM/14/GoR/8.1.

[13] TM/14/GoR/8.2, Thomas to Gordon, 11 December 1920.

[14] TM/14/GoR/9.4a.

[15] Ibid.

[16] R M Gordon & C J Young, 'The feeding habits of *Stegomyia calopus*, Moigen', *ATMP*, 15, 1921, 265–268; R M Gordon, 'The susceptibility of the individual to the bites of *Stegomyia calopus'*, ibid., 16, 1922, 229–234; *idem* & A M Evans, 'Mosquitoes collected in the Manáos region of the Amazon', ibid., 315–338; R M Gordon, 'Notes on the bionomics of *Stegomyia calopus*, Moigen, in Brazil, Part II', ibid., 425–439.

[17] R M Gordon, 'Ancylostomes recorded from 67 post-mortems performed in Amazonas', *ATMP*, 16, 1922, 223–228; *idem*, 'The occurrence of ancylostomes resembling *Necator americanus* amongst domestic pigs in Amazonas', ibid., 295–296; *idem* & C J Young, 'Parasites in dogs and cats in Amazonas', ibid., 297–300; *idem*, 'A further note on the occurrence of ancylostomes resembling *Necator americanus* amongst domestic pigs in Amazonas', ibid., 17, 1923, 289–298.

[18] TM/14/GoR/114.26.

[19] J Procopio, 'Harold Wolferstan Thomas: Cientista canadense a servicia da medicina no Amazonas' *Revista Brasiliera de Medicina*, 10, 1953, 371–373.

[20] C W Brown, 'Historical notes on Freetown Harbour', *Sierra Leone Studies*, 20, 1936, 96–122.

[21] M Havinden & D Meredith, *Colonialism and development: Britain and its tropical colonies 1850–1960*, London: Routledge, 1993, p. 70.

[22] L Spitzer, *The creoles of Sierra Leone: responses to colonialism, 1870–1945*, Madison: University of Wisconsin Press, 1974, p. 14.

[23] Ibid., p. 15.

[24] *Idem*, 'The mosquito and segregation in Sierra Leone', *Canadian Journal of African Studies*, 2, 1968, 49–61.

[25] T S Gale, 'Official medical policy in British West Africa, 1870–1930', PhD thesis, University of London, 1973.

[26] M C F Easmon, 'Sierra Leone doctors', *Sierra Leone Studies*, 6 (n.s.), 1956, 81–86.

[27] TM/13/3.

[28] TM/13/151.

[29] TM/13/59/11/1.

[30] TM/13/42.

[31] G MacDonald, 'Malaria in the children of Freetown, Sierra Leone and five other papers', MD thesis, University of Liverpool, 1932.

[32] TM/13/77/37, Davey to Yorke, 6 April 1938.

[33] TM/13/76/10, Davey to Yorke, 26 September 1937.

[34] TM/13/62/15/2, Blacklock to Yorke, 2 June 1929.

[35] Ibid.

[36] TM/13/62/11/1, Blacklock to Yorke, 4 April 1929.

[37] TM/13/62/24/3, Yorke to Blacklock, 12 August 1929.

[38] TM/13/70/4/2, Yorke to Gordon, 26 January 1937.

[39] TM/13/56/33, Suggestions for the development of medical research in West Africa.

[40] TM/13/63/23/3, Gordon, Proposed transference of Sir Alfred Lewis Jones laboratory from Tower Hill to Mount Aureol and the taking over by them of the work at present performed by the Government pathologists.

[41] TM/13/76/31/3, Davey to Gordon, 12 December 1937.

[42] TM/13/56/33, Suggestions for the development of medical research in West Africa.

[43] TM/13/59/17/1, Yorke to Blacklock, 2 February 1922.

[44] TM/13/68/15; TM/13/70/29/3; TM/13/76/1/9.

[45] TM/13/69/17, Adams to Gordon, 2 December 1936.

[46] TM/13/59/7/5, Yorke to Miller, 12 May 1920.

[47] M Kingsley, *Travels in West Africa: Congo Français, Corisco and Cameroons*, London: Macmillan, 1897; F Pedler, *The lion and the unicorn in Africa: a history of the origins of the United Africa Company, 1787–1931*, London: Heinemann, 1974; D K Fieldhouse, *Unilever overseas: the anatomy of a multinational, 1895–1965*, London: Croom Helm, 1978.

[48] TM/13/70/4/2, Yorke to Gordon, 26 January 1937.

[49] TM/13/56/8/1, Blacklock to Danson, 7 December 1923.

[50] TM/13/1, Report for the period 1 December 1922 to 30 April 1923. The laboratory was expected to 1. act as consultants in cases of difficulty arising in the course of routine laboratory examination; 2. identify flies, worms and other

zoological specimens of medical importance or interest; 3. undertake or assist in
medico-legal investigations in cases of particular difficulty or when suitable
apparatus is not at the disposal of the Medical Department; 4. examine and
report on pathological material other than routine blood, sputum, faecal and
urine specimens.

[51] TM/13/56/8/1, Blacklock to Danson, 7 February 1923.

[52] TM/13/63/23/3, Gordon, Proposed transference of Sir Alfred Lewis Jones
Laboratory.

[53] TM/13/60/17, Blacklock to Yorke, 28 March 1927.

[54] TM/13/65/20/3, Gordon to Blacklock, 31 December 1932.

[55] TM/13/64/1–10.

[56] TM/13/63/27/2, Yorke to Gordon, 19 November 1930.

[57] TM/13/64/8/1, Fiddian (CO) to Yorke, 11 September 1931.

[58] Havinden & Meredith, *Colonialism and development*, pp. 140–148.

[59] TM/13/64/9/3, Yorke to Gordon, 17 September 1931.

[60] TM/13/65/20/9, C E Cookson, memorandum on medical research, 9
November 1932.

[61] TM/13/65/20/12, Report of a meeting of the Governor, Gordon and DMSS.

[62] TM/13/65/20/5, Annual address delivered by His Excellency the Governor,
Sir Arnold Hodson KCMG, opening of the Sierra Leone Legislative Council,
Session 1932–1933.

[63] TM/13/72/4/2, Gordon to Davey, 26 September 1934.

[64] TM/13/67/17/1, Gordon to Yorke, 19 September 1934; TM/13/126/9/3,
Davey to Gordon, 5 December 1935.

[65] TM/13/67/18/1, Yorke to Gordon, 20 September 1934.

[66] TM/13/1–2, Half-yearly reports from the Director of the Laboratory to the
LSTM; TM/13/104/12, Pathological records, 1935–1941.

[67] TM/13/1–2, Half-yearly reports.

[68] D B Blacklock, 'Report of an investigation into the prevalence and
transmission of human schistosomiasis in Sierra Leone', *Annual Report of the
Medical Department of Sierra Leone*, 1923.

[69] TM/13/1–2, Half-yearly report from the Director of the Laboratory to the
LSTM, 1 November 1923 to 30 April 1924.

[70] TM/13/11P.

[71] TM/13/60/3/1, Blacklock to Yorke, 12 May 1926.

[72] TM/13/38X.

[73] Ibid.

[74] TM/13/131/1/2.

[75] TM/13/54, Proposed investigation into the ecology of rats and other rodents in
relation to the incidence and spread of plague in West Africa.

[76] TM/13/54, Gordon to Yorke, 16 July 1935.

[77] TM/13/70/8/2, Gordon to Yorke, 10 February 1937.

[78] TM/13/54, Yorke to Henry Dale, 12 October 1935.

[79] TM/13/67/7/1, Interim report on a rat survey of Freetown from the Sir Alfred
Lewis Jones Research Laboratory, 1 March 1936.

[80] TM/13/54, Yorke to Davis, 10 July 1937; Davis to Yorke, 3 October 1937.

[81] R Hankins, 'Medical science in a colonial context: the work of the Sir Alfred Lewis Jones Research Laboratory, Freetown, Sierra Leone, 1922 to 1940', MSc thesis, University of Manchester, 1985.

[82] S Adler, 'Malaria in a chimpanzee in Sierra Leone', *ATMP*, 17, 1923, 13–18; D B Blacklock & S Adler, 'A malaria parasite of the chimpanzee', ibid., 18, 1924, 1–2.

[83] TM/13/1, Report of the Sir Alfred Lewis Jones Tropical Research Laboratory, Freetown, Sierra Leone for the period ending 31 May 1922.

[84] TM/13/56/7, Blacklock to Yorke, 20 September 1922.

[85] D B Blacklock, 'The development of *Onchocerca volvulus*, in *Simulium damnosum*', *ATMP*, 20, 1926, 1–48.

[86] D B Blacklock, 'The further development of *Onchocerca volvulus* (Leuckart) (1892) in *Simulium damnosum* Theo', *ATMP*, 20, 1926, 203–218.

[87] TM/13/35, Report on a sleeping sickness survey of the eastern border of Sierra Leone; TM/13/58/3; TM/13/58/16; TM/13/81/16.

[88] D B Blacklock, 'Report on the effects of bush clearance in reducing *G. palpalis* in the Cape Lighthouse Peninsula', *Annual Report of the Medical Department of Sierra Leone*, 1923; *idem* & A M Evans, 'Breeding places of Anopheline mosquitoes in and around Freetown, Sierra Leone', *ATMP*, 20, 1926, 59–84; R M Gordon, E P Hicks, T H Davey & M Watson, 'A study of the house-hunting culicidae occurring in Freetown, Sierra Leone and of the part played by them in the transmission of certain tropical diseases, together with observation of the relationship of anophelines to housing and the effects of anti-larval measures in Freetown', ibid., 26, 1932, 273–345.

[89] TM/13/144, D B Blacklock, Report of the Military Cantonment, West African Frontier Force Headquarters, Daru, Sierra Leone.

[90] Ibid., p. 17.

[91] Ibid., p. 18.

[92] Ibid., p. 30.

[93] TM/13/95; TM/13/86.

[94] TM/13/104/6/7.

[95] TM/13/126/13/1, A F Richards to Yorke, 20 December 1935.

[96] TM/13/130/23, Yorke to A F Richards, 2 October 1936.

[97] TM/13/126/27, Yorke to Gordon, 4 February 1936; TM/13/130/13/1, Council, Special Meeting, 10 February 1936.

[98] TM/13/126/29/2, Memorandum on the future policy of the School with special reference to the Sir Alfred Lewis Jones Laboratory and The Gambia scheme.

[99] TM/13/57/15/2, Davey to Yorke, 20 March 1940; TM/13/83/20 Davey to Yorke, 12 April 1940.

[100] Metazoa, parasitic worms and the larvae of certain flies. The larvae cause myiasis, an infestation of living tissue by maggots, amongst man and domestic stock.

[101] A G Adebayo, 'The production and export of hides and skins in colonial northern Nigeria, 1900–1945', *Journal of African History*, 33, 1992, 273–300.

[102] D B Blacklock & M G Thompson, 'A study of the Tumbu fly *Cordylobia anthropophaga* Grunberg in Sierra Leone', *ATMP*, 1923, 17, 444–501.

[103] D B Blacklock & R M Gordon, 'The experimental production of immunity against metazoan parasites and an investigation of its nature', *ATMP*, 21, 1927, 181–224 & *Lancet*, i, 1927, 923–925.

[104] TM/13/12/12/9, 'Complement fixation and precipitation tests were negative; the whole blood and serum of immune animals possessed not larvicidal properties *in vitro*; whole blood defibrinated, and active and inactivated serum of immune animals were neither lethal to larvae living in contact with them for several days, nor did their influence prevent the development of such larvae in a normal manner when subsequently placed on non-immune animals'.

[105] TM/13/12/12/9.

[106] Ibid.

[107] A Besredka, *Local immunization: specific dressings*, London, 1927.

[108] TM/13/12/1/12.

[109] TM/13/12/12/9.

[110] See R Hankins, 'Between tropical disease and veterinary medicine: the development of immunological studies of parasitism 1900–1970', PhD thesis, University of Manchester, 1998, pp. 81–172.

[111] TM/13/12/12/9, Memorandum for the Imperial Agricultural Research Conference: 'The experimental production of immunity against metazoan parasites and an investigation of its nature', 1927.

[112] Havinden & Meredith, *Colonialism and development*, p. 150.

[113] TM/13/12/1/2.

[114] TM/13/12/2, Blacklock to Gordon, 1 March 1927.

[115] TM/13/12/24/2.

[116] TM/13/12/50, Blacklock to Gordon, 25 May 1927.

[117] TM/13/12/50.

[118] TM/13/12/14.

[119] TM/13/63/6/2, Gordon to Yorke, 5 March 1930.

[120] TM/13/63/17, Gordon to Yorke, 15 July 1930.

[121] TM/13/63/32/2, Gordon to Topley, 5 December 1930.

[122] TM/13/12/29, Gordon to Yorke, 25 September 1927.

[123] TM/13/138/1.

[124] H Bell, 'Medical research and medical practice in the Anglo-Egyptian Sudan' DPhil thesis, University of Oxford, 1996.

[125] TM/13/84/5/1, Yorke to Blacklock, 12 December 1940; TM/13/85/3/1, Davey to Yorke, 27 February 1941.

[126] TM/14/GoR/124, *Irish Times*, 6 July 1929, 'The Warble fly ravages: £200,000 loss to Irish cattle exporters'.

# 3

# DRUGS FOR THE TROPICS

## INTRODUCTION

The LSTM re-opened on 24 July 1920 in new premises on Pembroke Place. The new building visibly reinforced its position as one of the premier institutions for the study, research and treatment of tropical diseases. The School had established a reputation for promoting improvements in health in the tropical colonies through teaching and research work. The overseas interest, beginning with the expeditions, extended in the inter-war period to permanent laboratories in Brazil and West Africa. In different ways, the laboratories affected medical practice in the informal and formal empire but neither could provide a comprehensive health service to the local population.

Organised independence movements in South Africa, Egypt and India directly challenged the principle of colonialism. Increasingly nationalists and reformers questioned the validity of the medicine practised in Britain's colonial regimes. The new international health agencies employed a different ideology from the CO and Colonial Governments.[1] They began to raise questions about the methodology, scope and aims of colonial medicine. After World War II, the School had to respond to these developments. In the inter-war years, the changes were subtle. New directions related to developments in medical science and the funding of research in British medicine.

This chapter concentrates on the development of drugs against tropical diseases, an area of work within the LSTM that was innovative and added considerably to the national and international reputation of the School. At Runcorn, staff of the School investigated the chemotherapy of parasitic infections. This work did not receive a priority within the School. For instance, it did not receive significant amounts of dedicated funding, nor were special facilities established. It was not recognised nationally as a specialist centre, although scientists in Europe held the laboratory in esteem. World War I provided opportunities to establish a reputation. By the start of World War II,

79

the School had achieved recognition for its work. Chemotherapy became the priority research field at the LSTM by the end of the war.


## THE 'NEW' SCHOOL AND ITS TROPICAL MEDICINE

From the outside, the School enjoyed an impressive if rather lop-sided appearance. Before the outbreak of war: only half of the architects' original plans were complete.[2] The sandstone and brick building was four storeys high. Iron railings and gates provided a secure frontage. Inside the building was light and airy, a central skylight bringing daylight to all the floors including the ground level.

Students and staff benefited from the enhanced features included in the new School. On the second floor, a teaching laboratory (sixty-nine feet by fifty-eight feet), with an adjoining preparation room, provided individual bench space for DTM students. The lecture theatre on the ground floor seated seventy students. The roof space housed a post-mortem room, insectarium, mosquito-proof house and additional preparation rooms for the maintenance of parasite strains by passage through animals and the breeding of vectors. This brought together in one site the facilities previously divided between Runcorn and Liverpool. Skilled laboratory technicians Frank Swain and A E Goodrich provided a valuable service looking after the raw materials of teaching and research besides their other multifarious contributions to the smooth running of the new School.

Several new features indicated the LSTM's maturity, self-sufficiency and international reputation. Miss Dorothy Allmand now had charge of a proper library facility based on the original subject catalogue of Drawz. A valuable journal exchange system traded copies of the *ATMP* for a range of British and overseas publications. Over one hundred current medical journals were available along with an extensive reprint and monograph collection. Gifts from staff and others around the world regularly enlarged the collection. On the clinical side, the Tropical Ward at the LRI was once more restricted to special cases as the need for general accommodation abated. In 1926, new private wards paid for by the Chairman of Council, Sir Francis Danson, supplemented accommodation in the open ward. The private beds replaced the teaching laboratory attached to the main ward. Laboratory work and teaching were now centralised within the Pembroke Place building.

The specimen collection previously stored in a sectioned off part of the laboratory was re-configured as a permanent teaching museum. Charts, diagrams and models augmented the original display. Miss Maude Brown, assistant in the Department of Entomology, made large-scale wax models of arthropod vectors and was responsible for photographic work and other illustrations. In the basement, the School provided her with microphotography facilities and a dark-room. Newstead (1926–1929) and Dr Mary Blacklock (1932–1945) acted as curators for short periods. Both added to the value of the museum displays according to their own particular interests.

The allocation of space within the building reflected the organisation of tropical medicine at the LSTM. The School was divided into Departments of Tropical Medicine, Parasitology and Entomology. These were initially under Professors Stephens, Yorke and Newstead, holders of the respective chairs in these fields.[3] Each department had dedicated laboratories and the use of additional research rooms on the second and third floors. The Departments of Entomology and Parasitology had sufficient space to maintain their own library collections. The Department of Parasitology was not restricted to human diseases. Research in veterinary parasitology occupied the staff, often with outside funding. The School also gave lectures and demonstrations to the University's MRCVS and BVSc students.

The creation of departments in the School effectively dismantled the discipline of tropical medicine into its constituent parts. Discreet research projects on different facets of the same disease were pursued, as the complicated life cycles of tropical diseases were teased apart for more detailed study. The smallness of the institution in the inter-war years and the personalities involved united disparate work as and when necessary.

The arrangement of the departments was fluid. The Dutton Memorial Chair of Entomology and the Walter Myers Chair of Parasitology merged in 1941. Gordon (previously Professor of Entomology) became the first Dutton and Myers Professor in charge of the Department of Entomology and Parasitology. In 1943, the Department of Tropical Medicine split into two sub-departments to meet the increased demands of clinical work.[4]

In addition to tropical medicine, parasitology and entomology, the LSTM developed its interest in tropical hygiene. The School introduced a DTH in 1926. This was not as popular as the DTM. The Department of Tropical Hygiene, first described as such in 1929, consisted of only a temporary external lecturer. In 1934, Blacklock became the new professor of Tropical Hygiene, vacating the chair of Parasitology. Dr Thomas Southwell, the assistant lecturer in parasitology, became Lecturer in charge of the Department of Parasitology, but to his disappointment, the School did not appoint him professor.[5] With minimal resources, Blacklock improved the standard of teaching. The award of a Leverhulme Travelling Fellowship to the Far East in 1935 and 1936 acknowledged his expertise in housing, rural sanitation and hygiene.[6]

Separate departments characterised the internal organisation of the LSTM from 1920 until the 1990s. A combination of changes in medical science, successive re-definitions of health and severe financial constraints brought moves to reunite the School and hence the discipline. The School could absorb and initiate development while maintaining what it perceived to be the core activities of tropical medicine. Within a single institution, a considerable range of expertise functioned side by side. In a climate of financial stringency, differences of opinion were particularly destructive. Internal competition rarely promoted collegiality.

The internal arrangement of the School reflected changes in government policy toward the colonies and the role of medicine and development within these territories. However, changes in the funding of basic medical science were also significant. The financial crisis of the inter-war years affected the fortunes of the LSTM. Philanthropy in general suffered as the world economy contracted. Early in 1931 the Treasurer warned that 'we are, and have been, living beyond our income for years and though we could continue the process at a reduced rate without coming to an end for a year or two, yet it is absolutely necessary to stop it at the earliest possible moment'.[7]

While there was an attempt to maintain existing facilities under Yorke's leadership, it became clear that the School must take forward its work in a definite direction. This attitude had not been so apparent before. Yorke chose to limit expenditure on the laboratory in Sierra Leone, despite its association with the founding fathers, in order to strengthen the chemotherapy side. This created tension within the professional staff. In other instances, there were tensions between the professional staff and Council. Council wanted to lose the tropical hygiene lecturer to save money. The staff argued successfully that such a loss would 'leave the School without an authority on a subject of ever increasing importance'.[8]

The School was a victim of its success. The gains made in the health of Europeans in the tropics dulled the need of the commercial community in Liverpool to provide further assistance. Attempts at developing the processing of natural products overseas were a failure for reasons other than the health of the native work force.[9] The provision of treatment in Britain and some improvement in therapies also contributed to the illusion that tropical medicine was the preserve of laboratories at home and colonial governments overseas. Government moneys in one form or another became the single largest annual payments into the general funds. However, this represented commitments to the universities, higher education, and government sponsorship of research rather than the cause of tropical medicine.

Some limited financial support from the CO reached British-based schools of tropical medicine following the establishment of the Colonial Medical Research Committee in 1927. The CMRC, jointly appointed by the MRC and the CO, advised the Secretary of State for the Colonies on research in the empire.[10]

Stephens represented the LSTM on this body. Yorke replaced him after his retirement in 1928. The CMRC lasted until the end of 1930 when it disbanded.[11]

In 1936, a new initiative, the Tropical Medicine Research Committee, presided over the award of MRC grants for work in the tropics and at home. It was also responsible for a scheme promoting research through the appointment of a 'small staff of highly-qualified workers' as Junior and Senior Fellows who would work in Britain or overseas as their research demanded.[12] The holders of such fellowships could look forward to permanent and pensionable appointments for research work in tropical medicine in Britain. Unlike the CMS, there would be no administrative duties. Equally, MRC staff would not have teaching duties, as would other employees at a school of tropical medicine. The aim was to attract quality researchers to a field lacking an attractive career structure. The background of the appointees supported the MRC's earlier view that

> the time has gone by for usefully thinking of 'tropical diseases' as a separate subject of medical research...the stage is set for intensive laboratory investigation wherever that can best be done, whether in bacteriology, or in biochemistry or in the difficult study of 'viruses'.[13]

The MRC fellowships began with a year of training at either School of Tropical Medicine and Fellows often continued working in these laboratories. There was no requirement for overseas experience or previous specialist knowledge in the discipline.

The LSTM was keen to accept MRC Fellows. Their award either relieved the School of existing expenditure or created new appointments they could not otherwise afford. In the first round, Dr G B Ludlam came as a Junior Fellow in 1936 and Dr Frederick Murgatroyd, already working in Liverpool, was appointed a Senior Fellow. In the second round, Dr J L Dales arrived as a Junior Fellow. Scott G Cowper and W H R Lumsden joined them in 1938. The MRC were keen to utilise the fellowships to promote research in chemotherapy. In addition to work in Britain, the recipients were able to go overseas conducting tests with new and improved compounds. In the later 1930s, there was considerable overlap between the MRC's interest in chemotherapy and tropical medicine. Liverpool replicated this interest.

The MRC's tropical medicine initiatives signalled the end of the brief hegemony of the two Schools in Britain. Nothing compelled MRC staff to stay at a school of tropical medicine after initial training. The universities of Cambridge, Edinburgh and Glasgow all had parasitology laboratories. In effect, this diluted tropical medicine. As resources dwindled, this would become an important issue.

The optimism that tropical medicine generated at the turn of the century and the novelty of its contents receded in the inter-war years. The exotic diseases of nineteenth century tales of adventure and exploration were reduced to laboratory investigations. This was yet to become the subject of popular fiction. Much of the innovation in the pre-war era became routine work in the inter-war years. In the 'discovery era' of tropical medicine the initial identification of parasites and vectors occurred at a rapid rate. Reports of new parasites and vectors continued. Stephens announced a new malarial parasite, *Plasmodium ovale*, in 1922 and Blacklock identified *Simulium damnosum* as the vector of *Onchocerca volvulus* in 1926.[14] However, the careful study of known parasites and vectors and the development of further techniques for their investigation replaced discovery.

It was essential to understand the processes by which parasites caused ill health in their human hosts. The complex relationship between an organism that had evolved to live inside another required basic research into the pathology and physiology of infection and immunity. Techniques to determine this knowledge were not necessarily particular to tropical medicine. Their study relied upon the integration of research in a variety of disciplines exploring how organisms and cells functioned.

Beyond the laboratory, the implementation of relatively simple preventative measures in the colonies was pressing. Money for public health measures was difficult to come by, but this was not the remit of the School of Tropical Medicine. By the 1930s, the School could not subsidise colonial governments and run free public health programmes overseas as it had once flirted with under Ross and Boyce. In this period, the laboratory dominated the School's view of tropical medicine. Its most innovative work in this sphere lay in the development of tropical chemotherapy.

## CHEMOTHERAPY

The twenty years either side of the foundation of the LSTM saw significant changes in the means to deal clinically with infectious diseases. This was due to several factors. First, the honing of germ theories of disease explained the way micro-organisms caused disease and the body's response to infection. Research in immunology offered prophylactic and therapeutic advances for bacterial infections such as diphtheria and typhoid. Initially it was much less successful in treating viral diseases, with the important exceptions of smallpox and rabies, and had no effect on protozoal conditions.

Second, cell theory had demonstrated that cells functioned as the smallest unit of life. The application of chemistry and physics to understanding life processes led to the discipline of biochemistry. Biochemistry reduced the processes of life to chemical reactions and the structure of the body to an atomic level. The investigation of treatment by chemicals used this model and its language. The study of pharmacology investigated the interaction of drugs and living material at the biochemical level.[15]

Third, there were changes in drug production. In the earlier part of the nineteenth century, drug production was characterised by small-scale extraction and purification of the active part of plant substances and the use of some minerals and animal products. Pharmacopoeias relied upon empirical research in the treatment of symptoms and current theories of disease causation. The European use of quinine extracted from cinchona bark dated back over two centuries.[16] Often administered as part of a more complex treatment regime, its specific role, as understood later, was not significant in initial usage. Its use as a symptomatic drug continued in the early years of the twentieth century despite some arguments that it was selectively efficacious in malaria. It was used to treat fever in conditions in which it had no tangible effect, giving it a mixed reputation.

Research in Germany in the 1860s and 1870s initiated the production of drugs based on rational understanding of their action in the body. The production of disinfectants such as phenol, useful for killing germs outside the body but too irritating for internal use, promoted research. In the twentieth century, large-scale industrial synthesis of chemical compounds produced for their selective active on specific germs radically altered the treatment of many infectious diseases. The involvement of industry, concerned primarily with profit, was a vital factor. These three activities, linked with clinical medicine, formed the basis for the chemotherapy of the inter-war years.

Chemotherapy was initially most successful in the treatment of parasites, particularly trypanosomes and spirochaetes, rather than bacterial infections. Pessimism surrounding the treatment of bacteria until the 1930s and then the dramatic effects of penicillin after World War II has encouraged historians to ignore much of the German work and inter-war research carried out in Britain.[17] However, there were significant advances in the treatment of protozoan diseases in the first half of the century. This was important for its intrinsic benefits to tropical medicine although many early drugs had serious side effects. History read as Euro-centric progress has ignored this work. It was also significant for the basic scientific research it promoted. In the transition from empirical chemotherapy to one driven by a theoretical model, linking structure with activity, it was necessary to understand the way drugs interacted with the target organism and the host it infected.[18] This involved developing techniques to measure precisely and explain the effects of drugs *in vitro* and *in vivo*. Despite the fact that they could not be cultured, larger more easily observed parasites were useful experimental tools. As single celled animals, parasites had the additional advantage of providing a means to study cell life and the effects of drugs on these processes.[19] Maintenance of trypanosomes in rats was relatively easy. The use of malaria to treat advanced syphilitics, accepted in 1917, provided a useful means of preserving strains of human malaria parasites.[20]

New models of disease causation and explanations for the way cells functioned were generated in the arena of academic medicine, but drug development and production tended to be the preserve of industry. Research in academic laboratories was not an instant marketable product even with the assistance of industry.[21] Industrial patents covered the process of manufacturing a reliable and uniform product but not the chemical or biological products. Industry could foster research either in its own laboratories or by forming alliances with academic institutions. Germany's exploitation of the coal tar derivatives for synthetic dyestuffs made this country the leader in pharmaceuticals in the early years of the twentieth century because these were the basic materials for a number of anti-parasitic drugs.[22] Their advantage lay not only in what they produced but also in the way they used technological innovation and human resources. Industrial laboratories provided training and promoted curiosity driven science and research. At the same time Britain's over commitment to staples such as coal, textiles, iron and steel became more noticeable. Britain had a good reputation in certain areas of industrial chemistry: fertilisers, soap and heavy inorganic chemicals but lagged behind in areas such as fine chemicals. Ironically, Britain exported the intermediary products used in the production of the coal tar derived drugs. With exceptions such as Burroughs Wellcome, the promotion of links between science and industry was poor.[23]

Wartime necessity promoted the Government to take a far greater interest in industrial manufacturing. Drugs were among the list of essential products that Britain had imported from Germany. Government intervention in the production of war goods increased efficiency, productivity and consolidated business interests. In the field of drug manufacture, it promoted moves towards quality and consistency controls. All salvarsan produced by Burroughs Wellcome and May and Baker, instead of the German imports, was subject to biological testing. This alliance dissolved after the war ended. The Government was primarily concerned with putting Britain back on the Gold Standard, achieving a balanced budget and servicing debts. Not until 1925 was a Therapeutic Substances Act passed which allowed British manufacturers to endorse their products with Government approval as their German and American competitors had been able to do for some years.[24]

New industry in this period was less dependent on the export market and more reliant upon domestic sales for its success.[25] Except for veterinary preparations that had a large potential market in Britain, anti-parasitic drugs bucked the trend. The primary market for human anti-parasitics was the tropical colonies. If successful, these drugs would be export products albeit within the empire trading block.

In the history of chemotherapy, the links between academia, industry and the Government were spasmodic and problematic. Government sponsorship of academic medical science came through the MRC. This was both a blessing and a hindrance. An advantage of the MRC was its access to other useful Government bodies. The Chemotherapy Committee, established in 1926, was jointly appointed with the Department of Scientific and Industrial Research who collaborated on the chemical side.[26] Disadvantages included the relationship between the MRC and industry. The MRC hesitated if industrial links threatened to compromise academic research. Besides work at the NIMR, the MRC funded external research and supported projects by awarding grants. In their own laboratories, it was easy to exert control in potential conflicts. Elsewhere this required negotiation. The involvement of industrial sponsorship in laboratories receiving assistance from the MRC was a major cause of concern. The Chemotherapy Committee worried that industrial pressure for patents would suppress publication of research findings. They submitted a memorandum to the Board of Trade in 1929, outlining proposals to change the patent rules for discoveries made under their sponsorship, but this was shelved.[27]

The development of pharmaceuticals represented a significant growth area within the chemical industry. It relied, as did much of the new industrial output, upon exploiting relatively new technology and concentrating output in the hands of a few large producers. However, in the case of anti-parasitic chemotherapy there were additional hurdles. Despite financial resources, commercial companies were unlikely to have sufficient biological knowledge of parasites, or the abilities to maintain strains for experimental purposes. Such facilities were available in only a few laboratories including the Schools of Tropical Medicine. Industry was also unlikely to have the facilities for clinical testing either in tropical cases in Britain or overseas. Legitimate channels for such work were restricted to the CO, and the Schools of Tropical Medicine.

## CHEMOTHERAPY AT LIVERPOOL

In the inter-war years, the MRC funded research in a number of areas relevant to tropical medicine and chemotherapy.[28] At the NIMR, arising out of work started during World War I, Clifford Dobell worked on intestinal parasites and Harold King continued the synthesis of arsenical compounds begun by George Barger and Arthur James Ewins. The MRC continued to support Barger's work, by the award of grants, after he moved to Edinburgh as professor of Medical Chemistry in 1919. At Glasgow, the professor of Bacteriology, Carl H Browning, investigated the bactericidal activities of organic compounds prepared by Professor J B Cohen at Leeds. There was also support for studies into quinine and the gold treatment of tuberculosis. Professor R T Leiper at the LSHTM received grants for helminthology. At the Molteno Institute in Cambridge, the MRC supported research under Nuttall and then Dr Keilin into metazoa and other aspects of parasitology, some tropical in nature. It was relatively late that the LSTM began to benefit directly from MRC support for tropical medicine and chemotherapy, when Yorke began to receive support for testing drugs after the establishment of the Chemotherapy Committee in 1925.

The early work in chemotherapy at Runcorn provided a useful training for those members of staff who were starting their careers at this time. Yorke was the only one, however, who remained in Liverpool and maintained his early interest. In 1914, he gave up the Directorship of the Runcorn Laboratory following his appointment to the Walter Myers Chair of Parasitology. He spent the first part of the war seconded to the military in Malta. Upon his return to Liverpool in 1916, he joined Stephens' research project on malaria at the military hospital in the School. In 1920, he became assistant physician to the Tropical Ward of the LRI and in 1926, consulting physician in tropical diseases for the Ministry of Pensions Hospital at Childwall in Liverpool. Besides the valuable clinical experience these positions offered a professor of parasitology, they also enabled him to maintain an interest at least in the chemotherapy of malaria.[29] His other research concerned the pathology of blackwater fever, trypanosomiasis and amoebic dysentery.

Stephens retired from the Alfred Jones Chair of Tropical Medicine in the autumn of 1928. Some members of the selection committee of the University expressed their concern that Yorke lacked sufficient clinical experience to succeed him in this post. A testimonial by Andrew Balfour in support of his application spoke of his considerable intellectual abilities. He made direct reference to Yorke's position on the Chemotherapy Committee of the MRC and that, he was 'highly esteemed by men who count'.[30] These considerations were appealing. Yorke became Professor of Tropical Medicine on 30 December 1928.

From now onwards his control of the LSTM's internal affairs increased. In 1934 this was formalised with his election as chairman of the Professional Sub-committee. His stature beyond the School also increased. In 1935, the League of Nations Health Commission invited him to become a member of the Malaria Commission. A year later the MRC invited him to sit on the new Tropical Diseases Research Committee. In 1937, he joined an informal group of malarial experts collected together by the Minister of Health. In 1938, at the third International Congress of Tropical Medicine and Malaria, he acted as a representative of the British Government.

With Yorke at the helm, the LSTM would prove to be well equipped to deal with the biological side of chemotherapy research. It also proved particularly adept at co-operating with industry and in this Yorke was a useful figurehead. In 1916, he married Elizabeth Annie Greening. The Greening family ran a wire-manufacturing firm. Amongst other products they made wire mesh for screening buildings in the tropics. His interest in the business proved to be more direct than one might expect from a medical son-in-law. In 1930, Yorke, apparently dissatisfied with the management of the family business, took on the directorship of N Greening & Co. He was therefore aware of the financial difficulties facing British exporting firms at this time. In 1940, he became a Director of the West African Drug Company. In 1942 shortly before his death in 1943, he became director and chairman of the Dressing and Screening Company. His scientific prowess and business acumen earned him a place on the advisory board of ICI (Dyestuffs Group) Medical Products Panel in 1940 following a nudge from Sir Henry Dale.

After Thomas' work at Runcorn, the laboratory received samples of drugs to test.[31] This was a common practice among drug producers, who lacked biological laboratories. The skill of maintaining parasites in experimental animals was a painstaking process. Moreover, academic institutes could gain the Home Office licences for animal experimentation more easily than commercial laboratories.[32]

Further publicity for the activities of the LSTM followed research into quinine treatment during World War I. The treatment of military casualties, pensioners and the use of malaria in GPI cases maintained a viable clinical base for experimental work. It also brought in periodic samples of drugs for clinical as well as animal testing.[33] It was spasmodic work such as this which became more organised into a programme of research at Liverpool in the late 1920s. It was a proactive move by Yorke to take the LSTM along this route. The chemotherapy work of the 1930s amounted to more than individuals working on a range of subjects. It represented a group activity with a clear leader and a planned research agenda. By the 1940s, the LSTM had become a premier institution for research into aspects of parasite chemotherapy. After Yorke's death, his plans for a department dedicated to this work continued as a memorial. When the School returned to normal work in 1945, plans for the Department of Tropical Chemotherapy showed this as the largest of those forming the LSTM.

## YORKE'S PROGRAMME

In 1927, the MRC Chemotherapy Committee decided to give a small sum of money to the LSTM to assist with the 'testing of anti-malaria remedies and potential trypanoicides'.[34] This biological research continued the organic chemistry conducted elsewhere. The grant covered the half-time salary of two research assistants already employed by the School in various capacities. The School appointed Alfred Robert Davies Adams Lecturer in Protozoology in 1925 and Frederick Murgatroyd Assistant Lecturer in Protozoology in 1927.[35] The MRC also granted Yorke's request in 1929 for an additional annual sum of £50.0.0 against expenses for mice, cages and animal food incurred as part of this work.

With this limited external support, Yorke began diverting resources within the LSTM towards chemotherapy research. As Professor of Tropical Medicine, he was able to direct his department. The *Annual Report* for 1930–1931 described research as 'almost entirely confined to the subject of chemotherapy'.[36] As the holder of the chair of Tropical Medicine appears also to have unofficially assumed control of the School, it was not surprising that Yorke appropriated the newly instituted Caton Memorial Fellowship.[37] Frank Hawking, a recent graduate of Oxford and St Bartholomews Hospital Medical School, became the first Fellow on 20 August 1930. On Adams' secondment to Entebbe, Hawking took up the vacant MRC post. Yorke continued to fill the Caton Fellowship with those who would assist with chemotherapy research.[38]

Yorke's team carried out the routine testing of compounds sent to the LSTM by the Chemotherapy Committee of the MRC. In 1934, clinical testing began. He made arrangements with the local health authorities to treat neurosyphilis patients with new compounds. Dr Lester, in charge of the Sleeping Sickness Investigation in Nigeria, conducted complementary tests using the same drugs.[39] In 1935, they began testing a new series of compounds produced in Professor Morgan's laboratories at the Department of Scientific and Industrial Research at Teddington. The product was marketed as Neocryl. This link demonstrates the ethos of the MRC in the inter-war years. They facilitated the development of products of potential industrial importance (Morgan's research) and the testing of these products (Yorke's research) in a hands off but controlled way. Importantly for the LSTM, the service role Yorke provided for the MRC brought far greater benefits.

Adams, Murgatroyd (and their successors) and Yorke began a series of investigations concerned with techniques of parasite research for use in chemotherapy work. They investigated the development of drug resistance in parasites and used resistance as a means to understand the action of drugs and the host-parasite relationships.[40] This utilised the remaining time and resources of the staff funded by the MRC. This work appeared as series of papers, 'Studies in Chemotherapy', in the *ATMP*. The aim of this research appears to be a systematic study of current knowledge of drug resistance. Much of the other work in this field came out of European laboratories and appeared in German or French journals.

The initial methodological investigations established a technique to maintain trypanosomes *in vitro* 'alive, in undiminished numbers and in a condition of unlowered vitality, for a period of at least twenty-four hours at 37°C'.[41] Although the maintenance of trypanosomes in laboratory animals was now a skilled routine practice, Yorke considered this insufficient for chemotherapy research. The host environment of the laboratory animal was subject to uncontrolled variation. Moreover, the full role of the host in infection, immunity and resistance to drugs was undetermined. Removal of the host from the experiment reduced the number of variables. Yorke's team frequently used this method. It was particularly useful in combination with simultaneous *in vivo* studies. By the later 1930s, Miss Strangways at the NIMR was using the technique in her trypanosomiasis research.[42]

The *in vitro* technique was also important because it allowed the researcher a greater degree of confidence when pronouncing a strain of parasites as resistant. Much of the previous literature on the nature and effects of resistance was contradictory. This led to confusion and dissension among the researchers and clinicians faced with untreatable cases. In Yorke's opinion it was not clear from published reports that genuine resistance occurred. He claimed that the *in vitro* method gave certain proof of resistance measurable by titre.

Proof of resistance made resistant strains of parasites of value in further experiments. The nature of resistance, its passage from one generation to the next through the normal insect or arthropod intermediary, and the factors responsible for producing resistance were important unresolved issues. Yorke's publications indicate that he attempted a systematic approach to these questions.

The study of resistance had immediate practical ramifications. If, as Yorke argued, resistance was a stable characteristic passed from one generation of parasites to the next, care in the use of drugs in mass disease prevention or treatment campaigns was a pressing public health issue. Resistance was also significant for the knowledge it yielded about how parasites functioned within hosts and how hosts mediated immune responses. This was basic research into the mechanism of parasitic infection in man. It was in addition to the knowledge gained about the potential for a chemical compound to exert a non-toxic effect on the host and a lethal effect on the parasite. Hawking's 1933 MD thesis discussed induced drug resistance in trypanosomes. It also dealt with associated topics of immunology, host specificity and quantitative studies on the uptake of acriflavine by parasites.[43] The last point was particularly important methodologically, as it determined the mechanism by which certain chemicals were effective in treating parasitic infections.

Hawking's thesis was therefore part of the project led by Yorke which hoped to advance the theoretical understanding of the action of drugs. Parascandola claims 'Ehrlich felt that the phenomenon of drug resistance would play an important role in the development of "therapeutic biology" and would help to bring order and light to the chaos of drug action'.[44] From his publications, it is clear that Yorke perceived his own work in this way. It was an attempt to transform chemotherapy from an empirical science to one based upon theoretical models.[45] The routine testing and research enhanced Yorke's reputation with the MRC and brought him to the forefront of parasite research in Britain.

In the first instance Yorke's team concentrated on exploring these broad questions by investigating the parasites causing trypanosomiasis and Kala-azar. The known organic arsenicals, the mainstay of tropical chemotherapy, were often the object of study. The aim was advancement of knowledge concerning these drugs and the search for more efficient drugs with fewer side effects, more easily administered, and showing greater activity against the parasites without harming the host. In 1936, the collaborative work of Dr Harold King of the NIMR, Yorke and Emmanuel M Lourie resulted in a new synthetic substance active against trypanosomes, 'sythalin'. Although itself too toxic for clinical application, it indicated a new direction for development in the shape of aliphatic and aromatic guanidine and amidine compounds.

In 1933 Lourie joined Yorke's team and became an author on the 'Studies in chemotherapy' series. Appointed to the School in September 1930 as Assistant Lecturer in Protozoology, following the award of a Beit Memorial Fellowship, he began his own research on bird malaria: 'Studies on chemotherapy of bird malaria' in the *ATMP*. The publications are significant because they point to the increasing profile of the LSTM in this field and the growing diversity of diseases under active study by the chemotherapy group. Yorke was consciously building up a research culture within the School.

In 1936, the Government earmarked an additional £30,000 for the MRC 'with a special view to the development of research in chemotherapy'.[46] The aim was furthering medical research, boosting British industry and improving the conditions of health in the colonies. In this scheme, the money was to be paid at the rate of £10,000 over three years. The first year's funding would be devoted to the provision of buildings and equipment. In the absence of industrial biological and chemical laboratories, the government via the MRC was seeking to establish a central laboratory to bring together the chemists and the biologists to work on the same problem at the same time. The aim was to promote integrated research with interaction between workers in these disciplines rather than chemical production followed by biological testing in a linear fashion. The central laboratory functioned without pressures associated with profit. Select academic units would assist with specific projects.

In 1937, Yorke, aware of these developments through his seat on the Chemotherapy Committee, approached the MRC. His aim was to have the LSTM become the premier centre for biological research in chemotherapy. The MRC were not willing to fund proposals for enlarging the LSTM to meet this initiative, but increased their existing support for research staff. In October and November 1937, Lourie and Dr J Devine, a biochemist from the Physiology Department at Manchester University, joined the School as full-time researchers for a period of five years.

Yorke persuaded School Council to complete the building as originally intended. In 1938, the builders cleared the site and construction started. This coincided with the fortieth anniversary of the School. The LSTM paid for building and equipping the extension at a cost of seven thousand pounds. The extension relieved overcrowding in other departments, especially Tropical Hygiene. The number of students had increased to the extent that additional cloakroom facilities were required. The extension also provided the new facilities for chemotherapy. To recoup the capital outlay the School launched an appeal including a circular to local pharmaceutical firms.

An annual subvention of £400 from May and Baker offset some of the running costs. This represented an offer of money to a laboratory conducting MRC sponsored work but not under MRC control. In 1929, May and Baker gave £150 to the NIMR for biological work. Liverpool would now offer the same kind of service on an expanded scale. Such a policy was palatable to industry, but the MRC were more cautious. They were worried that commercial concern with patenting would hamper the free flow of information necessary for scientific progress. Yorke proved able to negotiate such obstacles or at least impress those who counted on the Chemotherapy Committee that he would act in the accepted spirit of scientific endeavour and not sell out to commercial pressures.[47] Yorke saw the sponsorship as a lifeline for his own research. He also recognised it represented a diversification of the traditional links with commerce and potentially would assist the development of British industry.

The credibility of the other members of the alliance between the School and May and Baker reassured the MRC. 'Synthalin' was developed in collaboration with Harold King of the NIMR and Ewins of May and Baker. The two had worked together at Mill Hill during World War I before Ewins moved onto the commercial post. They were keen for Yorke to continue the biological side of this work, extending the informal network of chemotherapy research in Britain.

The success of the arrangement with the LSTM encouraged Ewins to pursue it further. In July 1939, he visited Yorke at the School proposing to extend the collaboration and establish a unit 'for the testing of compounds for possible anti-malarial action'. Yorke insisted May and Baker pay the recurrent expenses of the unit. He and Ewins agreed that this would mean taking on a further 'mutually acceptable qualified worker, the wages of a laboratory attendant, and the sum required for the maintenance and cost of the animals required'. This amounted to £750 per annum.[48]

The interest of two further manufacturers in the special facilities the School offered strengthened the links with industry. The first came from Messrs Evans Sons Lescher and Webb. In July 1939, their chief scientific adviser wrote in response to the appeal circular suggested a future collaboration between his industrial laboratory and Yorke's department.[49] The second link came through less pleasant circumstances. After the outbreak of World War II, Sir Edward Mellanby of the MRC wrote and asked Yorke if he could test atebrine and plasmoquine produced by ICI. Imports from Germany were impossible, and ICI was one of the companies chosen by the Government to produce equivalents.[50] Yorke readily agreed. A year later in September 1940 he was asked to join ICI's (Dyestuffs group) Medicinal Products Panel. This personal link brought benefits to the LSTM. By November, he was able to report a grant of £200 assisting with the costs of tests. In 1942 by arrangement with the WO and ICI, Gordon supervised tests for a new anti-scabies product. ICI offered a grant of £500 for additional laboratory expenses. The tests involved the use of Army personnel and conscientious objectors.

ICI also offered to provide specialist staff from their plant to work at the LSTM as part of the chemotherapy research team. In return, they received training in the techniques of parasite biology. Dr J R M Innes came for a month at the end of 1940 and Dr H O J Collier from March 1941 until the end of the war. Later ICI sent two lady technicians to assist Adams in the Paludrine work.[51] The death of Yorke on 24 April 1943 affected ICI's relationship with the School. Adams replaced him as acting head of the Department of Tropical Medicine, but School Council decided to leave the chair vacant until the end of the war. Adams withdrew from active involvement in the chemotherapy research in June 1938. He took on the routine management of the Department of Tropical Medicine after construction of the new extension. Adams picked up some of the research burden following Yorke's death, running the clinical tests of anti-malaria drugs in conjunction with his appointment to the Tropical Ward and Emergency Medical Service. Lourie continued the laboratory research side of the programme collaborating on the malaria work but also developing other anti-parasitics. No immediate replacement from the LSTM joined the ICI Medicinal Products Panel.

Yorke's death brought letters of condolence from around the world. The School, already committed to a separate Department of Chemotherapy, launched a memorial appeal. In November 1943, Lourie became the Director of the department for a period of three years starting in the New Year of 1944.[52] Dr J C E Simpson, an ICI Research Fellow of the University, joined him on 1 January 1945. This was a significant appointment. It indicated the willingness of the University to support the initiatives of the School in this subject. To some, his appointment diluted the interests of the School. Simpson had graduated with a first-class degree in organic and inorganic chemistry.[53] His background prompted comments from Hobhouse on his suitability as an Assistant for the Chemotherapy Department.[54] The other members of the department would be James Williamson, an MRC fellow, and Mr J R Keneford seconded from ICI. In February 1945, Ewins wrote in reference to previous correspondence and offered to pay a sum in the region of £1,000 per annum in addition to the £400 currently paid. The additional money was to be utilised to pay the salaries of two researchers or a more senior person and a technical assistant. The money would be given on condition that 'their work would, at least in part, be directed to some branch of chemotherapeutic investigation in which this firm could afford effective co-operation or in which it was directly interested'.[55] By August of that year, Lourie had already found additional laboratory space and a member of the University staff to fill it. He asked Dr G T Mills, presently in the Department of Biochemistry, to join as a research assistant.

## THE SCHOOL AT WAR (AGAIN)

When World War II broke out in 1939 there were a number of unpleasant parallels with the previous international conflict. The School hurriedly put to use the new extension completed in July 1940. They abandoned plans to furnish the Tropical Hygiene Museum and altered the plans for chemotherapy in line with the demands of warfare. The normal functions of the School broke down and various emergency teaching programmes for members of the armed forces started in June 1940. The London School closed temporarily in 1939 and students came to Liverpool. Several members of staff proceeded overseas at the request of the CO and WO.

Along with the rest of the Liverpool, the School instigated air-raid precautions. Valuable equipment was stored in the basement and a fire-watching rota established. The School suffered some bomb damage in December 1940 and March and May of 1941, but nothing serious enough to prevent work continuing. Other buildings nearby were not so lucky. In March 1941, a bomb fell on the Pathology Department. The blood transfusion service operated from these laboratories. The School offered temporary accommodation in the new extension until the end of that year. The May blitz closed the Tropical Ward at the LRI.

As in the previous war, Liverpool became a centre for military causalities. Tropical cases were concentrated in several hospitals around the city. The EMS brought together the municipal and voluntary hospitals to provide a comprehensive service using existing resources. Members of the Merchant Marine suffered from tropical diseases particularly malaria. The School provided what assistance it could, treating the men free of charge and providing the necessary drugs. Unable to meet the expenditure they persuaded the City Council to meet the cost of anti-malarial drugs for seamen whose home-port was not Liverpool. They continued to provide their clinical care without charge and advertised the service for those arriving in Liverpool for the first time.

In the Department of Chemotherapy, work on a range of anti-parasitic compounds continued with the previous emphasis on resistance and developing techniques for testing drugs in the laboratory. The School's role in the development of ICI's anti-malarial Paludrine was part of the special relationship Yorke established with that company. It also formed part of the clinical work of the EMS. The pre-war planning for chemotherapy ensured that Liverpool was poised to play a fundamental role in the development of new anti-malarial drugs. With the outbreak of World War II, it became essential to produce drugs previously imported from overseas. There was clear rationale to start production of synthetic anti-malarials as these were all made in Germany.[56] After the fall of Java in 1942, quinine supplies were minimal, and it became a priority to produce synthetic alternatives. Liverpool's reputation and enhanced facilities made it sensible to concentrate work in the North West of England. Dr James D Fulton, an MRC worker in chemotherapy at the London School, was transferred in October 1939. A further MRC Junior Fellow, appointed to the Tropical Hygiene Department, later became involved with the clinical chemotherapy work in Liverpool. Arrangements between civilian public health and military medical officers were co-ordinated to maximise use of resources.[57]

The EMS dealt with civilian casualties and members of the fighting services. Liverpool was part of Region 10 of the EMS, under the charge of Group Officer K W Monsarrat.[58] In 1940, Adams and Yorke joined the EMS as medical officers. Adams also provided yellow fever inoculations for employees of the CO and others proceeding to the West Coast of Africa. In December 1943 he was elected to membership of the Royal Liverpool United Hospitals' Medical Board and in February 1944 appointed as a Ministry of Health Physician-specialist in Tropical Diseases for Region 10 of the EMS.

In 1943, one thousand four hundred inpatients and three thousand outpatients passed through the city's hospitals. The laboratories at the School received twenty thousand pathological samples requiring specialist analysis from around Britain. In order to deal effectively with the increased case-load and to select and monitor patients for tests of various anti-malarial compounds, service casualties were concentrated under EMS care at Walton Hospital. Yorke had used Walton Hospital for tests involving neurosyphilis cases and William Frazer the MOH happily offered beds at Walton.[59] A further concentration of malarious casualties occurred at the small eighty-four bedded City Hospital South in Grafton Street.[60] In June 1943, Dr Gerard Sanderson joined as a clinical assistant and helped Adams with the clinical tests of a series of compounds produced at the Blackley ICI laboratories. The final compound was subsequently tested by Neil Hamilton Fairley in Cairns, Northern Australia and marketed as Paludrine.[61]

A further clinical facility opened in June 1944 following a request from the Ministry of Health to provide hospital accommodation for 'difficult and obscure cases of tropical disease'.[62] The WO were no longer confident that they could deal with the increased number of cases returning from Eastern theatres of war. Beds were not the problem but expert clinical and technical staffs were in short supply. The proposal was for three centres in Liverpool, London and Edinburgh.[63] One hundred and sixty beds were set aside at the Smithdown Road Hospital and the cases transferred from Walton. The Grafton Street facility remained open and continued to house malaria cases undergoing treatment and forming part of the drug tests. As the number of malarious casualties dwindled, Grafton Street closed towards the end of 1945. The Smithdown Road Tropical Diseases Centre remained open and provided a service after the end of the war. Initially there was a shortfall in qualified nursing staff and Adams ran courses to remedy this. Later nurse education played an important part of the work of the Centre.[64]

Despite the difficulties in keeping an institution such as the LSTM running during the war years, School Council actively planned for the future after the end of the war. The next chapter considers these plans. They were the inheritance of the new leader of the School, Brian Maegraith. The School appointed him Professor of Tropical Medicine on 24 October 1944 and the army released him from his commission to take up the appointment on 6 March 1945.

CONCLUSION

In 1920, the School began again in its new laboratories. As is the case with many facets of life in inter-war Britain, the trend was not initially to create something new, but to return to pre-war practices. The construction and staffing of the Sierra Leone laboratory preoccupied the School. Afterwards, the staff focused on creating an organised structure for the School based on a series of departments.

The departmental structure acknowledged the composite elements of tropical medicine as conceived at the turn of the century. In the absence of money for expansion, the departments consisted of the professorial staff with perhaps one assistant or junior lecturer. As vacancies occurred at the senior level, existing staff replaced them according to seniority not expertise in the particular subject area. With the exception of Walter Scott Patton, Dutton Professor of Entomology from 1927 to 1937, there were no outside appointments at the professorial level.

Within the departmental structure staff continued to explore the natural history of parasites and vectors. Output increased because of the improved laboratory facilities, the additional support staff of technicians, and the library and librarian. After Yorke's appointment to the chair of Tropical Medicine the profile and function of the School gradually changed. Yorke developed an interest in chemotherapy as a means to explore the relationship of the parasite and the host. In comparison with other research, this involved more analytical techniques and the use of methodologies developed in other disciplines. Besides this shift in scientific emphasis, he created a sense of priority within the School and a clear direction.

To fund this research Yorke attracted the attention of the MRC. This organisation increased its interest in chemotherapy and tropical medicine research in the inter-war period. Yorke's presence on the Chemotherapy Committee of the MRC indicated the potential for integrating this discipline with other areas of biomedical science. The other source of funding for chemotherapy at Liverpool came from the interest of British chemical and pharmaceutical companies in producing new drugs. Yorke traded the traditional link between tropical medicine in Liverpool and commerce, for a growing interest in manufacturing firms.

Yorke promoted the School as a centre for the biological side of parasite chemotherapy supported by the MRC and by industry. He managed this project well and it yielded appreciable results, although he did not live to see the fruition of all his plans. Despite the disruption caused by World War II, the School was poised to continue his vision of its future, creating a separate department, the largest in the School and planning for a chair in Tropical Chemotherapy.

The 1920s were characterised by adjusting to the decline of Britain's international position, while attempting to support an extended network for the laboratories of the School. In the 1930s in the face of further retrenchment, Yorke manufactured a particular direction for the LSTM. He achieved this by tapping into networks beyond the School and the discipline of tropical medicine. This was a new clarity of purpose within the older diverse goal of improving health in the tropics. The concentration or perhaps the retreat to the laboratory undeniably brought results. It did not address the non-medical causes of much ill health in the tropics, such as poverty and a lack of education, inherent in the colonial system. These were not part of the discipline of tropical medicine at this time.

The appointment of Brian Maegraith as Professor of Tropical Medicine and Dean of the LSTM brought to Liverpool a man with a different vision of tropical medicine and the future of the School. Yorke had seized initiatives that others may not have followed to the same extent or with the same success. However, he functioned in an environment receptive to his style. If Maegraith's style was different, so too was his era.

NOTES

[1] P Weindling (ed), *International health organisations and movements 1918–1939*, Cambridge: CUP, 1995.

[2] *40th Annual Report of the LSTM, 1938–1939.*

[3] Stephens retired in 1928 and was replaced by Yorke as Alfred Lewis Jones Professor of Tropical Medicine. Yorke resigned from the Walter Myers Chair of Parasitology and was replaced by Blacklock who returned from Sierra Leone. Newstead retired in 1926 and was replaced by Walter Scott Patton in 1927 as Dutton Memorial Professor of Entomology; Patton retired in 1937 after the death of Miss A M Evans; Gordon returned from Sierra Leone and replaced Patton in 1938.

[4] Stephens' work on Blackwater fever and the malaria research of Yorke et al., benefited from clinical work at the LRI Tropical Ward and elsewhere in the Northwest. Many papers in the *ATMP* reported clinical findings from the Tropical Ward, written by the clinical pathologists, D Uvedale Owen and Frederick Murgatroyd. Murgatroyd also acted as Assistant Physician and was replaced by Alfred R D Adams, who also contributed clinical papers.

[5] TM/3/1.5b, Council Minutes, Southwell to Chair of Council, 11 May 1939.

[6] D B Blacklock, *An empire problem: the house and the village in the tropics*, Liverpool: LUP, 1932.

[7] TM/4/2.2, Professional Committee Minutes, 1927–1936, Memorandum, 11 May 1931.

[8] TM/4/2.2, Professional Committee Minutes, 1927–1936, 27 May 1931.

[9] A Phillips, *The enigma of colonialism: British policy in West Africa*, London: James Currey, 1988.

[10] *Annual Report of the MRC, 1926–1927*, p. 9.

[11] J Beinart, 'The inner world of imperial sickness: the MRC and research in tropical medicine', J Austoker & L Bryder (eds), *Historical perspectives on the role of the MRC*, Oxford: OUP, 1989, pp. 109–136.

[12] *Annual Report of the MRC, 1935–1936*, p. 36.

[13] *Annual Report of the MRC, 1926–-1927*, p. 9.

[14] J W W Stephens, 'A new malaria parasite of man', *ATMP*, 16, 1922, 383–386; D B Blacklock, 'The development of *Onchocerca volvulus* in *Simulium damnosum*', ibid., 20, 1926, 1–48.

[15] C D Leake, *An historical account of pharmacology to the twentieth century*, Illinois: Charles C Thomas, 1975, p. 146.

[16] See for instance, M Dobson, 'Bitter-sweet solutions for malaria: exploring natural remedies from the past', W F Bynum & B Fantini (eds), *Strategies against malaria eradication or control?*, *Parassitologia*, 40, 1998, 69–83.

[17] P Hayes, *Industry and ideology: I G Farben in the Nazi era*, Cambridge: CUP, 1987.

[18] For discussion of early theories of chemotherapeutic action see W F Bynum, 'Chemical structure and pharmacological action: a chapter in the history of nineteenth century molecular pharmacology', *BHM*, 44, 1970, 518–538; J Parascandola & R Jasensky, 'Origins of the receptor theory of drug action', ibid., 48, 1974, 199–220; J Parascandola, 'Carl Voegltin and the arsenic

receptor in chemotherapy', *JHMAS*, 32, 1977, 151–171; *idem*, 'The theoretical basis of Paul Ehrlich's chemotherapy', ibid., 36, 1981, 19–43.

[19] See for example the work of Clifford Dobell at the NIMR on *Coccidia*.

[20] W Yorke & W Rees Wright reported on strains that had been maintained in the human host for three and a half years: 'The mosquito infectivity of *P. vivax* after prolonged sojourn in the human host', *ATMP*, 20, 1926, 327–328.

[21] P Neushul, 'Science, Government and the mass production of penicillin', *JHMAS*, 48, 1993, 371–395.

[22] J J Beer, 'Coal-tar dye manufacture and the origins of the modern industrial research lab', *Isis*, 49, 1958, 123–131.

[23] E M Tansey & R C E Milligan, 'The early history of the Wellcome Research Laboratories, 1894–1914', G J Higby & E C Stroud (eds), *Pill peddlers: essays on the history of the pharmaceutical industry*, Madison: American Institute of the History of Pharmacy, 1990, pp. 91–106.

[24] J Liebanau, 'The MRC and the pharmaceutical industry: the model of insulin', Austoker and Bryder, *Historical perspectives on the role of the MRC*, pp. 163–180.

[25] T May, *An economic and social history of Britain 1760–1970*, London: Longman, 1987, p. 332.

[26] The Department of Scientific and Industrial Research was established in 1916.

[27] *Annual Report of the MRC, 1929–1930*, Appendix A, pp. 130–135.

[28] Beinart, 'The inner world of imperial sickness', p. 126.

[29] W Yorke & J Macfie, 'Observations on malaria made during treatment of general paralysis', *TRSTMH*, 18, 1924, 13–33; W Yorke, 'Further observations on malaria made during treatment of general paralysis', ibid., 19, 1925, 108–122, Discussion, 123–130.

[30] TM/14/YoW/4.3.

[31] TM/11/2/1–2.

[32] E M Tansey, 'The Wellcome Physiological Research Laboratories 1984–1904: the Home Office, pharmaceutical firms and animal experiments', *Medical History*, 33, 1989, 1–41.

[33] S Adler, 'The trypanocidal effect of phenylglycine amido arsenate of sodium on *T. brucei* in rats and *T. rhodesiense* in mice', *ATMP*, 15, 1921, 427–432, [sent by May and Baker]; *idem*, 'Note on bismuth as a trypanocide', ibid., 433; J W W Stephens & W Yorke, 'A case of sleeping sickness (*T. gambiense*) treated with "Bayer 205"', ibid., 16, 1922, 421–424.

[34] MRC records: FD1/4275 I, Letter, Landsbough Thomson to Yorke, 15 November 1927.

[35] TM/14/AdA, Adams was an ex-DTM student and winner of the Alan Milne Memorial Medal in 1925; TM/14/MuF.

[36] *32nd Annual Report of the LSTM, 1930–1931*, p. 8.

[37] Fellowship founded in 1929 to commemorate the late Dr Richard Caton, original member of the Governing Body of the LSTM and a Vice-chairman from 1913.

[38] Hawking succeeded Adams to the part MRC funded post. He was replaced as Caton Fellow by Dr Helen Russell in September 1933 until December 1934. Russell was replaced by G R Walker until July 1935. Walker was replaced by Dr

R J O'Conner in September 1935. He stayed at the School until December 1936. Murgatroyd was awarded a Senior MRC fellowship in October 1935 and his part MRC funded post was filled by Adams who returned to the School from secondment in Uganda.

[39] W Yorke, F Murgatroyd, F Glyn-Hughes, H M O Lester & A O F Ross, 'A new arsenical for the treatment of syphilis and trypanosomiasis', *BMJ*, i, 1936, 1042–1048.

[40] Within this context 'resistance' meant that doses larger than the previously lethal dose would fail to cause the death of a parasite.

[41] W Yorke, 'Drug resistance', *British Journal of Venereal Diseases*, 9, 1933, 83–97, p. 85.

[42] *Annual Report of the MRC, 1936–1937*, p. 48.

[43] Obituary, *BMJ*, 293, 1986, 455.

[44] Parascandola, 'The theoretical basis of Paul Ehrlich's chemotherapy', pp. 36–37.

[45] M Weatherall, *In search of a cure*, Oxford: OUP, 1990, pp. 141–160.

[46] *Annual Report of the MRC, 1936–1937*, p. 9.

[47] TM/4/2.3, Professional Committee Minutes, 1936–1942, Ewins to Yorke, 10 May 1938 & 29 June 1938.

[48] TM/4/2.3, Professional Committee Minutes, 1936–1942, Ewins to Yorke, 18 July 1939.

[49] TM/4/2.3, Professional Committee Minutes, 1936–1942, 24 July 1939.

[50] TM/4/2.3, Professional Committee Minutes, 1936–1942, Mellanby to Yorke, 22 September 1939.

[51] TM/4/2.4, Professional Committee Minutes 1942–1946, 31 January 1944.

[52] TM/4/2.4, Professional Committee Minutes 1942–1946, 6 November 1943.

[53] Simpson graduated from the University of Liverpool, 1929; post doctoral research under Professor Heilbron, Liverpool and W A Jacobs, Rockefeller Institute, New York; Assistant Lecturer Organic Chemistry Kings College, London; Lecturer in Chemistry, Durham University.

[54] TM/3/1.5b, Council Minutes, 4 September 1944.

[55] TM/4/2.4, Professional Committee Minutes 1942–1946, Ewins to Lourie, 6 February 1945.

[56] H J Power, 'Malaria, drugs and World War II: the role of the LSTM in the development of Paludrine', paper presented at Symposium, Malaria & War, Wellcome Institute for the History of Medicine, London, 6 May 1994.

[57] TM/4/2.4, Professional Committee Minutes 1942–1946, Meeting 26 November 1943.

[58] TM/13/143.

[59] TM/4/2.4, Professional Committee Minutes 1942–1946, Frazer to Blacklock, 15 October 1943.

[60] TM/4/2.4, Professional Committee Minutes 1942–1946, 31 January 1944.

[61] M Harrison, 'Medicine and the culture of command: the case of malaria control in the British Army during the two world wars', *Medical History*, 40, 1996, 437–453; A W Sweeney, 'The malaria frontline, pioneering malaria research by the Australian Army in World War II', *Medical Journal of Australia*, 166, 1997, 316–319.

[62] *45th Annual Report of the LSTM, 1934–1944*, p. 8.

[63] TM/4/2.4, Professional Committee Minutes 1942–1946, Fraser to Blacklock, 8 May 1944.

[64] TM/4/2.4, Professional Committee Minutes 1942–1946, Meeting, 28 August 1944.

# 4

# A BRAVE NEW WORLD?
# THE LSTM AFTER WORLD WAR II

## INTRODUCTION

After World War II, the discipline of tropical medicine would be remade. In the years up to 1945 it was fashioned by the demands of constructive imperialism and reacted to developments in medical science. After 1945, colonialism gave way to a new style international politics and a new perception of health and medicine in the Third World emerged. Problems of disease could now be solved on a grand scale. On the new global map the LSTM appeared as a small speck, however, it continued to mould tropical medicine in Britain and in those parts of the world where it made its presence felt. Despite the end of the formal British empire the number of overseas contacts has increased from the end of the war to the present day.

The LSTM rose to the challenges of decolonisation and international health. It reshaped itself from a colonial institution and found a new identity moving between government, non-government and international organisations. This was not an easy path and involved selective decisions about the identity and mission of the School. The Pasteur Institutes spread around the French Empire make an interesting comparison. As private institutes they were not necessarily part of French Imperialism, but in effect they were actively its tools. In the post-war era they rewrote their past as independent networked institutes which practised international health rather than tropical or colonial medicine.[1] The LSTM with its teaching history could not so easily do this. The second half of this book looks at this changing identity and its influence on tropical medicine. This chapter looks in detail at the years 1945 to 1955. The theme is the emergence of a new identity for the School linked with the figure of Brian Gilmore Maegraith.

The disparate historiography of British decolonisation analyses the transition from colonies to the Commonwealth. This history is significant for the history of tropical medicine. A greater emphasis on social development, including health and welfare policies, characterised this final phase. In the case of Africa, there were tensions between implementing welfare policies and developing the machinery for government. A close analysis of the historiography of decolonisation with that of tropical medicine is beyond the scope of this chapter. What is crucial is to understand that the uncertainties during the final phase of colonialism affected the nature of tropical medicine and the identity of the LSTM.

Conflicting decisions over the future of the colonies and the role welfare policies would play in developing these territories created an unsettling atmosphere. An uncertain future affected the membership of the CMS. Decolonisation would cause greater disruption still. Each year fewer CMS officers came forward to take the diploma course at Liverpool. On the research side, valuable CO consultancies testified to the expertise of individual members of staff. Links with the CO were strengthened by the reinstatement of CO representation on School Council, which had been in abeyance since 1925. Dr William Henry Krauntz, Chief Medical Adviser to the Secretary of State for the Colonies, was appointed to the vacant position on 21 May 1946. The School looked for new directions to work within the revised role of the CO. Despite these opportunities the years after the war served as a valuable notice period for the LSTM. There was concern that the LSTM would not necessarily be able to sustain its programme of research without colonies in which to work. It could no longer self-finance regular expeditions nor reopen the overseas laboratory.

Changes in the post-war world economy affected Liverpool. Some members of the commercial community continued their traditional support for the LSTM. Several large companies made covenanted gifts for specific projects.[2] Much as it liked its past association with commerce the LSTM was now dependent not upon their generosity but upon a formula driven grant from the higher education budget of the Treasury.[3] The UGC now maintained the LSTM, providing as much as two-thirds of the recurrent income in any one year. For the LSTM to qualify for UGC funding it was required to establish stronger ties with the University authorities which hinted at a potential future loss of autonomy. The School's accounts were to be presented to the University Council annually and estimates of expenditure prepared and transmitted to the University for transmission to the UGC. Although this did not mean that the University Council and Senate were directly involved in the financial accounting of the School or in determining its research policy, it forced the LSTM to become more transparent in its administrative affairs. University representation on School Council and the Professional Committee were both increased after the Articles of Association were changed accordingly. A successful drive for funds in 1954 restored the balance between School and UGC money to more equal proportions. Further regular subscriptions very gradually reduced the accumulated deficit. The LSTM was shaken a little but remained committed to its independence.

## A FUTURE FOR THE COLONIES AND COLONIAL
## TROPICAL MEDICINE?

During World War II, debate on the future of the colonies reached a new level. Discussions on colonial development were focused by the issues raised for example in the report of the West India Royal Commission and Hailey's *An African Survey*.[4] The colonies provided sources of raw materials, labour and military strength during the war. Although the British tried to present colonialism as good propaganda, it also provided a rationale for attacking the British. Before the attack on Pearl Harbor, overtures to secure American intervention were clouded, among other things, by hostility to British imperialism. This was based on ideological and economic grounds.

Impressions of the economic development policies introduced in the 1930s were unfavourable. The emphasis on improving markets for British manufactures effectively continued the inherent exploitation of the imperial relationship. The CO tried to recast these programmes as neglectful rather than exploitative but acknowledged the need for change. New programmes were to redress the neglect of social development and welfare policies. Such policies should be integral to economic development rather than something that would follow in time.

The CDW Act of 1940 redefined trusteeship: colonies would no longer 'live of their own' instead 'a new conception of responsibility [ensured] Britain undertook to finance and help forward the development and welfare of the colonies'.[5] The discourse became that of 'constructive colonialism', 'partnership' and the 'transformation of Empire into Commonwealth'. Suitably educated local people could expect adequate representation and opportunity for active involvement in the various public services of their country. The time-frame for attaining this goal was vague. There was also no comprehensive plan for the colonies as a whole: the internal arrangement of the CO, with its regional divisions, and tensions in the colonies tended towards a piecemeal approach.[6]

If the CDW Act of 1940 was born of pre-war concerns and war-time necessities, the act of 1945 cautiously planned post-war reconstruction.[7] The Treasury provided one hundred and twenty million pounds over a ten-year period from March 1946. Colonial governments were to draw up a ten-year development plan encouraging the participation of indigenous people. In theory, machinery for colonial social and economic development had been inaugurated. The Labour Party, committed to removing freedom from want by its creation of the Welfare State, formed their first government in July 1945. They extended the same ethos to the colonies while preparing the way for self-government. Labour considered 'it is a truism...particularly applicable to Colonial societies that good health and education are pre-requisites to the practice of democratic government'.[8] They appeared to be honouring their commitment with two further CDW Acts in 1949 and 1950.

Achieving the laudable goals of colonial development proved to be difficult. Governments operate through intermediary bodies, in this case the CO. The CO had its agendas. The CO officials found greater difficulty in administering their plans than anticipated. In the later 1940s, problems in financing the home economy dissuaded the Government from rapid decolonisation. The politics of the cold war validated a revised colonialism. For all the rhetoric, welfare remained overshadowed by economic and political development policies.

Exposure to the rhetoric of their right to self-determination and anti-Nazi propaganda rejecting ideas of a master-race, left nationalists expecting more than they gained after the war ended. The United Nations, with its emphasis on equality of membership, reminded them of their inequitable position. Haqqi argues that the native leaders of the colonies perceived industrialisation rather than reliance upon export of raw materials as the way out of poverty. Britain often 'bought at fixed prices on long-term contracts': a system prejudicing the producers.[9] Rapid industrialisation was hard to realise in a short period given the circumstances in the tropical colonies. They lacked the basic infrastructure of modern industrial economies: adequate transport and energy resources, appropriate mineral and land usage, provision for the needs of an active labour force, and access to credit and banking facilities. Moreover, the CO did not encourage industrialisation. Instead, they tried to focus on programmes encouraging the dissolution of these ideas and the co-operation of the native people, particularly in Africa, by concentrating on agriculture: most famously in the ill-fated groundnut scheme. Communities were to be strengthened by improvements in health and education with an emphasis on infant and maternal welfare, sanitation and water supplies.

Britain's plans for colonial development coincided with other plans for economic and social development. The Marshall Aid plan launched in April 1948 addressed the immediate problems in Europe. The Point Four programme of President Truman of the USA relied upon the new principles of unity and equality among nations. The Colombo Plan for South East Asia, started in January 1950, aimed to bring two thousand million pounds over a six-year period to assist the development of this area of the world. There was no shortage of idealism and appreciable amounts of funding were forthcoming.

At a level above the bilateral and multilateral projects were the UN's specialised agencies for health, and social development: WHO, UNESCO and UNICEF. These agencies had a mandate to define health. Many programmes they inaugurated, particularly vertical disease programmes, imposed this definition on countries applying for aid. There was no shortage of applicants. Newly independent India and Pakistan led the chorus of those claiming the resources of WHO.[10] These international developments were not of immediate concern to the LSTM. It was not clear initially what kind of role an institution such as the School of Tropical Medicine in Liverpool could play in the machinery of global organisations. This was a difficulty shared with other much larger organisations such as the Office International d'Hygiene Publique and the Pan-American Sanitary Organisation, though they did not have the same colonial inheritance as the LSTM. These events reshaped the discipline of tropical medicine. However, the LSTM still played a crucial role in this not only in the British and colonial contexts, but as the second half of this book shows, increasingly in the international arena.

The importance of the changing face of colonialism and the challenge of the international organisations affected the School in a number of ways. First, the curtailment of their stock in trade: preparing CMS officers for overseas service. The student body taking the diploma courses was quite different to the pre-war cohorts (see chapter 7). Second, projects under the umbrella of welfare development introduced by the CO and the MRC affected the way the LSTM worked, particularly in the case of research overseas. Third, the role of the 'international expert' became increasingly popular in the colonial context. The staff of the LSTM largely ignored by WHO in the early years later found themselves greatly in demand for commissions, committees, overseas visits and as part of dedicated research projects.

The LSTM was no more able to redress the health problems of the colonial empire after the war than it had been before. However, those leading the School needed to find how it could represent a useful resource in the long term. 'Partnership' in the colonial relationship would be promoted by improvements in higher education in the tropics and the establishment of centres of excellence. It also worked at the level of village hygiene, where the partnership was still less equal and more paternal, but at least the concern was with the health of the indigenous population as a whole. School staff sat on a joint committee of the MRC and the CO, the Colonial Medical Research Committee. This was one of a series of 'welfare' committees formed during the war and immediately afterwards and aimed to co-ordinate and fund research in tropical health.[11] While it had to make immediate contributions, the LSTM needed to decide its future in changing circumstances.

## CHANGES AT THE LSTM: THE BUILDING AND THE ETHOS

Physically the LSTM emerged in reasonable shape at the end of the war. The building hastily completed in 1940 and pressed into immediate service needed refurbishing. The general shortage of materials delayed the outstanding work, but considerable internal alterations began in 1947. These changes accommodated the enlarged teaching and research programmes. Research rooms and offices were provided for the increasing number of post-graduate students. The expansion in staff, facilitated by the MRC's programme of Junior and Senior Fellows, was interrupted by war service. Thus, Scott Gladstone Cowper, D S Bertram and Ronald Seaton had to be 're-housed' upon their return to the LSTM.

The Museum had played an important part in teaching after the new building opened in 1920. In 1947, part of the space it occupied became the insectaries and an aquarium room. The new insectaries housed an expanded range of species. The maintenance of snail colonies and strains of schistosomes were also a new feature of these living collections. Active methods of investigation using live or recently killed specimens gradually replaced static models and exhibits in the study of entomology and parasitology. On the second floor, a new annexe stored the material used in these classes. New animal houses in 1950 completed these improvements. The wider range of insect and parasite species offset the lack of a permanent base in the tropics.

As the size of the Tropical Medicine museum declined, the Hygiene museum expanded. The range of material from around the world – photographs, models, and reference collections of food – increased. The field station in the grounds of Fazakerly Hospital, closed for the war, did not reopen. The displays therefore emphasised practical instruction on a wider range of topics for the new DTMH. A small printing press eased the preparation of teaching material. In December 1946, Dr Norman Lace Corkill became lecturer in Tropical Hygiene and curator of the museum. His appointment doubled the permanent staff of the department. Tropical Hygiene at Liverpool consisted of Davey as professor and Cowper who upon repatriation from a POW camp had returned to Liverpool to complete his MRC fellowship. In 1947, a bequest of £20,000 left in the will of the late John Middlemass Hunt in 1932 partly endowed the chair of Tropical Hygiene.

A new waiting room for out-patients on the first floor helped the consulting staff. The clinical work continued as an important feature of the School's work. After Yorke's death in 1943, the Department of Tropical Medicine had been divided into two sub-departments dealing with (a) teaching and research, and (b) clinical tropical medicine, which covered out-patient, in-patient and consultations. Adams, acting head of the Department of Tropical Medicine, remained in charge of Clinical Tropical Medicine after Maegraith's appointment.[12]

In the final year of the war over three and half thousand outpatients came to the LSTM. Approximately half of this number were servicemen and another five hundred belonged to the merchant navy. This case-load continued for several years. New illnesses appeared in those infected overseas who had initially not sought treatment, had been misdiagnosed or in whom the infections had been latent. These included the POWs who returned from the Far East. The figures for inpatients were similarly large. Liverpool's role as one the three centres of clinical tropical medicine in the country ensured a steady stream of cases and pathological specimens after the end of the war. The Smithdown Road Centre treated over two thousand in-patients in 1946. Although the smaller facility at Grafton Street closed in 1946, on 1 May that year the School's ward at the LRI reopened. Clinical cases were again available next door for students and city-wide the variety of cases was a great improvement on the pre-war situation.

Finance and management of the Tropical Diseases Centre at Smithdown Road, albeit in reduced form, became the responsibility of the Corporation after the EMS disbanded in July 1947.[13] Twelve months later it transferred to the care of the National Health Service. The involvement of British troops in the Korean conflict in 1950 and their later deployment in Malaya brought an influx of fresh cases, particularly *vivax* malaria. Consultations for the CO, the Ministry of Pensions and the resumption of trade with the tropics continued to bring new cases. Adams had inoculated several hundred people each year against yellow fever. This important preventative role continued and diversified. In 1946, over two thousand people came to the LSTM for inoculations against yellow fever, typhoid, typhus and smallpox. A year later the figure was one and half times greater. The LSTM now concentrated on promoting individual preventative medicine. The Travel Clinic awaited mass participation in exotic foreign holidays, but the escalation of air-travel increased the need for vigilance. The School was also keen to ensure that non-specialist practitioners were alert to the possibility of tropical infections should preventative measures fail and sought ways to increase the awareness of imported diseases. Thus in subtle ways the LSTM adapted to changes and gradually carved out new roles amidst the faster pace of life in post-war Britain.

New incumbents of key positions are held responsible for all that occurs from the date of their appointment. This is unfair: often they implement policies agreed before their arrival. However, they may be able to exercise considerable discretion in the manner in which they implement previously agreed programmes, reflecting their views on the institution's future. This was the case with the appointment of the new senior staff member at the LSTM.

Formal discussions on the post-war future of the LSTM appear to have begun with a circular issued to the professional staff by John R Hobhouse on 29 April 1942.[14] Hobhouse urged, on the issue of future staff, 'we should make up our minds now what staff we shall require after the war, so that we may recruit the right men as soon as they become available'.[15] The minimum requirement for each of the established Departments of Tropical Medicine, Tropical Hygiene and Entomology and Parasitology was a professor and a senior lecturer. In the case of Entomology and Parasitology there would be two senior lecturers.

Hobhouse was clear on the future of chemotherapy research at Liverpool: 'it is very desirable for the School to continue its work'. He ascribed success in this to Yorke and urged recruitment of someone capable of living up to his reputation. He indicated that this research could no longer be run from the Department of Tropical

Medicine, but should form its own department and the University be prevailed upon to create a chair of Chemotherapy. The new department would have a professor, 'a deputy' and a senior assistant, complemented by assistants from the MRC and industry. In a letter requesting support from the Nuffield Trust to endow the chair of Tropical Medicine in 1943, the School reaffirmed its commitment to establishing Chemotherapy on an independent basis.[16]

Hobhouse urged against reopening the laboratory at Freetown: recurrent expenditure was more than the School could bear. However, he considered it most desirable that staff spend time in the tropics and proposed a scheme whereby the senior staff could spend time overseas. To realise this he suggested that the LSTM and the LSHTM in collaboration with the MRC should develop a scheme co-ordinating tropical medicine research on an empire-wide basis.

Hobhouse's memorandum highlights key factors in the post-war management of the LSTM. First, there is no conception of the end of empire. Second, co-operation with government agencies, the MRC and CO, and the London School was a priority. The School would not benefit from being run in intellectual isolation. The relationship with the MRC had been useful. Their commitment to areas of research relevant to the tropics had expanded rapidly before the outbreak of war. There was every indication that this would continue. The link with the LSHTM had not always been smooth but the war had facilitated a pooling of effort, which Hobhouse wanted to extend in peace. He also urged the School to 'increase mutual assistance' with relevant faculties of the University. After the war, there was little indication that Hobhouse's hopes were realised.

On the general administration of the School, he indicated that this should 'not necessarily be handled by the senior professor'. He referred here to the default system that had evolved whereby the professor of Tropical Medicine took on responsibilities such as chair of Professional Committee and ambassador for the LSTM. Hobhouse suggested appointing a Dean who was above the departmental structure and free of departmental duties. The finances of the School were unlikely to permit such a luxury. As a compromise, the office of Dean could be revived and filled by a professor in return for an honorarium. This reference to the salary of the Dean was the only mention of finance in the memorandum. There was no indication that the LSTM envisaged a change in the style of funding. The contents of the circular met with general approval from the members of the Professional Committee. It was informally adopted, but left aside pending an appointment to the vacant chair of Tropical Medicine at the end of the war. In principle, the future ethos of the LSTM had been decided.

The leadership of Brian Gilmore Maegraith can be compared with the generally agreed plans on the running of the LSTM. His actions indicate how his plans for the future of tropical medicine and the role of the LSTM differed from those agreed previously.

## BRIAN GILMORE MAEGRAITH: 'HE MIGHT WELL TURN OUT TO BE A REAL WINNER.'[17]

After Yorke's sudden death the School waited before appointing a new professor of Tropical Medicine. However, early in 1944 a University Selection Committee met to consider suitable candidates. Tropical medicine was a small world. The post was not advertised. The committee and its external advisers, Edward Mellanby of the MRC, and Charles Wenyon, Director of the Wellcome Laboratories, agreed that the eight men suggested included all those suitable for the post. There was a clear British bias in the candidates. Lt-Col Brian Gilmore Maegraith, the youngest at thirty-seven years of age, was the 'strongest' contender, reservations on his background and experience notwithstanding.[18]

Maegraith, an Australian by birth, qualified MB BS from the University of Adelaide in 1930. Later that year a Rhodes scholarship brought him to the University of Oxford. In 1932, he won a Beit Memorial Fellowship that tided him over until 1934. In that year, he was elected a Fellow of Exeter College and made College tutor in physiology. He excelled in this discipline and the related field of pathology. In 1938, he became Dean of the Medical School at Oxford. At this date, he had an excellent research and administration background, but no tropical experience or evidence of interest in the problems of tropical medicine. He had served no apprenticeship in the CMS nor been exploring in the tropics in search of parasites and vectors. This had benefits. He was not hidebound by the pressures of colonial service. He was probably ignorant of the difficulties that faced an average member of the CMS pre-war or a member of staff in an institution like the LSTM. In the extraordinary circumstances of war, some of this changed.

On the outbreak of World War II Maegraith joined the RAMC, and, attached to the Advanced Air Striking Force, took charge of a mobile pathology unit in France. In August 1940, after his evacuation from Europe, he went overseas again. This time it was as Area Pathologist for Sierra Leone. As army laboratory facilities were not yet properly established in Freetown, he benefited from the offer of bench space and support from the School's laboratory and staff. This was the first contact with the LSTM, and he clearly made a lasting impression. When Davey fell ill, Maegraith repaid his kindness by taking on the additional pathology work including routine examination of specimens and post-mortems for the colonial government. He apparently enjoyed the post-mortem work. In 1941, he was promoted Assistant Director of Pathology for the West African Command. The work was well within his capabilities, although the material must at first have been unfamiliar. His time in West Africa, the experience of tropical diseases and their pathology, changed the course of his career.

Maegraith returned to Britain in 1943. He joined the MRC's Malaria Committee and took charge of the WO's Army Malaria Research Unit at Oxford. In three years, he had clearly gained a reputation in tropical medicine at least in military circles. His involvement with the MRC pointed towards expertise in malaria. In West Africa, he had taken an interest in the pathophysiology of malaria, blackwater fever and its association with quinine. The work for the AMRU continued his interest in the pharmacology and therapeutics of malaria. His team carried out a programme establishing the efficacy and safety of mepacrine as the drug of choice for treatment and prophylaxis in the military context. It was from the AMRU that he came to Liverpool, supported by recommendations from Edward Mellanby and Howard Florey of the Sir William Dunn School of Pathology, University of Oxford.

Referees were asked to comment on a candidate's clinical skills. The University Selection Committee were at pains to find an appointee with sufficient clinical expertise. In Maegraith's case they felt that his strong background in physiology and limited work in the tropics might make him unsuitable for Liverpool despite his reputation. This was similar to the reservations voiced against Yorke's appointment in 1928, but the situation had now intensified.

Florey wrote privately to McNair, the vice-chancellor of the University, but cautioned that the letter 'had better not be waved in front of [your] clinical colleagues'.[19] He urged that clinical ability should not be the main criteria used to assess Maegraith's candidature. He admitted that this was not where his current strengths lay but saw this as an advantage. Regardless of whether Maegraith was ultimately appointed, he urged McNair not to follow a current trend in pathology. Innovative experimenters lost university chairs because key clinicians wanted very skilled technicians rather than independent researchers. He considered that the 'chair of Tropical Medicine will unquestionably have an increasingly important role to play if what the Government says about colonial policy is not mere verbiage'.[20] Florey's public reference also alluded to Maegraith's administrative experience and his personal qualities. He particularly recommended Maegraith's ability to fashion individuals into a team working under his direction. Mellanby commented that 'he would undoubtedly prove to be at least up to the average of most professors in this subject', indicating a general low opinion of the discipline. He finished by saying that he thought Maegraith 'might well turn out to be a real winner'.[21]

In March 1945, Maegraith took up his appointment at the LSTM. He spent what remained of that year settling in and taking up associated positions within the University and city. He was appointed Honorary Consulting Physician for Tropical Diseases at the LRI on behalf of the Royal Liverpool United Hospitals Board and assumed responsibility for clinical work at the Tropical Diseases Centre. He continued research on the pharmacology of anti-malarial drugs assisted by staff in the department and Surgeon-Lieutenant R E Havard whose transfer from Oxford he had arranged.

In January 1946, Gordon resigned as chairman of the Professional Committee. Maegraith took his place. At the same time, he became Dean for two years in line with Hobhouse's earlier suggestion. Maegraith held the position until 1975 being re-elected every two or three years. The office of Dean became a key position. This marked a return to the days of Boyce rather than the hands-off style of John Middlemass Hunt, the previous Honorary Dean. As Dean and professor of Tropical Medicine Maegraith would lead the LSTM very visibly from the front.

In the ten years following Maegraith's arrival in Liverpool he gradually created an external network of influence. Some contacts he made because of his position as Dean and acted as the LSTM's representative, others reflected his research interests: all validated his position as leader of the LSTM.[22] This was important for he tried, as his predecessor Yorke had done, to channel the energies of the School along a path that suited his research interests and his vision of tropical medicine. It is unlikely Maegraith saw his project in any way similar to that of Yorke but both were trying to bring the basic biomedical sciences to bear on tropical diseases. Entomology and parasitology supported clinical tropical medicine which, in itself, did not attract experimental research. What Maegraith did was to bring tropical medicine to the forefront of current physiological research. Unlike Yorke he did not rely upon the results of new drugs to legitimate this. He extolled the virtue of pure science for its sake: 'fundamental work is often regarded as academic and unsatisfying from the point of view of spectacular results in the attack on human disease, but this is a narrow view'.[23] What stands out most about Maegraith, however, was the strength of his views on the future of the tropical medicine and how the LSTM could realise this vision during his long period of leadership.

External appointments allowed Maegraith to extend his influence beyond Liverpool in ways that were just beginning for Yorke in the inter-war years. The agenda of many of the committees on which Maegraith sat was implicitly one of reshaping tropical medicine in line with changing circumstances of its practice overseas. He was therefore privy to the views of other bodies and virtually in control of his own. He attempted to turn tropical medicine into a much more rigorous experimental science and gradually realigned the LSTM in this direction. He was most successful initially in taking control of the Departments of Tropical Medicine, Clinical Tropical Medicine and Chemotherapy. He came up against equally strong personalities in the Department of Entomology and Parasitology where proto research schools were emerging. He exerted much less control here. As Dean he was able to note with satisfaction that a productive and diverse research culture developed along the corridor albeit less dogmatic in style than his own.

## EXPERIMENTAL PHYSIOLOGY IN TROPICAL MEDICINE

Maegraith's familiarity with malaria and blackwater fever was apparent from the papers published after he joined the School. His research at Oxford and latterly in Liverpool had been subject to wartime publishing restrictions. With these lifted, a backlog of material came out in two collections of papers. One dealt with the development of Paludrine[24] and the second covered the results of the AMRU's investigations.[25] The emphasis on malaria chemotherapy, apparently complementing the LSTM's work, belied his overriding interest. Of much greater importance to Maegraith were the processes by which the normal functioning of the body became compromised in ill health. His application of pathophysiological methods to tropical diseases was an accident of fate, but he found a field ripe for investigation.[26] Despite its record of achievement, the LSTM had no reputation for tackling disease problems in this way and it was far from usual within the discipline.

His commitment to methodology over discipline is apparent in other early papers on conditions such as tropical sprue. This 'prolonged small-intestinal diarrhoea accompanied by a failure to absorb certain nutrients', was, at the time, understood to be a metabolic breakdown rather than the result of a specific infecting micro-organism.[27] What could be a better disease for a physiologist to tackle?[28] Later he would turn to conditions associated with malnutrition and deprivation: social diseases of tropical medicine. He was perhaps at his happiest breaking down what he regarded as artificial distinctions created by disciplinary boundaries.[29]

Maegraith's programme of pathophysiological research received a boost with the £10,000 received from the Board of Messrs John Holt & Co in April 1948. This firm had been among the LSTM's first group of supporters. The *Annual Report* described their motivation as a desire 'to do something in a practical way' about the malaria affecting their African and European staff. They considered that 'there was much to be learned on the pathophysiological level'.[30] It is highly unlikely that a commercial Board of Directors would have chosen a specific research methodology as the means of achieving their 'practical' result without help. As Yorke had persuaded commercial firms to use the LSTM's laboratories for biological research in chemotherapy, so Maegraith commanded the ear of Messrs John Holt & Co. He could now dictate the research of the leading department in the LSTM. The language of the annual reports and paper titles from the Department of Tropical Medicine changed radically under Maegraith's leadership. His public pronouncements on the future of the discipline and the School were repeated in private correspondence within the management structure of the LSTM.[31]

The Fund bought new equipment for the laboratories. It also paid for the salary of a research assistant for three years. When the initial grant expired, Messrs John Holt & Co agreed to fund a further programme of research. In the *Annual Report* for 1953–1954, Maegraith referred to a working hypothesis formed during the war. His observations on liver damage, associated with blackwater fever and malaria, were very similar to those previously seen when active substances circulated in the blood stream and passed through the liver.[32] Maegraith not only conducted a review of the literature, but began a programme of experimental work establishing a new baseline of knowledge in this field.[33]

Maegraith's opportunities for research were constrained by administration and external responsibilities. He increasingly relied upon research students and technicians to take forward his ideas along with their own. By default and by design he created a research school investigating the pathophysiology of tropical diseases. Florey's reference had mentioned Maegraith's ability to lead a research team and create an environment in which people worked well together. One of the key features of the Maegraith research school was an insistence on team work to answer certain fundamental questions in the pathophysiology of malaria. He set out six points in a memorandum to the Treasurer in 1948, one month before the announcement of the Holt Fund.[34] This can be read as Maegraith's manifesto on the LSTM and tropical medicine:

> we are dissecting malaria as a problem of living tissue subject to normal physiological reactions and faced with severe competition from the invading malaria parasite. It is amazing that this has never been done in malaria or for that matter in any *other disease as a whole*. No one for instance has taken pneumonia and tried to find out why exactly the patient fails to use oxygen or what happens in his tissue as a result of this failure. The implications of this research are of course much wider than simply clearing up the problems of malaria, but in this particular disease it has become clear that the approach is a profitable one. It is important to progress for the sake of knowledge alone, but it is gratifying to have early practical results...I regard this physiological approach as fundamental.[35]

It was both the contents of this statement and the strength and certainty with which he made it that demonstrates his vision of the LSTM and tropical medicine.

The international nature of the LSTM's students ensured from the beginning that Maegraith's research school had an international basis. International did not mean the usual North American and European networks or the international agencies. It referred to links with developing countries and encompassed the new role of the LSTM as an institute primarily providing recognised qualifications in higher education, not preparing practitioners for the colonial service. For instance

Chamlong Harinasuta, Maegraith's first PhD student, started work at the LSTM on 1 October 1951 funded by the British Council. He chose to work on amoebiasis rather than follow Maegraith's suggestion of malaria. The research determined the factors underlying liver abscess and the antigenic structure of *E. hystolytica*. The guinea pig served as a model, and parasite strains were established. The disease may not have been Maegraith's first choice, but his ideas inspired the methodology. Dr Kanjika Devakul, from the University of Bangkok, arrived in 1954 to replace Harinasuta. She worked on haemolysis in protozoal infections.

Maegraith's research school also attracted specific kinds of funding and interaction with other groups. Mrs B Glocking, funded by the MRC through the CMRC, represented the first appointment under this scheme in the UK rather than an overseas laboratory. She joined the research team in 1954. The LSTM gained valuable experience in the field through their links with the MRC and their laboratory at Fajara in The Gambia. The School returned to the extended laboratory network, characteristic of years up to 1914. However, this time the LSTM was now helping to form networks with other organisations rather than being independent. Clever links, not isolationism, pointed the way forward.

## CHEMOTHERAPY: MAEGRAITH TAKES CONTROL OF THE LSTM

This chapter has reviewed the status of the LSTM at the end of the war, the appointment of Maegraith and his approach to tropical medicine. The fate of the Department of Chemotherapy is an excellent example of the way Maegraith controlled the LSTM. It sets in context pronouncements such as the 'energy of the School research staff can be concentrated where they are most efficient – the study of fundamental problems' and 'fundamental work...is a primary function of the School'.[36] It shows that his definition of 'fundamental' prioritised physiological research in tropical medicine. It did not necessarily refer to fundamental work in disciplines likely to have an immediate bearing on health in the tropics.

From the School's point of view, Yorke's initiative, continued on the clinical side by Adams and on the chemical and biological side by Lourie and his department, had brought considerable kudos. Financially the department was relatively secure. The appeal to create a department in Yorke's memory received generous support: £46,000 of the required capital sum of £60,000 had been raised. Hobhouse's wartime memorandum considered it essential that the LSTM continue with chemotherapy research. There was no evidence of dissent by other members of staff. The response to memoranda from the University's Post-war Planning Committee indicated that the already large Department of Chemotherapy was likely to grow, crowding other departments. Estimated staff numbers from 1944 showed the Departments of Tropical Medicine and Chemotherapy leading the way with thirteen members of staff each. Entomology and Parasitology would have ten, and Tropical Hygiene, five members of staff.[37] The estimate of annual staff costs for Tropical Medicine was £6,100 and for Chemotherapy, £5,200. Estimates of likely capital costs included a sum of £750 for equipment.[38] However, £3,100 of the Chemotherapy costs were recoverable from outside sources.[39]

The Department of Clinical Tropical Medicine under Adams assumed responsibility for the majority of drug testing. The success of preliminary trials of Paludrine set a precedent. Besides clinical care, drug tests such as those establishing the efficacy of new antibiotics in amoebic dysentery were part of the work of the department. Adams and later Maegraith's clinical appointments made testing a matter of routine and not dependent on special arrangement with hospital authorities. Lourie's work on out-patient administration of penicillin for syphilis aside, the Department of Chemotherapy concentrated on pure chemical and biological research.[40]

Lourie continued work on Paludrine. He focused on human malaria following the announcement of parasite resistance in birds.[41] This was a collaborative project with Bertram in the Department of Entomology and Parasitology. They jointly demonstrated the persistence of parasite resistance after passage through mosquitoes. Simpson continued his work with cinnolines. He investigated the mechanism by which this group of compounds worked in trypanosomiasis. Williamson concentrated on the idea of chemotherapeutic interference. This occurred after the simultaneous administration of two compounds. One would annul the effect of the other. Such research projects were a continuation of Yorke's interests and methods.

Yet, Lourie's penicillin study was significant. It was the first trial commissioned by the MRC Penicillin Trials Committee, therefore confirming his high standing, and that of the LSTM, in the eyes of the MRC. In the 1920s, the MRC tested arsenical compounds as anti-syphilitics, but did not commission the LSTM. Yorke had an excellent record in the malaria therapy of GPI patients and could have performed interesting comparative experiments. Penicillin treatment of syphilis did not appear as a priority in tropical medicine. It may have fuelled Maegraith's argument that this was not work for the LSTM. He extolled 'discovery of the processes at work in the disease' while dismissing 'ad hoc successes such as...the clinical trials of Paludrine'. The Paludrine work attracted useful publicity, but greater value lay in the School's 'fundamentalist outlook...that has given it the very great name it possesses in the scientific world'.[42]

His justification for supporting the closure of the Department of Chemotherapy was the enhancement of the work of the Department of Tropical Medicine. In his report to the Treasurer in March 1948, he mentioned a recent paper on physiological research in tropical medicine at the RSTMH. The 'team' presentation, well received by a prestigious audience, persuaded him to 'devote all available space and staff in the department to the work of clearing up as much as possible of the outstanding problems of malaria over the next five years'.[43] Recent American interest in his work threatened the LSTM's pre-eminence in this field. Expansion by the Department of Chemotherapy might restrict his plans. On a mundane level, the animal houses on the roof urgently needed rebuilding to avoid an official complaint from the Home Office inspector. With limited funds, there was direct competition between plans for Chemotherapy and Tropical Medicine. If the endowment for Chemotherapy was transferred to Tropical Medicine this would materially aid the physiology research projects. The appropriateness of chemotherapy work within the LSTM would have to be challenged if Maegraith were to realise his plans. The tensions of running an institution and running personal research in an essentially under-funded environment came to the fore in this episode.

At the end of September 1948 Lourie tendered his resignation from the Directorship of the Department of Chemotherapy and the LSTM. At the end of the year J C E Simpson, J S Morley, J McIntyre and P E Macey also left. Ian M Rollo and Williamson had left by the end of July 1949. In the *Annual Report* for 1949–1950 there was no longer a Department of Chemotherapy listed in the opening pages. Lourie's resignation was apparently prompted by the University's failure, after protracted discussions, to meet his demands that they offer him a chair in Chemotherapy instead of the proposed readership. He had approached the University in January 1946 to clarify their position on the department's future, arguing that he could not plan its strategy without knowing their views.[44] This overture formed part of general discussions on the relationship of the LSTM and University referred to above. There was some initial sympathy to expanding the University's interest in this field and particularly as this potentially involved the transfer of the endowments attached to the department. Maegraith's notes show his decision not to lose this funding if Chemotherapy changed to a department of the Faculty of Medicine located in the LSTM.[45] He was confident that Council would not allow the University to 'accept a successful department, £46,000 and accommodation for an indefinite period in return for recognising the department in the University so long as they don't have to pay for it'.[46] He considered it was better for the LSTM to lose Chemotherapy than the money raised. The University's attitude convinced Maegraith that a safe distance between the University and the LSTM was in the best interests of the School. He would sacrifice chemotherapy and Lourie if it ensured no deeper involvement between the two institutions.[47]

The University's rationale behind this decision apparently lay in uncertainty over the true independence of chemotherapy as distinct from pharmacology and bacteriology. They were therefore reluctant to establish a chair in a subject that might prove to have no legitimacy. Lourie regarded the interdisciplinary nature of the subject as its greatest strength. He warned the University that unless they appointed at the professorial level the subject would fail to attract bright post-graduate students necessary to develop this field. A readership sent out the message that this was a career path limited to the medium levels of academic life. Lourie called the bluff of the Faculty of Medicine and lost: resignation was then his only option.[48] It appears that Maegraith failed to communicate the seriousness of Lourie's intentions in writing to the University's Standing Committee on Chairs when they met on 12 May 1947. Undoubtedly Lourie had a difficult personality. This was evident during his time in West Africa in the late 1930s. It is also apparent from some of the correspondence concerned with the Department of Chemotherapy. However, his academic standing was clear. After a short period in Oxford, Lourie joined the WHO secretariat as Chief of the Section of Biological Standardisation.

When the Department of Chemotherapy disbanded, the School had a large sum of money but no one to lead the department it had been raised to support. The best option appeared to be reabsorption of the activities and attached endowments of Chemotherapy into the Department of Tropical Medicine. Maegraith's forceful memorandum to the School's Treasurer provided the impetus. There was some concern over the legality of closing the Department of Chemotherapy. It took some time to contact the benefactors and obtain their consent.[49] A meeting of the professional staff on 4 June 1949 decided to re-endow the chair of Tropical Medicine with the Warrington Yorke Fund. Maegraith became the Alfred Jones & Warrington Yorke Professor of Tropical Medicine in 1951.

## OTHER RESEARCH SCHOOLS AT THE LSTM: ENTOMOLOGY AND PARASITOLOGY

Maegraith's emphasis on fundamental research and on team work were not the exclusive preserve of the Department of Tropical Medicine. In contrast to his style, however, members of staff did not publicly articulate their activities in the same manner or to the same degree. The Department of Tropical Hygiene was small and not research driven. The LSTM could not claim much of a reputation in this field in the immediate post-war years. Besides the teaching for the Diploma course, Davey's main work was as an international consultant. The role of ambassador and expert enhanced the School's visibility overseas. His work for the Inter-University Commission on Higher Education in the Colonies is reviewed in chapters 5 and 7. Long periods away from the School on behalf of this Commission and his involvement with other CO committees made sustained research difficult.[50] Davey became involved with debates on the population explosion in developing countries and the risks of preventative medical intervention in these circumstances.[51]

121

On the other hand the Department of Entomology and Parasitology under Gordon's lead was very much research driven. The unification of these disciplines came to fruition only after the war. The idea of bringing together study of the vector and parasite as a complex, rather than studying such elements in isolation, was an important innovation for the LSTM. The internal organisation of the department also reflected new directions in these subjects. It involved none of the machinations that faced the Department of Tropical Medicine.

The number of staff and the diversity of projects in Entomology and Parasitology increased in the years following the war. Besides Gordon as professor, William Edgar Kershaw joined the department in August 1946 as the first lecturer in medical parasitology. After 1953, this position became the Leverhulme Lectureship in recognition of their generous funding. This complemented the lectureship in medical entomology. The School's long-standing interest in veterinary parasitology continued with the appointment of Reginald Bark Griffiths in January 1949 as a replacement for Kenneth Unsworth. The University's Veterinary Pathology laboratories conducted work on insecticides relevant to animal health.[52] The relationship between the Faculty of Veterinary Medicine and the LSTM appeared to be a good deal smoother than between the Faculty of Medicine and the LSTM. The veterinary connection also involved the LSTM in parasitology and entomology of direct relevance to British veterinary medicine. The Agricultural Research Council supported work in the department on bovine cysticercosis. Gordon and Griffiths established this programme, but the study was carried out by the American zoologist, Paul H Silverman.[53]

The external interest and funding were a characteristic of the joint department. For instance, the MRC funded research in schistosomiasis and filariasis in the department. The CO also funded an overseas project in Kumba in British Cameroon supervised by Gordon. Kershaw and Crewe worked for varying periods on aspects of loiasis under the same scheme: Kershaw as a member of LSTM staff and Crewe under an appointment of the CMRS. This was large scale, networked research: the MRC and CO facilitated frequent interchange between Kumba and Liverpool. Staff shared similar interests but worked less obviously as a team. Gordon and Kershaw made no public show of joint research interests.

The reputation of members of staff created frequent requests for their service as consultants, particularly in West Africa. Gordon chaired the Helminthiasis Sub-Committee of the CMRC in 1951. A year later Kershaw joined him on the Committee. The loiasis work in the Cameroon expanded into studies of filarial infections and their vectors in other parts of the British colonies: a CMRC project.

The quality of work notwithstanding, the Department of Entomology and Parasitology was less proactive than Tropical Medicine. It successfully responded to new opportunities created by the expansion of medical research in the colonies. It did not seek to send out a different message about its activities from the conservative excellence in this field that the School had demonstrated before. There is less of a sense that the staff in this department attempted to redefine the contents of tropical medicine by institutional alignments or the style of their work.


## CONCLUSION

Amidst the uncertainties of the colonial situation, the LSTM had to consider how it would continue its activities. Moves to reshape higher education, in particular the teaching of medicine, through the Goodenough Committee and the provision for scientific training, via the Barlow Report created a further set of uncertainties. The LSTM was affected by debate on the future of higher education because it increasingly taught by research and because its independence from the University was threatened by lack of finance from private sources. The Hobhouse memorandum suggested a continuation of all the pre-war work with expansion where possible.

This was the situation which the new professor and Dean, Maegraith, inherited. His views on tropical medicine and the role of the LSTM were quite different to anything the LSTM had experienced before. Maegraith promoted fundamental research. He considered this was the most appropriate use of the skills of the staff, the resources of the LSTM and its location outside the tropics as part of British higher education. His views developed during 1945 to 1948: the years between his arrival at the LSTM and the publication of his seminal work on the pathophysiology of malaria. He was not content to let parasitology and entomology, although becoming increasingly more sophisticated, be the leading sciences of the discipline of tropical medicine. He was determined that the process of disease in the human body caused by infectious organisms should have a proper scientific basis alongside entomology and parasitology. His non-tropical background and belief in the results of properly applied experimental physiology ensured that he perceived tropical medicine differently.

The discipline of tropical medicine, created in part with the foundation of the two Schools, represented parasitology and helminthology, as variants of bacteriology, applied to ill health in the tropics. There was initially an emphasis on the fevers and bowel diseases. The established and successful empirical observation of sickness overseas became clinical tropical medicine. The complicated life cycles of parasites and worms required an additional supporting science – entomology. In this 'new' discipline, the process of disease in the body was not investigated with the same rigour as the supporting sciences of parasitology, helminthology and entomology. Yorke used ideas of infection and immunity to introduce scientific methods into tropical medicine. He still concentrated more on the parasite than the host. He also worked with the goal of producing drugs in the background. Maegraith ignored this tradition of the discipline. He advocated physiological research for its sake, investigating the process of disease in the body with and without reference to the parasite. The role of the human body in disease was no longer a passive element triangulating entomology and parasitology.

The LSTM emerged from the end of the war with limited options and a need to find a new position in the local, national and international contexts. Maegraith would not squander his research for the sake of the institution. He took a pragmatic look at the structure of the LSTM and decided that Chemotherapy was the least useful of the composite elements that formed the School. To justify this he referred to its marginal connection with the discipline and moved centre-stage his research agenda. His skills as an administrator, his force and his drive were no match for Lourie. Chemotherapy was easily marginalised. Maegraith now used his position as clear leader of the LSTM to direct the School and its view of tropical medicine.

## NOTES

[1] A M Moulin, 'The Pasteur Institutes between the two world wars. The transformation of the international sanitary order', P Weindling (ed), *International health organizations and movements 1918–1939*, Cambridge: CUP, 1995, pp. 244–265.
[2] ICI donated money for the Department of Chemotherapy and later for research in the Departments of Tropical Medicine and Entomology and Parasitology; May & Baker supported biochemical research in the Department of Tropical Medicine; United Africa Company sponsored filariasis research in the Department of Entomology and Parasitology; Messrs John Holt & Co. established a fund for malaria research in the Department of Tropical Medicine.
[3] TM/8/F.5.1, University Estimates Committee.
[4] W M Hailey, *An African survey: a study of the problems arising in Africa south of the Sahara*, London: OUP, 1938.
[5] S A H Haqqi, *The colonial policy of the Labour Government (1945–51)*, Aligarh: Muslim University Press, 1960, p. 12.
[6] A N Porter & A J Stockwell, *British imperial policy and decolonization, 1938–1964*, Macmillan: Basingstoke, 1987, pp. 32–38.
[7] Ibid., p. 41.
[8] A Creech Jones, *Labour's colonial policy*, London, 1947, p. 11.
[9] Porter & Stockwell, *British imperial policy*, p. 49.
[10] S Lee, 'WHO and the developing world: the contest for ideology', A Cunningham & B Andrews (eds), *Western medicine as contested knowledge*, Manchester: MUP, 1997, pp. 24–45.
[11] Other committees: Development and Welfare Advisory Committee, Colonial Products Research Council, Colonial Primary Products Committee.
[12] Adams was appointed Consulting Physician for the CO, and Honorary Physician in charge of the Tropical Diseases Department at the LRI in 1945.
[13] TM/8/F.1.
[14] TM/14/HoJ, John Richard Hobhouse served as a representative of the University's Council on the Council of the LSTM from 1932–1934. He was made Honorary Treasurer a year later and held this post until 1942 when he was made a Vice-Chairman. He served in this position until 1949 when he was made Chairman. From 1955 until his death in 1961, he was President of the LSTM.
[15] TM/3/1.5a, Council Minutes, 4 May 1942.
[16] TM/3/1.5a, Council Minutes, 4 October 1943, 20 September 1943.
[17] TM/14/MaB/8–10, Report on the Selection Committee for the chair of Tropical Medicine, 2 October 1944.
[18] Ibid.
[19] TM/14/MaB/8–10, Florey to McNair, 23 June 1944.
[20] Ibid.
[21] TM/14/MaB/8–10, Report on the Selection Committee for the chair of Tropical Medicine, 2 October 1944.
[22] 1944, Tropical Diseases Hospital Committee. 1945, ICI Fellowships Committee University of Liverpool. 1946, Malaria Sub-committee, CMRC; Council & Policy Committee of the RSTMH; Member of the Board of

Veterinary Studies, University of Liverpool. 1947, British West African CMRC. 1948, Committee of the International Congresses of Tropical Medicine & Malaria. 1949, Member of the Nuffield Panel of Consultants to the CMS. 1950, LSTM representative Advisory Committee of the Empire Medical Advisory Bureau. 1951, LSTM representative West African Standing Advisory Committee Medical Research. 1953, West African Council for Medical Research; Chemotherapy Committee, MRC; Management Committee, MRC's laboratories at Fajara, The Gambia.

[23] TM/8/F.2, Rawlings, Mr H J (Treasurer), Correspondence 1948–1952.

[24] For instance, B G Maegraith, A R D Adams, J D King, M M Tottey, D J Rigby & R A Sladden, 'Paludrine in the treatment of malaria', *BMJ*, i, 1946, 305–309; A Spinks, M M Tottey & B G Maegraith, 'The pharmacology of Paludrine and some other new antimalarials', *Proceedings of the Biochemical Society*, 40, 1946, i–ii.

[25] For instance, AMRU, 'Determination of plasma mepacrine: a note on the anticoagulant', *Lancet*, 249, 1945, 144–145; *idem*, 'Factors effecting the excretion of mepacrine in the urine', *ATMP*, 39, 1945, 53–60; *idem*, 'Mepacrine in animal tissues', ibid., 40, 1946, 174–180.

[26] *DNB 1986–1990*, pp. 283–284.

[27] G C Cook, 'Tropical sprue', F E G Cox (ed), *The Wellcome Trust illustrated history of tropical diseases*, Wellcome Trust: London, 1996, pp. 356–369.

[28] B G Maegraith, A R D Adams, R E Havard, J D King & R F Millett, 'Carbohydrate absorption in sprue', *Lancet*, 249, 1945, 635; B G Maegraith, 'The diagnosis and treatment of sprue and associated syndromes', *Medical Press*, 216, 1947, 297–305.

[29] *54th Annual Report of the LSTM, 1952–1953*, p. 12.

[30] *49th Annual Report of the LSTM, 1947–1948*, p. 18.

[31] TM/8/F.2, Rawlings, Mr H J (Treasurer), Correspondence 1948–1952; TM/8/G.2, Tropical Diseases Hospital Committee 1945–1947; TM/8/F.20.1, May & Baker Ltd 1938–1961; TM/8/F.20.2, May & Baker 1944–1949; TM/8/D.15, Chemotherapy I; TM/8/F.13, Warrington Yorke Memorial Fund 1944–1951.

[32] *55th Annual Report of the LSTM, 1953–1954*, p. 26.

[33] B G Maegraith, *Pathological processes in malaria and blackwater fever*, Oxford: OUP, 1948.

[34] The six questions to be answered by this research were: 1. How does the parasite exist in relation to the host? 2. Why does anaemia develop in severe malaria? 3. Why in malaria and blackwater fever does kidney failure supervene and how should it be treated? 4. Why does the liver so often fail in malaria and blackwater fever? 5. What kills the patient in acute malaria? 6. What initiates the clinical picture in malaria?

[35] TM/8/F.2, Rawlings, Mr H J (Treasurer), Correspondence 1948–1952, Research in the Department of Tropical Medicine, Maegraith to Rawlings, 18 March 1948.

[36] *53rd Annual Report of the LSTM, 1951–1952*, p. 13; *52nd Annual Report of the LSTM, 1950–1951*, p. 8.

[37] TM/8/U.6.1, Planning School, Future of, 1944.

[38] TM/8/F.5.1, University Estimates Committee, 1945.

[39] TM/8/U.6.2, Planning School, Future of, 1946.

[40] A O F Ross, R B Nelson, E M Lourie & H O J Collier, 'Treatment of early syphilis with penicillin', *Lancet*, 247, 1944, 845–848; E M Lourie, H O J Collier, A O F Ross, D T Robinson & R B Nelson, 'Ambulatory treatment of early syphilis with penicillin: rationale, experimental basis and preliminary results', *Lancet*, 249, 1945, 696–701.

[41] J Williamson, D S Bertram & E M Lourie, 'Acquired resistance to Paludrine in *P. gallinaceum*: effects of Paludrine and other antimalarials', *Nature*, 159, 1947, 885–886.

[42] TM/8/F.2.

[43] Ibid.

[44] TM/8/D.15, Chemotherapy I 1946–1948, Lourie, Memorandum, Warrington Yorke Department of Chemotherapy, 2 January 1946.

[45] TM/8/D.15, Chemotherapy I 1946–1948, Meeting, Subcommittee of Chemotherapy, 3 March 1947.

[46] TM/8/D.15, Chemotherapy I 1946–1948, Maegraith to Burford, 12 February 1948.

[47] TM/8/D.15, Chemotherapy I 1946–1948, Notes of a conversation between the Vice-chancellor and Maegraith, 22 April 1948.

[48] TM/8/D.15, Chemotherapy I 1946–1948, Lourie to Gordon, 14 November 1947.

[49] TM/8/F.13, Warrington Yorke Memorial Fund 1944–1951, Burford to Hobhouse, 4 November 1948 and 19 June 1951.

[50] 1946 Colonial Advisory Medical Committee; CO Tsetse Fly & Trypanosomiasis Committee; Inter-University Council for Higher Education in the Colonies; Council of Gordon Memorial College Khartoum.

[51] T H Davey, 'Population growths in the tropics', *Health Education Journal* 6, 1948, 150–154.

[52] Trials of Gammexane were made against mite infections in domestic poultry.

[53] Personal Communiction, R B Griffiths, 3 April 1997.

1.   Exterior of Crofton Lodge: the School's research laboratory at Runcorn, c. 1905.

2.   Assistants with infected animals in the paddock at Runcorn, which provided facilities for keeping larger experimental animals.

3.  Interior of the monkey house at Runcorn, c. 1905.

4.  Interior of a workroom at Runcorn, c. 1905.

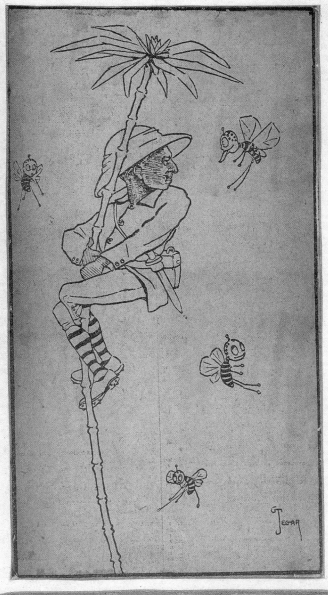

Sir Rubert Boyce leaves Liverpool to-morrow for Sekondi to devise means of stamping out the yellow fever outbreak.

5. Anonymous cartoon - 'Sir Rubert Boyce leaves Liverpool for Sekondi to devise a means of stamping out the yellow fever outbreak' - refers to the 25th expedition to Sierra Leone and the Gold Coast, June 1910.

6. 'A Gold Coast Road'. Members of the LSTM staff on expedition, c. 1904.

7. The School's 22nd expedition visited Barbados in 1909 to advise on anti-malaria measures. Sir Rubert Boyce, tenth from the left, watches the street clearing designed to remove mosquito breeding sites.

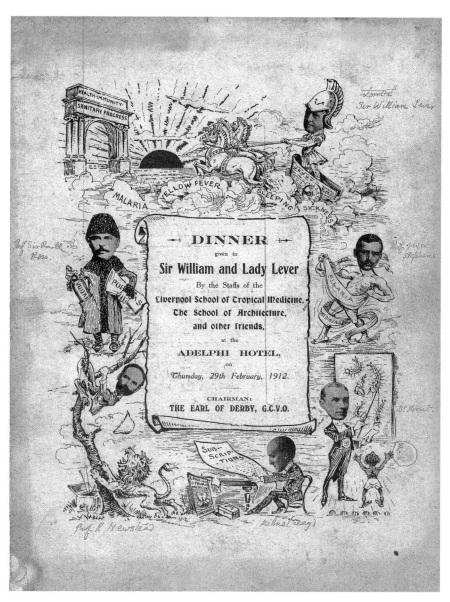

8. Dinner menu, 29 February 1912. Sir William Lever was the second Chairman of the LSTM, 1910-1913.

9.  The DTM class, December 1914. Front row from the left: Sir Ronald Ross, John W W Stephens, Warrington Yorke. Second row centre: Donald B Blacklock.

10.  Nursing and military medical staff who worked at the temporary military hospital at the LSTM during World War I.

11.  Exterior of the School's laboratory and the Santa Casa
     Hospital in Manáos, Brazil.

12.  Interior of the main laboratory in Manáos, Brazil.

13. Dr Harold Wolferstan Thomas, director of the Manáos laboratory, c. 1920.

14. The Eleanor Rice floating laboratory, presented to Dr Thomas in 1920 by Dr and Mrs Hamilton Rice.

15. Front of the Sir Alfred Jones Laboratory, Freetown, Sierra Leone, showing the projecting kiosk for microscopy and the living accommodation above.

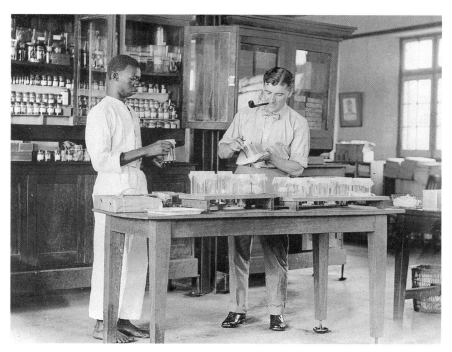

16. Interior of the Freetown Laboratory, Donald B Blacklock with one of the native assistants.

17. HRH The Prince of Wales inspecting material at the Freetown
    Laboratory during his visit to West Africa in 1925.

18. Native assistant and George MacDonald at work in Freetown,
    c. 1925.

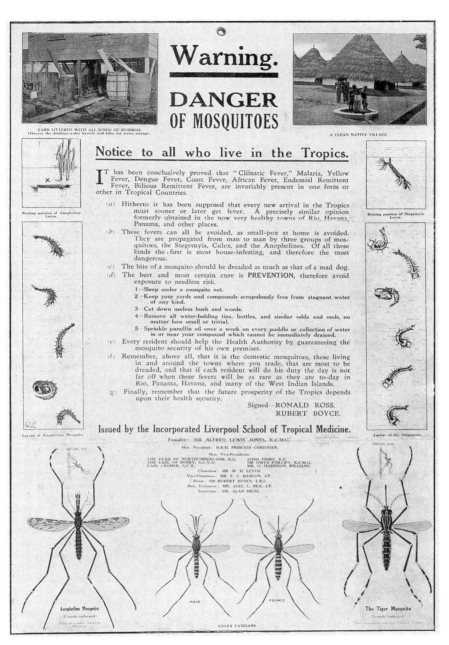

19. A notice issued by the LSTM in 1910 to advise the general public about the danger of mosquitoes in the tropics.

20. Entrance Hall of the LSTM's purpose-built building in Pembroke Place, c. 1920.

21. The animal houses on the roof of the LSTM, c. 1939, against the smog of Liverpool's skyline.

22. The library of the LSTM, c. 1939, with the skylight which illuminated all the floors of the building.

23. The first cohort of the new combined DTMH, autumn 1946.
Front row from left: Dr D S Bertram, Dr E M Lourie, Dr A R
D Adams, Professor B G Maegraith, Dr W H H Andrews,
Miss E W Roberts, Dr W E Kershaw.

24. DTMH class autumn 1953. Front row from left: Mr G B
Griffiths, Dr R Seaton, Dr W Lightbody, Professor T H Davey,
Professor B G Maegraith, Dr A R D Adams, Dr M Lavoipierre,
Mr D Dagnall. Chamlong Harinasuta, Maegraith's PhD student
and founder of the Faculty of Tropical Medicine Bangkok,
second row, second from the left.

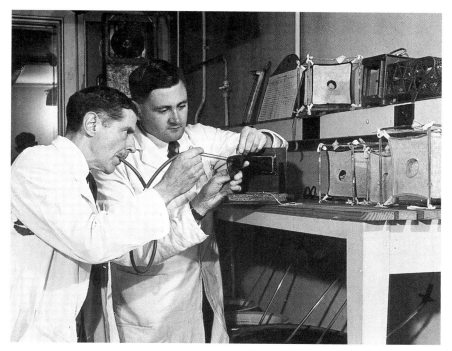

25. Professor R M Gordon working with sandfly larvae - the transmitter of Kala-azar - assisted by Dr O'Rourke, c. 1951

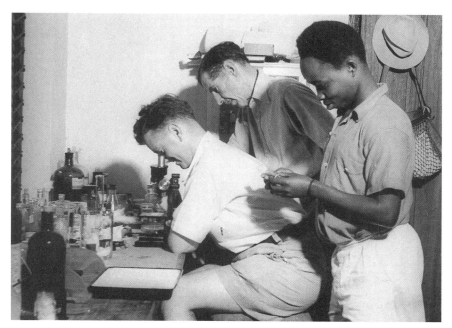

26. Dr W Crewe, Professor R M Gordon and Moses in the laboratory at Kumba, Cameroon, c. 1952.

LIVERPOOL SCHOOL OF TROPICAL MEDICINE

27. The LSTM in 1952 before the addition of the Nuffield and
     Maegraith wings.

# 5

# 'WE LIVE TO SERVE IN THE TROPICS': TEACHING THE TEACHERS.[1]

## INTRODUCTION

The years from 1955 to 1965 forced an identity crisis at the LSTM. Britain's association with certain parts of the empire ended. The Gold Coast became Ghana in March 1957: the first of the African colonies to gain independence. By 1966, the other West African territories joined Ghana as members of the Commonwealth. At the level of national policies for aid, there was a disjunction between the British and newly independent governments but individual links could still be fostered.

In Britain, the number of imported cases of diseases prevalent in the tropics increased. This reflected the greater use of air-travel and rising numbers of immigrants from the tropics. While transmission of malaria was extremely unlikely, 'cosmopolitan' diseases could be spread within Britain.[2] Adams reported a growing number of tuberculosis cases among immigrants, and commented that this 'non-tropical disease' now appeared with great regularity in his clinics and therefore overseas. It was a measure of the somewhat arbitrary creation of the discipline that the incidence of tuberculosis in the tropics was largely ignored until after World War II.[3] The humanitarian rationale for a specialist centre in Britain dealing with tropical medicine, broadly conceived, was apparent. How it would continue to function was less clear. It would become increasingly necessary to convince the British Government and civil service officers that despite the end of empire the problems of poor health in the tropics could not be forgotten. In this period, there were frequent debates on the rationale for and most effective provision of medical aid to developing countries. Before effectively convincing others, the LSTM had to settle on what their mission would be. This was a two-fold exercise: the home establishment and the overseas contacts.

Fundamental research at the School continued to flourish. Technological innovations in other fields of basic science brought increasing sophistication to the laboratory work in Liverpool. The transmission electron microscope, installed in 1963, and the routine use of radioisotopes, offered new ways of seeing disease causing organisms and changes inside the body. Advances in biochemistry further deconstructed the complicated processes of life, in this case the host-parasite interaction, to simple, reproducible elements. The host-parasite interaction referred to man compromised by disease. Significantly, it also referred to the effects of parasites on a range of arthropods and freshwater organisms hosting and transmitting the parasites. The mathematics of vector populations, the mechanisms that allowed some species to be carriers and not others, the genetics of the predisposition to carry parasites, all came under scrutiny as part of the applied biology in the Department of Parasitology and Entomology.

A serious lack of teaching and bench space was alleviated in 1966 by an extension on the left of the building. This provided a new lecture theatre and three floors of research rooms and teaching laboratories. The Nuffield wing was built at a cost of £200,000. Large donations from the Nuffield and Wolfson Foundations and an anonymous donor helped to realise this figure. An appeal for funds was successfully launched, but the LSTM was also forced to dip into its reserves. A continued short fall in recurrent funding obviously followed the realisation of assets. Moves were therefore also taken to establish a much larger invested capital.

The new wing doubled the number of DTMH students in each session. New University taught masters degrees, research masters, PhD students and technicians' courses could be accommodated more easily. This brought immediate benefits in increased income. The research rooms also increased the number of assistants attached to the departments, particularly that of Parasitology and Entomology. The diverse research methodologies employed in this department required an ever-increasing establishment. Physical space was also required for equipment.

Collaborations with other organisations continued to increase. Simultaneous programmes of research were established with colleagues overseas. The output of academic papers and personal tributes to members of staff belied concern over the School's overall mission. The School was proud of its status as an independent institution. Without colonies to serve, it might begin to look little different from a very successful University department with private endowment for research, anomalously offering rather more postgraduate than undergraduate education. What were the future roles of the LSTM?

These were not just private fears expressed in closed discussions. The Chairman's and Dean's speeches at the Annual General Meeting, reproduced in the *Annual Reports*, publicly focused on the crisis of identity the LSTM faced. Newly independent countries of the Commonwealth 'did not seek continuance of aid on the basis of a gift from richer Members of the Commonwealth'. Rather they looked in the words of Dr Nkrumah of Ghana for 'development expenditure...undertaken on the basis of equality and mutual benefit'. Despite new knowledge and technical innovations, health and disease problems in the Third World worsened as the 1960s progressed.

In the post-colonial era, the leaders of the LSTM were most vexed by the problems of maintaining the overseas contacts. A series of manoeuvres helped maintain and develop the School's position abroad as an independent and unique organisation: the one institution in Britain solely concerned with health overseas. The end of the colonial empire brought temporary difficulties for the LSTM but it was also liberating. There was no longer any need to restrict 'expansion of the School's activities...[to] countries of the Commonwealth but...to whatever parts of the world should seem to be best indicated for the purpose'.[4] The LSTM no longer needed to be British, it could become international.

To this end, along side the scientific research schools, models for education in tropical medicine were developed. The LSTM used several routes to offer advice on teaching tropical medicine at the undergraduate level. It was at the postgraduate level that the School's teaching model flourished. The LSTM offered a template suitable for export overseas and grafting onto the existing undergraduate medical education. The importance of an educational role for the first time transcended that of research in the conscious impact of the School on the tropics.

The two West African territories of the Gold Coast and Nigeria had different colonial histories, they participated in different styles of government albeit under colonial rule and faced different health problems because of their geography and level of economic and social development. If the differences between these two colonies were appreciable, the difference between West Africa and Thailand in Southeast Asia were even more striking. Thailand had retained its independence in a region with strong British, French and Dutch interests. Yet, it shared many of the tropical diseases and health care delivery problems of its colonial neighbours. All three countries were regarded as underdeveloped, but where the Gold Coast and Nigeria were subject to the policies of the British Government, Thailand could fish in 'international waters' for whatever aid was on offer in that larger arena.

What brings these three countries together in this chapter and links them with LSTM is the assistance which the School gave to plans to deal with the education of local doctors in tropical medicine, and to prepare these countries to teach their own students. This chapter aims to examine the transfer of education based on the Liverpool model in the three countries. Association with West Africa has been a cornerstone of the LSTM as other chapters have shown. The venture into Thailand represented a departure for the School, which was also part of a transition of tropical medicine away from the demands of colonialism. This is a tangible example of the kinds of disciplinary changes discussed for Liverpool in chapter 4.

This chapter discusses the overseas education policies of the School as it attempted to carve out a role in international health. This is informed by national initiatives which LSTM staff helped to shape, but highlights the strength of individual contributions by the School. From 1955 to 1965, the educational outreach policies of the School were most tangible in Ghana, Nigeria and Thailand. Of these the Thai connection was undoubtedly the most special, unique and prolonged. These innovations in teaching grew partly from the restyled overseas contacts in the post-war period.

## INTERNATIONAL CONSULTANTS, RESEARCHERS AND AMBASSADORS

The form of the School's tropical contacts was modified after the war. The overseas presence of the LSTM, starting with the expeditions followed by permanent laboratories, was replaced post-war by consultancies and collaborative research links. Staff also became more obviously ambassadors for the LSTM, promoting its work and ethos in research and teaching in an increasingly competitive market. The rise of air-travel greatly facilitated participation at international conferences and these meetings proliferated. The number of visits School staff made to such events, presenting their research, increased considerably. The contribution of the LSTM staff overall aided the reputation of the School. Certain strategic appearances at non-tropical conferences broadened the audience for research conducted in Liverpool.[5]

Staff travelled for themselves and the LSTM, but also as part of, or on behalf of other organisations. These were often what Martin Bulmer describes as intermediary institutions.[6] The role of the international expert, chosen for their abilities rather than their nationality, was one of the cardinal principles of the WHO. It became a popular vehicle for offering aid to developing countries. Initially these contacts were made through the colonial framework and later expanded to the Commonwealth. There were other programmes, such as the Colombo Plan, which brought Britain into contact with parts of the globe not touched by empire. However, this was the era of globalisation and international agencies.

Apart from the secretariat headquarters in Geneva, WHO represented a global network of experts. The WHO Regional Offices formed the nodes in this network. The concentration of expertise at the LSTM could not be immediately acknowledged because of its associations with colonial medicine: colonial did not translate automatically into international. The early papers of the WHO, and the Interim Commission, make virtually no reference to either of the Schools of Tropical Medicine in Britain. This is not surprising. The first goals of WHO and their methods of working were quite different to those of the LSTM and the CO despite the latter expanding its interest in tropical medicine research in the post-war era.

There was much concern at the UN level that the countries forming the British Empire would not be able to take their own place, but would be represented instead by their colonial overlords. Moreover, UN agencies' programmes would have to be accommodated initially within the colonial ethos. The LSTM still owed an allegiance to the CO. Members of staff were better represented among the activities of the CO rather than those of WHO. In the short term, this presented no problems.

In 1944, Davey was invited by the CO to return to West Africa and contribute to a report on the future of tropical medicine research. This included a possible role for the School's old laboratory in Sierra Leone. While the LSTM did not want to reopen it as their own overseas research station, it could serve as a base for a joint commission with the LSHTM, the CO or the MRC. This was the first of regular visits by School staff.[7] In 1957, recognising the long association between West Africa and the LSTM, the School was invited to nominate a representative for a permanent place on the West African Council for Medical Research. This was taken as a great compliment. The WACMR was disbanded in the early 1960s, as the independent states of former British West Africa did not feel the need to be linked in such a way. Long, but ultimately foreign traditions had short lives after the end of colonial rule. Changes such as these prompted the LSTM to adapt: 'Liaison with the WHO must be maintained actively. Our prestige if not our very existence as a world organisation depend upon the continued movement of our staff to the tropics and underdeveloped areas.'[8]

The worth of individual members of the LSTM was recognised in the period 1955 to 1965 with increasing regularity. Members of staff contributed to WHO Expert Committees on malaria, schistosomiasis, filariasis and the physiological effects of heat.[9] The renewed interest by WHO was partly linked to their increased interest in research. It also reflected the LSTM's disassociation from colonial medicine and the reputation they were building as leaders in medical education for the tropics. Survey tours on behalf of the WHO were extremely useful to the LSTM because staff were able to assess likely locations around the globe where their influence could be put to best effect providing money was forthcoming.[10]

At the start of the 1950s, Maegraith began to comment more frequently on the LSTM's role and the importance of overseas contacts. Without the money to fund its own overseas laboratory the LSTM now relied on other agencies:

> The vital thing is for the School to keep up its present intimate association with the tropical world and to strengthen the link between fundamental work going on in the home laboratories and medical problems in the field. These two complementary factors can be integrated with maximum efficiency only by institutions such as ours, where continuity is possible, not only of work, but of workers.[11]

Many of the projects linking the LSTM with the tropics continued in the 1960s. New and diverse initiatives partially satiated Maegraith's urges. In collaboration with the Kuwait Oil Company, which funded the project, a unit at Ahmadi, Kuwait began studies on the physiological effects of the climate in 1956. Dr C S Leithead and his wife, Mrs L A Leithead ran the unit. In 1959, in Liverpool, a hot room was constructed in the basement of the School for complementary and continuous research on this 'tropical' problem, when the Leitheads returned to this country. The RAF provided additional support, seconding a Flight Lieutenant to work on similar problems of heat exposure at the LSTM and Bahrain.[12]

The School used its reputation and the opportunities presented by inclusion on expert panels, study tours and conferences to sell its expertise in medical education. As government policy on tropical medicine increasingly looked towards medical aid as part of technical assistance the LSTM found itself with useful inside information. Davey's involvement as a co-opted member of the Inter-University Council for Higher Education in the Colonies and elected member of its Executive Committee opened the way for the LSTM to take informed initiatives on undergraduate medical education in the tropics and lead by example at the postgraduate level. A profile in these new areas greatly expanded the LSTM's position in international health and served to broaden still further the boundaries of the discipline of tropical medicine.

## DAVEY AND HIGHER EDUCATION FOR THE COLONIES

During the war, Government commissions investigated various aspects of colonial welfare. In 1943, a commission was appointed under Lord Asquith addressing the future provision of higher education in the colonies. Hobhouse, who oversaw planning for the LSTM's future during the years without a senior professor, suggested the School should contribute.[13] Davey, who held the largely redundant chair in Tropical Diseases of Africa, represented the School's views on the future of higher education in the colonies with special reference to medical research in overseas institutions to the Commission. A memorandum prepared for the Commission indicated that the School perceived itself to have a new role educating indirectly by example.[14] This stance fitted well with the plans for centres of excellence based on British models. It would prove a timely shift of emphasis. A new political correctness urged the development of indigenous education and after 1945 the number of diploma students intended for the CMS, who previously formed the bulk of each cohort, never returned to pre-war levels.

Under the recommendations of Asquith's report, British universities would provide a resource for colonial development. Some colonial students would continue to study in Britain. It was also envisaged that the staff would be seconded to the planned colonial colleges established as part of the development process. Where appropriate the colleges would include medical faculties. Davey considered the new emphasis on education offered opportunities for the LSTM to move towards closer co-operation with these colleges and the communities they served. He hoped for a gradual change in the focus of School's work, making it more responsive to the health needs of the local communities, rather the health of the ruling élite. Besides their undergraduate teaching, colonial colleges would take a lead in postgraduate education and begin to teach the teachers of the future.

In the short term, this proactive stance implied increased demands upon staff and in the longer term for additional personnel. Lecturers and possibly technicians from the School would be seconded overseas for lengthy periods. In addition to losing staff overseas the home teaching looked likely to expand. The diploma courses had traditionally accepted a small number from overseas. It was expected that growing numbers of DTMH students and those seeking other postgraduate training in entomology and parasitology as well as tropical medicine and hygiene would pressurise existing resources.

Davey's wartime involvement with higher education continued after he succeeded Blacklock to the chair of Tropical Hygiene in 1945. His contribution to the LSTM's redirection in this period lay not so much in research, but in the contributions he made to education in the LSTM and beyond. Davey initiated the joining of the two diplomas into a single integrated course. He argued that on 'economic and practical grounds preventative medicine claimed a higher priority than clinical medicine and could produce a greater saving of life'.[15] He argued that under him the 'emphasis of the department [changed] from sanitation to preventative medicine in the widest sense'.[16] His work in trying to introduce a more relevant undergraduate medical curricula overseas, bears this out. The Asquith Commission recommended that an independent body be established and take forward plans for creating six University Colleges in the colonies. These developments were overseen by an advisory body, the Inter-University Council for Higher Education in the Colonies.[17] The Council met for the first time in March 1946. Davey was co-opted and following the initial meeting elected to serve on the Executive Committee. He also acted as the Council's representative on the Council of Gordon College, Khartoum, holding both posts until his retirement from the LSTM.

The University Colleges of the Gold Coast and Nigeria were part of the post-war provision of higher education. In each case the LSTM was aware of the politics behind the colleges and advised on the medical education offered. With the exception of the Gold Coast, capital costs could be taken from the higher education allotments of CDW funds, but recurrent costs were fundable from local governments and private benefactors, if they could be found. The University College at Ibadan in Nigeria offered medical education from its inception in 1948. Clinical medicine was taught in a new five hundred-bed teaching hospital. The Ibadan Medical Faculty replaced the existing Medical School at Yaba. In 1962, University College became the University of Ibadan.

The majority report of the Elliot Commission, reviewing higher education in West Africa in 1945, advised that three colleges be established for West Africa in Nigeria, the Gold Coast and Sierra Leone. The minority report recommended that only Ibadan be built and serve as the college for West Africa. The signatories argued that there would be too few students to fill places in three colleges. When the Labour Government came to power in 1945, they adopted the minority report. The Gold Cost Government reacted strongly. They agreed to fund capital and recurrent expenditure for their own college. As this left CDW money free for Ibadan, the CO agreed in 1947 to allow the Gold Coast to go ahead. The University College of the Gold Coast was established in 1948 but had no medical faculty. In 1960, the Institute of Tropical Medicine and Endemic Diseases, a postgraduate centre, was founded in connection with the University and the National Research Council of Ghana.

The provision of higher education in West Africa was bound by certain principles. In all disciplines, an emphasis on maintaining a sufficiently high standard of staff and students dominated policy formation. This was to ensure that the qualifications from colonial colleges would enjoy international recognition and in time attract high calibre researchers from other bodies. The colleges were purportedly autonomous, receiving only advice from the Council. A 'special relationship' with the University of London allowed students to sit for degrees as external students until university status was achieved. The relationship with London University compromised the ideal of autonomy because the curricula were set in London and paid too little attention to the needs of the communities they served.

Medicine, acknowledged as one of the 'special problems involved in the provision of professional and vocational courses', was particularly vulnerable.[18] The accelerated development of colonial health and welfare required many more qualified practitioners than were currently available. British medical schools had argued that they could not take additional colonial medical students, because there was also a need to train future practitioners for Britain. The Medical Faculty of the University of London insisted that medical graduates from Colonial Universities be of a sufficient standard to be registered by the GMC. There was some discussion that greater attention could be placed on education in clinical tropical medicine rather than relying upon an extra postgraduate diploma to educate doctors about the endemic infectious diseases of their country. However, if the qualifications were to be registered in Britain, practitioners would require an adequate knowledge of general medicine besides their emphasis on problems of tropical health. Davey argued for a reorientation of the curriculum rather than additions to it. Moreover, it would be unfair if colonial graduates had to more qualified than their counterparts in Britain in order to be able to gain entry to the medical register.[19]

These well-intentioned ground rules established the principle of centres of excellence. There were disadvantages to the policy. A high initial cost of the decision to imitate exactly British standards and syllabi was the very limited number of graduates such a system could process. The number was certainly too few to meet the needs of a country preparing for independence. It also produced an élite not always interested in working in a developing country when their internationally recognised degree could bring them lucrative employment elsewhere. Those who remained in their country of origin tended to work in private practice or in well-equipped hospitals in the major cities rather than accepting employment from the government in rural areas. This was what the medical curricula of the University of London prepared them for, not to deal with public health and preventative medicine in a poorly equipped rural clinic. The new university colleges were independent of Government Medical Departments. Graduates were therefore under no obligation to work for the Government Medical Services, as had previously been the case for medical assistants in some colonies.[20]

The Inter-Departmental Committee on Medical Schools and the Planning Committee on Medical Education of the Royal College of Physicians reported in 1944 on medical curricula in Britain. The report referred to the need for a greater emphasis on nutritional physiology in the preclinical period and on social and preventative medicine during clinical training. In practical terms the need was even greater overseas and yet curricula tended to await metropolitan developments. It was the inclusion of these latter aspects that Davey championed. Ideologically modelling colonial universities on those in Britain continued a political message of dependence upon foreign practice.[21] Not creating institutions with equitable standards would have been a public admission of double standards and provoked a justified backlash by nationalists.[22] Any advice offered by the LSTM required careful packaging if it was to avoid these pitfalls.

Staff for these centres of excellence could not be taken part-time from the CMS, as had been the case with Government medical schools in the past. Full-time chairs in clinical as well as pre-clinical subjects were essential for high-quality teaching. They would be drawn in the first instance from metropolitan and dominion sources. Junior posts could be filled from the best among the first cohort of graduates, these people eventually replacing the senior ex-patriots. Thus the first generation of graduates could expect a double burden: a virtually insurmountable case-load and an urgent need to educate undergraduates, ancillary and support staff. In the teaching of endemic infectious diseases and their consequences, finding suitable staff was more difficult than in other parts of the medical curriculum. The number of qualified personnel in Britain was already insufficient. Medical practice and medical education were not the same thing, particularly when practice had been in the colonial context and education would be in the post-colonial era.

Davey continued to serve on the Council in the 1950s. His experience in this connection and at the LSTM led to various requests for advice. In 1956, he spent a month in the Gold Coast discussing a new medical school within the College. In July he returned to Africa for the third time that year as an adviser for the Nuffield Foundation. Proposals for a new University College of Rhodesia and Nyasaland included consideration of an undergraduate medical curriculum designed to serve the needs of the local community. In 1958, he spent five months as visiting Nuffield Professor at the Ibadan Medical School. The information he was able to feed back to the LSTM from constant contact with the problems of planning medical education helped formulate the LSTM's policy to 'foster medical education in under-developed areas'.[23]


## TECHNICAL ASSISTANCE AS GOVERNMENT POLICY

The policies establishing university colleges in the colonies were followed by programmes of 'technical assistance' to colonial and Commonwealth countries. Technical assistance referred to the provision of experts and the training and education within the UK for overseas subjects. This became a popular way of delivering aid to the developing world. National and international programmes such as the Economic Co-operation Administration of the USA and the Expanded Technical Assistance Programme of the UN emphasised economic development, but projects concerned with improvements in health were acceptable if appropriately drafted.[24] In March 1959, Britain set aside £150,000 under the new CDW Act for technical assistance. This was not publicised, preventing a flood of applications that could not be met from such a small sum. It was a gesture showing that international experts or consultants were not an invention of the UN but an established part of British policy. It also aimed at keeping potentially lucrative aid projects in colonial and Commonwealth territories in British hands if possible.

The Colonial Advisory Service, responsible for administering technical assistance programmes, served a greatly reduced population as decolonisation progressed. Its future was considered as part of moves to amalgamate the function and resources of the CO and the Commonwealth Relations Office into a single Commonwealth Office. This was the idea of Sir Hilton Poynton, Permanent Under Secretary of State for the CO, from August 1959. The merger proposal was rejected, and in its place the Department of Technical Co-operation was created under a junior Minister. The DTC administered Britain's technical assistance to what remained of the colonies and members of the Commonwealth who were eligible to receive assistance. [25]

Under the DTC employment overseas would be for limited periods and form part of a career based primarily in Britain or in the service of a British Institution. Many of the staff for the new department came from the CO and there was some concern that technical assistance would appear as neo-colonialism. The DTC was created on 24 July 1961 with Denis Vosper as Secretary for Technical Co-operation. The first task was to determine the existing arrangements and develop further initiatives. 'The supply of high-grade medical personnel and advanced medical training' was listed as one of twelve priority areas on which the DTC would concentrate.[26] Vosper suggested the DTC's effectiveness could be enhanced by persuading the corporate and university sectors to release staff for overseas service. The LSTM was ahead of the game.

## TECHNICAL ASSISTANCE AT THE LSTM: THE LECTURER-AT-LARGE

Alive to the rationale for creating technical assistance and the need for medical education to serve the communities in which it occurred, the LSTM created their Lecturer-at-Large scheme. The scheme relied upon Davey's immediate knowledge of medical education in developing countries and Maegraith's commitment to keep the LSTM independent, unique and at the forefront of international health.

The LSTM's scheme predated the initiatives of the CO and the DTC. Unlike a government department, the LSTM was not obliged to consider the effects of technical assistance as aid. Nor did it to try to use technical assistance as a means of securing financial benefits. The publicity value of the Lecturer-at-Large raised the LSTM's standing. Fundamentally, it was a means of expanding the work of the School overseas in new and innovative ways. The LSTM emphasised the flexibility of the scheme, the ability to respond to the changing needs of developing countries and the desire to meet the requirements of recipients. The scheme relied upon individual collaboration rather than government officers and therefore appeared more politically neutral. This helped to side-step concern over whether technical assistance was neo-colonial. The LSTM's scheme was designed deliberately to move away from colonial ties.

A sub-committee authorised by Council to consider expanding the interests of the School abroad asked Maegraith to prepare a memorandum for further discussion and ultimate presentation to the Professional Committee early in 1957. Maegraith recommended that the School create a new flexible appointment at the senior lecturer level. This was a home-based appointment offering the security of tenure, pension rights and career prospects of an equitable university appointment. The intention was, however, that the holder would spend the majority of this appointment overseas, seconded when local institutions perceived a need. A single appointment would not solve the political difficulties that at a national level 'may have closed certain areas of the world to us'.[27] There was optimism that if the scheme was a success it could be expanded by the University funding this and additional posts. When Maegraith became involved with discussions at the national level, the Lecturer-at-Large presented a model for a more ambitious scheme.

In October 1958, Herbert Gilles was appointed as the School's Lecturer-at-Large. Gilles was no stranger to Liverpool. From 1949 to 1951, he was House Physician at the Tropical Diseases Centre, during which time he took the diploma of the School and worked with Maegraith in the Department of Tropical Medicine, cementing a deep friendship. After leaving Liverpool, Gilles held increasingly senior clinical appointments in Oxford. In 1954, he joined Ian McGregor in The Gambia at the Fajara Laboratories as a member of the MRC's scientific staff and Physician in Charge of the attached ward.

As Lecturer-at-Large his first secondment was to University College Ibaban in Nigeria as lecturer in Tropical Medicine and Consultant Physician at the University College Teaching Hospital from January 1959. These positions allowed Gilles to continue his research on the relationship of renal dysfunction and malaria in children.[28] The Lecturer-at-Large scheme aimed to realise Davey's recommendations that the undergraduate medical curricula shift towards preventative and social medicine with a special emphasis on the endemic infectious diseases. From the point of view of the School, it was important if possible that the Lecturer-at-Large be able to establish future research links. In his five years in Ibadan Gilles achieved this. His success and the initiative of the LSTM helped to move tropical medicine away from its overtly colonial past.

In February 1959, Gilles opened negotiations with the Chief of Akufo village, ten miles from Ibadan. The object was to establish a broad study of the parasitological, genetic and economic background of the village, to observe how changes in preventative and social medicine could improve the health of the village community as well as individuals, and to use the village as a teaching station and research base. In this way, the direction of medical instruction could be gradually adapted to the problems of the country. If the undergraduate syllabus might remain tied to British medicine, at the postgraduate level such restrictions were less likely to apply. The smallness of the project was one of its strengths. It served as pilot study, open to contributions and criticism from local doctors, lecturers and development planners, and not thrust paternalistically upon the people.

Gilles' success as Lecturer-at-Large brought him to Ghana for a short period in 1962. Following independence and Nkrumah's explicit statements on aid, it was perhaps surprising that he should seek British assistance to establish a postgraduate centre at Accra. It was characteristic of the leadership of Ghana that they should push for educational development at the postgraduate level having taken the initiative in founding the University College of the Gold Coast. The LSTM could provide assistance by stressing its independence and desire for mutual co-operation: the lectureship at Ibadan apparently proving their good intentions. Davey prepared the ground, undertaking a study tour advising on plans for a medical school in the future. Nkrumah wanted to move more quickly and suggested establishing an institute with teaching facilities and a research unit emphasising environmental changes and their impact on health. The target group was doctors who returned from their basic, curative medical education outside of Ghana.[29] When it looked likely that the LSTM would be able to contribute 'as far as its funds, staff and facilities will permit', Maegraith formalised negotiations between the LSTM and the National Research Council of Ghana.[30]

The School offered general advice through Maegraith acting as a consultant to the NRC. They undertook to provide an information service during the establishment of the Institute and afterwards for research. The LSTM would act as a link for the recruitment of expatriate staff, and would deal directly with the government technical assistance programmes, where appropriate. Exchange and secondment of staff for specific periods or linked to specific projects could be negotiated. The LSTM offered to waive fees for up to three postgraduates who, on receipt of a higher degree from the University of Liverpool, would return to positions in the ITMED. A scholarship would be required to cover students' maintenance. The same arrangement would be offered for up to five technicians, although they would also work for the LSTM without payment during the period of their training. ITMED staff could apply for bench space on an occasional basis. These were significant contributions, but it was at the level of postgraduate teaching that the LSTM made an innovative offer. The School undertook to 'advise in the design of a suitable curriculum for postgraduate training in Tropical Medicine and Hygiene with special reference to Ghana', down to lists of apparatus to equip the Institute. They also offered assistance, writing examination papers and agreeing to act as external examiners. The course would prepare doctors who had qualified elsewhere for practice in rural Ghana. Later, 'refresher' courses for existing members of the country's public health services would be introduced.

In effect, the School offered to transfer a modified version of the LSTM's teaching role to Ghana in return for a subvention of £3,000 for a four-year period 1960 to 1963. It was selling its best asset, its cumulative experience in tropical medicine, on an expenses only basis as an aid to the development of a former colonial country. Maegraith summed up the significance of the Ghanaian project with the words 'we live to serve in the tropics'.[31] A similar offer was made to the Faculty of Tropical Medicine in Bangkok. However, the history of the political association of Thailand and Britain, and a special personal relationship between Maegraith and Chamlong Harinasuta created an institute of a different kind. By the time this scheme was coming to fruition, his dictum had become more forceful: 'we must accept that our impact on the tropics must be made in the tropics'.[32]

## THE FACULTY OF TROPICAL MEDICINE, BANGKOK, THAILAND

For many years, the LSTM had received diploma students from Siam. In 1888, as part of a careful reorganisation of aspects of Government policy, King Chulalongkorn (Rama V) ordered the construction of a permanent hospital in Bangkok, the Siriraj. This replaced the temporary buildings erected during epidemics. A medical school attached to the Siriraj offered a curriculum closely modelled on that taught in medical schools in the West, although there was some inclusion of Thai and Chinese materia medica. The first group of students graduated in 1893. On the advice of a Rockefeller Foundation Commission, in 1917, the Medical School amalgamated with Chulalongkorn University, granting its own degrees after 1928. In the same year a medical register was established for qualified doctors, but was only relevant in Bangkok where medical practitioners clustered around those who could afford to pay for their services. Nurses (initially all male) were trained at the Bangkok Nursing Home for Europeans which opened in 1898. Midwifery training for Thai women began in 1897 in a school under royal patronage. The absence of tropical diseases in the ordinary undergraduate curriculum in the West, copied to a high standard in Thailand, brought Thai graduates to Europe for postgraduate study. After the launch of the Colombo Plan, fellowships in tropical medicine for extended study abroad were popular.

As part of the deliberations on the expansion of the LSTM, the subcommittee considered which parts of the world could usefully provide future links with Liverpool. The School remained committed to members of the Commonwealth, providing postgraduate medical education and advice to those countries seeking to develop a health system based on the Western model in its contents and style. Other countries listed as potential future contacts were New Guinea and Thailand, respectively described as providing 'almost limitless' and 'very great' facilities for research. A likely strategy for Thailand was for a 'senior professional representative from the School to start a corresponding establishment in Siam and to wait there until it could be left to progress further by itself'.[33]

This casual statement belied the close informal links between Bangkok and Liverpool. Nor could it convey the national efforts in Thailand to improve the standard of public health in the country for economic and political reasons. Thailand had been one of the first WHO anti-malaria demonstration areas in 1949. This programme was expanded with the assistance of Food and Agriculture Organisation and aimed to reach five million homes by 1957.[34] The Thais were keen to utilise various schemes of technical co-operation and assistance for study abroad. A meeting of a Commonwealth Consultative Committee in Colombo, Sri Lanka in January 1950 launched the Colombo Plan for Co-operative Economic Development for South and Southeast Asia.[35] This emulated the Marshall plan for Europe.[36] The aim was for the more prosperous countries in Asia, and those interested in the region, to collectively improve the standard of living of the people of Southeast Asia.[37] Each member country drew up its own strategy for development. There was no central fund for projects. Limited money for technical assistance was available and a Council for Technical Co-operation formed by member countries to co-ordinate opportunities for training and education.[38] The British Council assisted with educational fellowships.[39]

In 1956, Maegraith had undertaken a study tour of the middle and Far East. In Bangkok, he met up with his former student Chamlong Harinasuta, lecturer in Tropical Medicine at the Siriraj Medical School and Hospital. There were four other Liverpool DTMH students in important positions.[40] During the visit, the Director General of Medical Services, Dr Luang Nityavejvisit, asked Maegraith directly what help the LSTM could offer if plans for a separate Division of Tropical Medicine in the Faculty were realised.[41]

Dr Kanjika Devakul and Dr Rawewan Juraliminta had both worked in Liverpool as John Holt Research Fellows, and the Colombo Plan regularly brought other Thais to Liverpool as visitors or students.[42] Maegraith and Harinasuta met again at the sixth International Congress of Tropical Medicine and Malaria in Lisbon. Besides the usual conference business, they discussed the possible future relations between Bangkok and Liverpool. Serendipity transformed these associations.

## THE FACULTY OF TROPICAL MEDICINE IN BANGKOK AND SEAMEO TROP-MED IN SOUTHEAST ASIA

Harinasuta nurtured the idea of a school of tropical medicine in Bangkok to serve Thailand and ultimately the whole of Southeast Asia. Maegraith provided encouragement, acting as a mentor and confidant during several abortive attempts to persuade the Thai Government to provide funding for a school. Financial considerations aside, by acknowledging the need for a postgraduate school the Government recognised that the national medical curriculum was flawed. As currently taught it did not equip medical practitioners to deal with the endemic diseases in rural Thailand. Its rectification, by a separate institution devoted to teaching and research into tropical diseases, again implied importing a model from outside. These considerations were swept aside by external events. In Harinasuta's words:

> In Thailand at that time there was a *coup d'état* led by Field Marshal Sarit Thanarat…in 1959…and I [Harinasuta] am the personal physician to him and so one day in the morning, eight o'clock he called me to his house, personal house, so he said to me Dr Chamlong I would like to make you…minister of public health of Thailand because you are close to me…and you are a doctor, I said I am sorry I am too young, at that time I was 38 or 39, I am too young to be the minister…you are silly he said to me I would like to make you a big man, but what do you want, I said I want a school of tropical medicine in Bangkok, what – I gave you the ministry and you want a school, a school small school…alright you go and carry on and do the work officially by your way, at that time the president of the university asked the WHO to give a fellowship for Professor Maegraith to be as a consultant to establish the

school of tropical medicine here, that is 1959, so he very glad you know he came and see and make the plan, and he went to see the Prime Minister and explain to him how to proceed further...and the faculty was established by the government in March 1960.[43]

Maegraith's formal and informal role in establishing the Faculty in Thailand proved useful for the LSTM. After the Faculty was established, the majority of senior members of staff came to Liverpool for postgraduate training in the 1960s and early 1970s. Some Thais also continued to take the DTMH at Liverpool. The close personal association, now formalised, enhanced the possibilities for programmes of simultaneous research.[44] The clinical facilities in the Hospital for Tropical Diseases, completed the year after the Faculty opened, were of great value in this respect. The Faculty also provided Maegraith with opportunities for further sojourns in Southeast Asia: for the next fifteen years he acted as a consultant, visiting Bangkok approximately every two years advising on curriculum development and specific research projects. On these occasions Harinasuta, the Faculty's first Dean, would give up his office to make way for Maegraith.

It was far from plain sailing for the newly founded faculty. Harinasuta continues:

> I am the first Dean of the Faculty...I am very happy in 1960, but unfortunately...at that time, 1960-66 we taught in Thai...and the student the first year is about twelve...but after one year, one year, one year because at that time...the new doctors after graduation they all go to USA to be the intern you know and get the big money you know and at that time they open for the foreigners to be the doctors...because they are fighting with communists at that time, so our students less and less and less until finally we have only four students for DTM...so in 1966 I would decide if we have less than four students we have to close...because we have no student doctors it is not worthwhile.[45]

The solution to this problem signified a break with the reliance upon Liverpool as a model, although it involved Maegraith's continued support as a consultant. It also represented a growing sense of inter-regional cohesion in Southeast Asia, despite political, cultural, religious and linguistic differences. It also indicated a diminution of reliance upon the West intellectually if not financially. In 1965, at a meeting of the Southeast Asian Ministers of Education Organisation, the Vietnamese delegate suggested that tropical medicine be included in plans for the regional co-ordination of educational facilities. Disciplines such as engineering and the English language were each to have a designated institution in one of the member countries. The difficulty in the case of tropical medicine was to choose which of the existing national centres, including the Faculty in Bangkok, should be the home of this initiative. An international task force advised on this issue, with Maegraith as one of the consultants. The task force diplomatically recommended that each of the national centres should be responsible for a specific sub-discipline of tropical medicine. However, the SEAMEO Tropical-Medicine project would require a secretariat to oversee planning, training and funding requirements. It was a further recommendation of the task force that this Central Co-ordinating Board be housed within the Faculty in Bangkok, with Harinasuta as its head.

Tranakchit Harinasuta explained the difference this made to the Faculty, 'At first since '60–67 we taught in Thai, and the course is for the Thai only, and from '67 onwards we will change to international with the emphasis for Southeast Asia.'[46] The shift from teaching on a national level (in Thai) to an international level (in English) indicated the pragmatism of the Thais. In the absence of colonialism, they accepted a transfer of technology from the West using it immediately to their direct benefit. As evidence of the 'brain drain' became evident, emphasis on the provision of training facilities within developing countries increased.[47] The Faculty introduced Masters and PhD programmes in the late 1960s, upgrading its status. The Faculty became a hub for postgraduate education in tropical medicine in the Southeast Asian region. These initiatives also benefited from the continued close association of Liverpool and Bangkok. The Thais who studied in Liverpool returned not only with additional qualifications and relevant laboratory experience, but also with a changed ethos.

The Thai people have a great respect for their teachers. As with all formal relationships in Thailand, that of student and teacher relies upon hierarchy. This can have negative effects, particularly at the level of higher research degrees,

> there is no doubt that the way in which people are taught in Asia or at least in Thailand particularly, does not lend itself to inquiry or questioning...suddenly as a postgraduate you are expected to start questioning everything and that is very difficult, so what people tend to do is find that transition difficult, and they just tend to copy.[48]

Study outside of Thailand therefore represented a liberating experience for the students who came to Liverpool. In effect they already represented a biased sample among their peers by demonstrating the independence to study overseas, but it is clear that despite this they maintained an intense sense of respect for their academic superiors and Maegraith in particular. In turn Maegraith was keen to have his PhD students work on areas of research which overlapped with his own interests in the pathophysiology of malaria, amoebiasis and more generally to work on schistosomiasis. While making arrangements for a visit by Maegraith in 1973 after the latter had suffered a bout of ill health, which necessitated his wife travelling constantly with him, he wrote, 'with regard to the finance...leave this to me, my dear Pappa'.[49] The idea of Maegraith as the intellectual father of Harinasuta and later to the whole faculty was genuine,

> Dr Chamlong was his student...and Professor Maegraith loved him so much, whenever Professor Chamlong need him he will call 'Pop will come and help me' everyone will call him 'Pop, pop, pop', he was very funny, when we were with him, we tell jokes and tell stories and sing songs.[50]

> We call Professor Maegraith father and Dr Tan his son.[51]

Individually those who studied in Liverpool reported how the experience had given them confidence in their own research, which they felt they would not otherwise have gained,

> I tell you what Professor Maegraith...taught me, he is very tough...he just said oh this is the subject to learn, you have to go and find yourself what would be the research question...so I have to take myself to the library, all the library research, documentary research, and then I came back to him and he said 'No no...if you did like this I wouldn't give you any degree', so I had to go back and do this again and again until he is satisfied and say ok this is the programme of work, a methodology and so on, and he had me do this work for few months and asked me to report to him what have I done...I learned it in a hard way I have to say, and this is good for me, because I know everything about it and when I came back here, and I taught my students, I said alright if you want a PhD from me you have to do the same way which my Professor taught me...so everyone here if they are my students have to work from the beginning, work it out and not like the other professors here who almost writing down everything and the student just do it, you have to do it from the beginning like Maegraith did...it give me good confidence in myself I came back here with good confidence in myself, I know something...and I used this for my career further you see, get more confident of course.[52]

The adoption of the Liverpool model emphasised tropical medicine as a subject for postgraduate study. It is very difficult in developing countries to attract enough high-calibre practitioners and medical scientists to work on endemic infectious diseases when a more lucrative career exists treating wealthier patients who suffer from complaints not associated with tropical medicine. It may be that offering tropical medicine as a postgraduate discipline reinforces this problem. The situation in Thailand differed from that in Ghana. There the University did not offer undergraduate medicine when the ITMED was established. In Ibadan the politics of equality between colonial and British curricula made radical change of the undergraduate curriculum extremely difficult.

In Thailand, without a colonial history, it would have been possible in theory to cut across the Liverpool/colonial model and greatly increase the exposure of undergraduates to the study of endemic infectious diseases and poverty-related health problems, as part of their basic medical education. A separate Faculty of Tropical Medicine ensured the 'Siriraj had lost two brilliant professors [the Harinasutas]'. As this was the main undergraduate medical faculty in the University, if they had stayed 'their influence could be felt by many of the medical students'. The limited time meant students 'barely felt the influence of the two leading professors'.[53]

Maegraith perceived the function of the Faculty was to provide the means for the country to catch up on missed undergraduate education and reorientate the emphasis on curative medicine apparent in doctors educated in Thai medical schools. It is not so clear that the Thais saw their Faculty in this way. They interpreted its foundation as a progressive step forward in academic medicine in Southeast Asia. Ironically, they utilised a Western model to cement their own hegemony in this region.

## MAEGRAITH AND TECHNICAL ASSISTANCE

The examples of Thailand and Ghana illustrate the proactive moves the LSTM made to changes in the perception of tropical medicine. This discipline was no longer the preserve of the CMS and British specialists, it had became part of national development created from within rather than imposed from above. While pursing their objectives, Maegraith also contributed to national schemes that ultimately fed into Government policy. By comparison, these proved much less successful in the short-term.

In April 1961, an informal group met in Birmingham to discuss ways in which the UK could provide trained clinical teachers for dependent and independent developing countries.[54] It was envisaged that the Inter-University Council for Higher Education Overseas would facilitate any additional support. There was no emphasis on tropical medicine or public health. On 27 July 1961,

Sir Arthur Porritt, President of the Royal College of Surgeons, invited Maegraith to a conference on medical and surgical aid to the underdeveloped territories. He joined the Working Party, created after the meeting. Professor E T C Spooner, Dean of the LSHTM, was also a member. Neither man represented his institution. Rather, they were experts with direct experience of these problems. Representatives were invited from the Ministry of Health and the DTC. The Working Party was a temporary body whose report would be passed to the DTC. The Medical Advisory Committee of the Department would then assess the report and implement what it considered to be suitable policies.

The Working Party considered the secondment of staff overseas and the practicalities of bringing 'selected medical graduates from overseas...to the United Kingdom for periods of study and training to qualify them to return overseas as medical teachers'.[55] Much of the Working Party's deliberations concerned the provision of a general medical education covering medicine, surgery, gynaecology, obstetrics and paediatrics, not tropical medicine and public health. The employment of overseas doctors in the NHS was a further important theme. A meeting on 3 January 1962 opened discussion on the provision of specialist help in public health and tropical medicine. Spooner pre-circulated a discussion paper. He referred to the outreach policies of the LSTHM such as Professor MacDonald's trip to Tanganyika and assistance with the training of medical assistants in Dar es Salaam.[56] At the meeting, Maegraith referred to the LSTM's experiences in Ghana and Thailand. Spooner closed his note with a warning that whatever schemes were established, 'priority should be given to assistance with the actual programmes drawn up by the countries concerned...and should not be allowed to divert funds from projects [which] in the long and short runs, may be more effective in maintaining the influence of British medicine'. This awareness of the need to work within the desires of the local community was a guiding principle of their efforts in steering the direction and mechanism for delivering medical aid. They agreed to put forward a joint submission based on the view of both Schools.[57]

At the next meeting, Spooner and Maegraith put forward four proposals. First, grants should be available to enable senior men with relevant experience to travel and offer advice on social and preventative medicine. Second and third, senior and junior lectureships should be created at the two Schools forming a 'pool for secondment' and a future cohort of trained staff. Fourth, fellowships could be created in the UK for overseas students. The Working Party endorsed these and concluded that the 'primary need in the field of public health is to teach the ordinary doctors in the developing countries how to deal with their own local health problems'.[58]

Maegraith was concerned that the Working Party and hence the final report for the DTC would focus on the provision of experts. The immediate needs of overseas countries might be overlooked. The first requirement was to listen to what developing countries wanted and then, by invitation, find means to reorientate 'basic' doctors towards thinking and practising social and preventative medicine at the community level.[59]

The final Report appeared to anticipate Maegraith's fears. However, international politics also underlay the recommendations. The authors of the Report saw fit to comment on Britain's relative decline in comparison with the USA and the USSR in promoting 'medical advance' in the developing countries of Africa, Asia and the Middle East. The cold war and Britain's continuing loss of prestige made medicine an overt part of neo-colonialism:

> While the Working Party is not primarily concerned with political objectives, it is unanimous in believing that the medical profession can play a unique part in the spread of British influence in the developing countries.[60]

The DTC was, not surprisingly, committed to such a policy. £50,000 offered to ITMED for apparatus and books specified that all books and journals must be either British or Commonwealth. At a stretch, they might accept South African journals. Such an attitude excluded the valuable publications from the USA.[61]

On 19 March 1963, the DTC issued its public response to the Porrit Report.[62] Under the heading 'Medical Aid in the Field of Public Health', the DTC applauded the recommendations of the report as 'most realistic and worthy of support'. They undertook to provide special funding for twelve senior and six junior lectureships in 1963–1964 at the two Schools of Tropical Medicine.[63] To keep the doctors involved, the DTC established a Medical Advisory Committee with membership incorporating a wide range of professional expertise.

Under the scheme, essentially what Maegraith read as a DTC version of the Lecturer-at-Large scheme, appointments were made at the LSTM over the next year. Lecturers would be paid from the budget of the DTC while working at their 'home' university. After a request for assistance, the lecturer would be seconded overseas. His salary, allowances and fares would then be paid from the appropriate Regional Programme Fund.[64] Where possible funding would be sought from the institution or government requesting assistance. Each Regional Programme Fund was limited, so governments bidding for assistance could choose between a DTC medical lecturer and another aspect of aid i.e. an engineer. Where countries could received medical aid at no direct cost they were likely to choose another source. Hence the fears over the aid from the USA and USSR and the allegiance of developing countries to these providers.

The DTC lecturers contributed to the home establishment in the Departments of Tropical Medicine and Hygiene, but it proved difficult to locate them overseas. As of 1965, only Alistair Reid had been seconded. He went to Bangkok, under the Colombo Plan as a consultant for four months. A longer posting was refused. The consultancy was regarded as a concession that would not be repeated. Dion Bell, appointed in June 1964, was expected to go to Ibadan. This was refused after Ibadan declined to pay a local salary. The same scenario occurred in the case of D R W Haddock and a posting to Ethiopia. D Scott was expected to proceed to Ghana because the authorities would pay a local salary. R Barclay had prospects of posting overseas.[65] The situation improved somewhat. However, correspondence between Maegraith and the DTC (later the Ministry of Overseas Development) testifies to the failure of the scheme to run smoothly and to the best advantage of the developing countries, in the eyes of the LSTM's Dean.[66]

On the other hand, Kershaw had been disappointed with what the scheme could offer to the LSTM from the outset, because it did not adequately support fundamental research.[67] He considered that this approach was vital and not sufficiently attended to under the DTC scheme. He concluded in October 1964 that it was impossible to appoint staff under the scheme as the type of staff he wanted to employ in his laboratories were dissuaded by the imposition of '*ad hoc* application in the tropics'.[68] Not all the staff shared Maegraith's vision of the new expanded role of LSTM. For many reasons, the LSTM would be obliged to rely on its own initiatives for connections with the tropics, should it be able to fund them.


## CONCLUSION

Immediately after the war, Maegraith consolidated the direction of research in his department and he tried to control the other departments. This identified the LSTM as an institute of higher education rather than an institute in the service of colonialism. By the mid-1960s, the LSTM had successfully extended its function beyond that of a fundamental research institute. The development of new functions in the tropics mitigated concerns over a clear identity for the School in Liverpool. During a period of uncertainty over the future of Britain's colonial empire the School looked for new ways to work in the tropics. Consultancies offered short-term opportunities for research. The export of technical assistance and medical aid was a common aim of health and development organisations. The staff at the School represented a resource for the developing world.

The teaching in Liverpool provided a further resource. The reoriented DTMH and the increase in research students at the School contributed to the intellectual capital of the developing world. However, in numerical terms this was a small contribution. In response, the School developed a complementary programme exporting its expertise in education. This provided opportunities to work overseas. It also offered a far greater potential to affect the fortunes of the developing countries than teaching in Liverpool could achieve. It formed part of the belief that developing countries could reach acceptable socio-economic levels by the rational application of select methods transferred from the developed world.

The contact with Nigeria, Ghana and Thailand provide three examples of the commitment to education in the tropics. The creation of the Lecturer-at-Large scheme represented a proactive move by the School to export individual expertise. The scheme and the quality of Gilles' work in Nigeria acted as a flagship. Later it served as a blueprint for the deliberations of the Porritt Committee. The politics of neo-colonialism initially interfered with the well-intentioned aims of the Committee realised through the DTC. The LSTM's initiatives, unlike those it facilitated for the DTC, were sufficiently free from such politics to succeed. The value of the LSTM's independence became apparent as political difficulties hampered national policies. Its relatively small size and limited finances were the disadvantages of this stance. This environment polarised differing perceptions of the relative importance of 'teaching the teachers' and fundamental research.

The involvement with the controversial leader of Ghana, Kwame Nkrumah and his plans for a higher education institute devoted to tropical and other infectious diseases and the project to establish a Faculty of Tropical Medicine in Bangkok, shared some similarities. Nkrumah's government asked the School to provide assistance and advice. The School drew up curricula for teaching, acted as on-the-spot advisers and external examiners. In Liverpool, they offered to teach technical and academic staff. The scheme worked well. Nkrumah's disinterest in retaining former colonial relationships thwarted hopes that the School, through the Foreign Office, could automatically offer assistance with development projects in Ghana.

Without the former colonial ties, the relationship with Thailand developed more successfully. Thailand gave the School the best opportunity to export a complete model of tropical medicine as practised in Liverpool to a developing country. Besides the different diplomatic relationship between Thailand and Liverpool that facilitated exchanges through formal channels such as the Colombo Plan, the personal relationship of Maegraith and Harinasuta linked Liverpool and Bangkok. The LSTM acted as mentor for the Bangkok faculty, extrapolating the relationship of PhD student and professor. The other Thai students who also studied in Liverpool continued the close association. For Maegraith, the Faculty in Bangkok personified his vision of 'One World'. The facilities of the Bangkok Faculty of Tropical Medicine, housing the CCB of

SEAMEO-Trop Med and the Hospital for Tropical Diseases, enjoy a record of original research. Expanded ranges of postgraduate courses testify to the Thais' success in importing and developing the discipline of tropical medicine. They adapted a colonial science into a non-colonial situation despite some significant problems.[69]

By the 1960s, few of the pre-war staff remained at the LSTM. A new generation with different views, many of them less attached to colonial ideologies, brought a different identity to the School. The School shed its colonial past and proved itself adaptable and responsive to the needs of the developing countries. The definition of tropical medicine began to change by attempting to meet the perceived health needs of the Third World. These connections were part of the post-war faith in science and medicine to improve the lot of human life on a global scale, because of its purported political neutrality. The problems attached to the endeavours of the School showed the fallacy of this stance.

## NOTES

[1] *61st Annual Report of the LSTM, 1959–1960*, p. 10.

[2] Manson referred to diseases of bacteriological origin commonly found in the tropics as 'cosmopolitan', P Manson, *Tropical diseases: a manual of the diseases of warm climates*, London: Cassell, 1898, p. xvi.

[3] M Harrison & M Worboys, 'A disease of civilisation: TB in Britain, Africa and India', L Marks & M Worboys (eds), *Migrants, minorities and health: historical and contemporary studies*, London: Routledge, 1997, pp. 93–124.

[4] TM/8/C.5, Interests of the School abroad, sub-committee meeting, 12 March 1957.

[5] 1956, Maegraith spoke at the US Naval Radiological Defense Laboratory on quantitative descriptions of liver function; 1957, Maegraith was a WHO Observer at an International Symposium on Abnormal Haemoglobins, in Istanbul.

[6] M Bulmer, 'Mobilising social knowledge for social welfare: intermediary institutions in the political systems of the United States and Great Britain between the First and Second World Wars', P Weindling (ed), *International Health Organizations and Movements, 1918–1939*, Cambridge: CUP, 1995, pp. 305–325.

[7] The Laboratory was not reopened, but sold to the University College of Sierra Leone.

[8] *60th Annual Report of the LSTM, 1958–1959*, p. 8.

[9] 1955: Maegraith, Expert Committee on Malaria; Gordon, Expert Panel Filariasis; 1957: Gordon, Advisory Panel, Parasitic Diseases.

[10] TM/8/C/5, Maegraith, Middle & Far East Tour, 1956. Preliminary report to Council.

[11] *53rd Annual Report of the LSTM, 1951–1952*, p. 14.

[12] The Kuwait project had an unexpected benefit for the LSTM. Mr J Friend was recruited by Maegraith from the Gulf to work at the School as Chief Technician in 1964.

[13] TM/3/1.5a, Minutes of Council, 4 October 1943.

[14] TM/3/1.5a, Minutes of Council, 20 March 1944.

[15] TM/14/DaT/6.1, Davey, Changes in the Department of Tropical Medicine between 1930 and 1960.

[16] TM/14/DaT/4, Davey to Smith, 5 November 1974.

[17] In 1955, 'overseas' replaced 'colonies' in the Council's title respecting the sensibilities of those whom it served.

[18] *Report of the Commission on Higher Education in the Colonies*, London: HMSO, 1945, p. 57.

[19] TM/8/G.24, Undated memorandum, T H Davey & J G Wright, The medical curriculum for tropical medical schools.

[20] N Okafor, *The development of universities in Nigeria*, Longman: London, 1971, p. 71.

[21] C K Eicher, 'African universities: overcoming intellectual dependency', T M Yesufu (ed), *Creating the African university*, Ibadan: OUP, 1973, pp. 27–36.

[22] Okafor, *The development of Universities in Nigeria*, pp. 70–77.

[23] *59th Annual Report of the LSTM, 1957–1958*, p. 13.

[24] D J Morgan, *The official history of colonial development 3: A reassessment of British aid policy, 1951–1965*, Basingstoke: Macmillan, 1980, pp. 236–270.

[25] In 1966, the proposed merger between the CO and the CRO took place: there was little left of the former territories by this time for the CO to work with. The DTC became the Overseas Development Ministry. After the amalgamation of the Commonweath Office and the Foreign Office, the ODM became the Overseas Development Administration under that amalgamated office. In 1974, Labour once more separated the ODA to become another ODM.

[26] Morgan, *The official history of colonial development*, p. 264.

[27] *59th Annual Report of the LSTM, 1957–1958*, p. 9.

[28] H M Gilles & R G Hendrickse, 'Possible aetiological role of *Plasmodium malariae* in "nephrotic syndrome" in Nigerian children', *Lancet*, i, 1960, 806–807.

[29] TM/8/G.22, Heads of understanding between the LSTM and the NRC, Ghana, in relation to liaison in the development and operation of the ITMED.

[30] TM/8/G.26, Undated draft of a letter discussing options for tropical medicine in Ghana.

[31] *61st Annual Report of the LSTM, 1959–1960*, p. 10.

[32] *64th Annual Report of the LSTM, 1962–1963*, p. 19.

[33] TM/8/C.5, Interests of the School abroad, 22 January 1957.

[34] H J Power, 'The role of chemotherapy in early malaria control and eradication programmes in Thailand', W F Bynum & B Fantini (eds), *Strategies against malaria, eradication or control, Parssitologia*, 40, 1998, 47–53; *idem*, 'Drug resistant malaria: a global problem and the Thai response', A Cunningham & B Andrews (eds), *Western medicine as contested knowledge*, Manchester: MUP, 1997, pp. 262–286.

[35] A N Porter & A J Stockwell, *British imperial policy and decolonization, 1938–1964*, Macmillan: Basingstoke, 1987, p. 63.

[36] *The Colombo Plan for cooperative economic development in South and South-East Asia*, London: HMSO, 1950.

[37] The original member countries were Commonwealth members in the area: India, Pakistan, Sri Lanka (Ceylon), Malaysia (Malaya) and outside members UK, Canada, New Zealand, Australia. However, all countries in the region were invited to join the Plan. Later the USA and Japan joined mainly as fund providers.

[38] The Colombo Plan, *The Colombo technical cooperation scheme*, London: HMSO, 1954.

[39] F Donaldson, *The British Council: the first fifty years*, London: Cape, 1984.

[40] Dr Kruatrachue, Lecturer in Medicine, Siriraj; Dr Kraivichien, Lecturer in Medicine, Chulalongkorn Medical School and Hospital; Dr Mantarbhorn, Chulalongkorn Medical School and Hospital; Surgeon Captain Sanid Poshakrishna, Royal Naval Hospital, Satterhib.

[41] TM/8.C.5, Maegraith, Middle and Far East Tour 1956, p. 22.

[42] For instance in 1958, Dr Chom Debyasuvarm and Professor Svasti Daengsvang visited the LSTM.

[43] Interview with Chamlong Harinasuta, 17 January 1995, recorded by H J Power.

[44] *64th Annual report of LSTM, 1962–1963*, p. 34.

[45] Interview with Chamlong Harinasuta, 17 January 1995, recorded by H J Power.

[46] Interview with Kunying Tranakchit Harinasuta, 9 January 1995, recorded by H J Power.

[47] Colombo Plan, *Brain drain: country papers, the working paper and the report of the special topic committee of the Colombo Plan*, Colombo: The Colombo Plan, 1972.

[48] Interview with Dr Nicholas White, 11 January 1995, recorded by H J Power.

[49] Private communication, C Harinasuta to Maegraith, 17 September 1973.

[50] Interview with Dr Pratin Visniyourith, 17 January 1995, recorded by H J Power.

[51] Interview with Dr Prakob Boonthai, 23 January 1995, recorded by H J Power.

[52] Interview with Prof Santasiri Sornmani, 13 January 1995, recorded by H J Power.

[53] Interview with Prof Nath Bhamaraprarati, 25 January 1995, recorded by H J Power.

[54] TM/8/G.26, Memorandum on medical technological aid to overseas countries.

[55] TM/8/G.26, February 1962, Allowance for doctors from overseas visiting the UK for study. Note by the DTC.

[56] TM/8/G.26, 2 January 1962, E T C Spooner, A note on 'public health' in relation to the contribution which the medical profession in the UK can make to the development of medical science in the developing countries.

[57] TM/8/G.26, Working Party on medical aid to the developing countries, 3 January 1962.

[58] TM/8/G.26, Working Party on medical aid to the developing countries, memorandum on proceedings to date, 31 January 1962.

[59] TM/8/G.26, Assistance to developing countries, undated memorandum.

[60] TM/8/G.26, Report of the working party on medical aid to the developing countries.

[61] TM/8/G.27, Notes of telephone conversation between Maegraith and Mr Mandeville, DTC, 11 January 1962.

[62] Department of Technical Co-operation, *Medical aid to the developing countries. Observations by HM Government on the report of a working party under the chairmanship of Sir Arthur Porritt*, London: HMSO, 1963.

[63] Ibid., p. 6.

[64] Regional Programme Funds: Colombo Plan, South East Asian Treaty Organisation, Special Commonwealth African Assistance Plan, Foundation for Mutual Assistance in Africa South of the Sahara, Central Treaty Organisation, Middle East Development Divison. Department of Technical Co-operation, *Technical Co-operation. A progress report by the new department*, London: HMSO, 1962.

[65] TM/8/G.33, Memorandum, Lecturers: Technical Assistance.

[66] TM/8/G.30; TM/8/G.31; TM/8/G.33.

[67] TM/8/G.27, *The Times*, 19 September 1963, Letters to the editor, W E Kershaw, 'Aid in the tropics. Science training a priority'.

[68] TM/8/G.32, Lecturers (Technical Assistance) Meeting 20 October 1964.

[69] Power, 'Drug-resistant malaria'.

# 6

# IN THE NAME OF THE CHILD: TROPICAL PAEDIATRICS

## INTRODUCTION

On 10 February 1966, the Director General of the WHO, Dr Marcolino G Candau, opened the new wing of the LSTM, confirming the international status of the School.[1] The new wing offered a public opportunity to move away from its past association with colonial politics and economics. The opening ceremony reinforced the image that the School was now an independent institution dedicated to global health care. The LSTM hoped that recognition at the international level would be rewarded by greater government support of the single institution in Britain concerned exclusively with tropical medicine.

Behind the new façade, the intellectual and operational management of the School was also reorganised. In his speech, Candau referred to the immediate problem posed by a new strain of cholera, the El Tor virus, and the implications of population growth. These were apposite tropics. They represented several general concerns in international health. First, there was a continuing need for biomedical and epidemiological research. Second, the increasing difficulty of controlling infectious diseases in times of rapid transit required greater consideration. Third, finding the means to provide a healthy start for new-borns and therefore slow the expansion of the world's population. Each of these was a significant issue in its own right. Their deliberate juxtaposition by the leader of the WHO at the opening of expanded facilities at the LSTM encapsulated the problems the School faced in the future.

The School had an established reputation in biomedicine with particular reference to infectious diseases. Epidemiology and the importance of paediatric and child health in relation to population presented new challenges. The need to strike a balance between public heath intervention and the increasing birth-rate created debate after the war as the fitness of national populations had in the inter-war years.[2] Davey had spoken several times on this subject and represented

159

the LSTM at meetings, but the School, as an institution, did not engage with the population question. The interest in the size of the total population coincided with a greater emphasis on the health of women and children and the need to deal more effectively with maternal and infant mortality.[3] This provided an expanded area of work in the Third World for non-tropical specialists, who tried to apply Western models of care overseas.[4] It attracted funding from a variety of government and non-governmental sources. A focus on the future generation was politically attractive to developing countries, as nation building had been to various European countries at the turn of the twentieth century.[5]

The discipline of tropical medicine only belatedly addressed the effects of an inadequate and/or inappropriate diet in children. Equally, the interrelation of malnutrition and infectious diseases excited little interest. In the inter-war years, the CO became aware of malnutrition in the colonies.[6] This was part of a wider realisation of the importance of dietary elements and the identification of the accessory food factors, the vitamins.[7] It also related to ethnographic studies of indigenous cultures, food habits and the disruptive effects of colonial rule.[8] The CO effectively dismissed Cicely Williams' work on kwashiorkor in the 1930s. This was typical of the minimal official interest in malnutrition as a medical problem and maternal and child welfare as a social problem.[9] Hugh Trowell, working in Uganda, chose not to publish his contemporaneous findings on protein deficiency in a British Protectorate.[10] Immediately after its formation, the FAO of the UN attempted to improve levels of food production. Later the 'green revolution' enjoyed some success before the negative effects of environmental degradation became apparent.[11] Meanwhile detailed understanding of the scientific basis for kwashiorkor and marasmus, suitable methods of treatment, social problems associated with infant weaning and education of mothers remained outstanding problems for paediatricians, medical scientists and social scientists. In respect to both research and practical provision in the tropics, the responses to these problems came from outside the discipline.[12]

The new wing at the LSTM offered much needed physical space for expansion of the existing research and teaching programmes in Liverpool. It also afforded intellectual space to develop the LSTM and the discipline of tropical medicine. The period from the opening of the Nuffield Wing in 1966 to 1990 was one of successive innovations, challenging institutes and organisations around the world to reconsider the discipline of tropical medicine. The emphasis on School staff being in the tropics as teachers and consultants, practising Liverpool's brand of tropical medicine, had to be accommodated alongside increasingly expensive fundamental science in the laboratory. Some members of staff perceived a tension between application and research. More importantly others questioned the desire to expand the range of applications and research interests that the School could realistically support. This chapter reviews the continued expansion of existing work at the School, but focuses on the first of these innovations, the Department of Tropical Paediatrics and Child Health.

The creation of the department acknowledged the gap in the education of those concerned with the health of infants and children in the tropics. The courses available for paediatricians from Europe wanting to practice overseas or locally educated physicians were inappropriate. Existing training relied on European models of paediatric care and failed to consider three central problems of child health in the tropics. First, the courses made no mention of the effects of tropical diseases during childhood. Second, the mistaken conception that there was a minimal incidence of common infections such as measles, diphtheria, mumps, poliomyelitis and tuberculosis meningitis had stultified interest in these conditions. Third, inappropriate and inadequate nutrition presented more widespread and fundamental problems than occurred in the wealthy countries of Europe. The effects of dirt, impure water, restricted access to education and employment interacted with the epidemiological profile, tying these issues together in a matrix of poverty and disadvantage. If the LSTM was not an appropriate organisation to remove the root causes, they could at least educate practitioners to deal with the problems. In 1970, with the support of the Ministry of Overseas Development, the LSTM offered its first new course since 1946: the Diploma in Tropical Child Health.

## NEW MANAGEMENT

The Nuffield Wing offered enhanced facilities for teaching and research. To make the best use of the new space the LSTM realised the necessity of upgrading the infrastructure. Increased activity brought a demand for additional support staff essential for the day-to-day work of the School. Miss J E Johnston became the first secretary appointed specifically to work for the *ATMP*. In 1907, the first volume of the in-house journal appeared with Ross as editor-in-chief.[13] Later, Fantham became the editorial secretary in 1912. At about this time the number of papers from authors outside the LSTM increased. Miss Gladys Phillips replaced Miss Twemlow as Librarian in 1931. Her position carried with it the additional responsibility of editorial secretary.[14] The appointment of a dedicated editorial secretary, for correspondence, copy editing and correction of proofs signified the expanding role of the journal and the library. A valuable member of staff, the chief technician, David Dagnall, died in 1966.[15] Jeffrey Friend was promoted to replace Dagnall. The teaching laboratory in the old building was named the Dagnall Laboratory out of respect for his long and dedicated service to the School. The new wing therefore not only provided new space, it also allowed space in the old building to be reorganised as the School embarked upon an further era of development. The library was enlarged by converting part of the old lecture theatre into a new reading room and creating a mezzanine floor for the periodicals. On the first floor, the small lecture theatre became a new photographic room. This facility, including the equipment for microphotography, now served the School as a centralised unit. The School acquired its first photocopier in 1967. This eased administrative work and allowed the library to copy material for inter-library loan rather than sending whole volumes. Members of staff found themselves gently encouraged to copy rather than hold bound volumes of journals in their offices.

In August 1965, a Management Committee replaced the Professional Committee. The Chairman of Council chaired the new committee and Maegraith, as Dean, became its executive officer. In October 1969 the scope of the new committee increased following a recommendation from Council and the title changed to Executive Management Committee, indicating its more dynamic role.[16] Under the Executive Management Committee were several sub-committees.[17] Council now met four times each year and reviewed the minutes of the monthly meetings of the Executive Management Committee and the Finance Committee. The Secretary of the Chamber of Commerce and Industry remained as the Secretary of Council after a review of the relationship between the two bodies. A reduction in the meetings of Council reduced the cost of using the secretariat at the Chamber. In 1973, the Articles of Association were revised to reformulate the Council. The number of elected members increased. This provided greater flexibility when making strategic elections to Council such as Dr J M Liston Chief Medical Adviser to the ODA. After Liston's retirement, his successor Dr Patrick Dill-Russell accepted election to the Council. Such a policy was useful in interesting the ODA in schemes of development and expansion which might attract funding from this source.[18]

The size of the staff had increased from the last revision of the Articles. Many now perceived themselves as members of a higher education institute. Changes in this area of employment warranted better representation for the School staff at the management level. Departmental heads became ex-officio members of Council. Two other teachers following an election among the staff joined them. As a body, the teaching staff formed a group meeting regularly to discuss teaching programmes, timetables and student issues. The intimacy of the pre-war years preserved to some extent by an initial continuity of the teaching staff was finally lost. The staff luncheon 'held weekly in the boardroom', replaced the sandwiches eaten in one of the professors' offices.[19]

Inevitably, the increase in size of the LSTM and the increasing complexity of employment contracts with outside organisations and fund providers added to the bureaucracy of the institution. The maintenance of dedicated facilities in the

LSTM, such as the library that could have been centralised within the University had the School not resisted closer links, would increasingly burden the recurrent budget. The realisation that the School, as a whole, represented a model for the developing world rendered the maintenance of the library a necessity. The later librarians assumed responsibility for explaining the techniques of efficient library usage. Students unfamiliar with these aspects of academic work learned how to compile bibliographies and plan research using abstracting journals, and later computer aided searches. This special service was of course in addition to regular duties of cataloguing, binding and dealing with outside requests.

The longer-term appeal for funds proved disappointing. The original plan, an appeal for one million pounds to create a capital sum sufficient to endow research and recurrent spending not provided for by the UGC grant, could not be realised. Money raised under this head was required for immediate needs. A realisation that raising money would not be time limited but a constant activity was carried forward with a deficit into the 1970s. The Voluntary Funds Committee issued mail shots, made direct requests and maintained a flow of publicity about the School. The Committee also liaised with fund providers on specific projects. A small budget and staff necessarily limited the activities of the committee.

To increase what the LSTM referred to as their 'asking power', two extra groups of interested people became formally linked with Council. First, under Brigadier Philip Toosey as President, a select group agreed to serve as Vice Presidents. Toosey and Council chose wisely: they were uniformly wealthy and/or well connected.[20] Besides the personal generosity and influence, the Vice Presidents also provided advice on how to best approach business firms which had a responsibility to shareholders. They employed an economic version of the discourse on health and development and avoided an unnecessary reliance upon humanitarianism. British support for development, for instance, prevented the spread of communism and maintained potential markets for manufactured goods. They were also able to dispel myths about the work of the LSTM and its impact on the developing world. The common misconception that promoting child health would abet the population explosion was countered with reliable information that the reverse occurred: people had fewer children if they believed they would survive.[21] The Vice Presidents' dinner provided an annual social occasion to discuss future planning and likely sources of support. The Patron, The Duke of Edinburgh, frequently attended. Second, the Associates of Council were prominent business and professional people in the region. A target of one hundred Associates was set. After an introduction to the activities of LSTM, interested individuals would use their personal connections at the local level to recruit small covenanted donations to the appeal. At the level of recruitment, the Associates scheme was initially successful, later the numbers declined. It is rather ironic that the initial success occurred when those who traditionally elected representatives to Council found it a difficult task to find individuals willing to serve. In 1969, the Merchant Bank of Baring Brothers assumed responsibility for the investment portfolio of the School. The Honorary Treasurer and Finance Committee had worked under the guidance of investment brokers, but as in other areas of the management, professionals that could be held responsible replaced volunteers.

## NEW DEPARTMENTS, NEW DIRECTIONS

The departmental structure established when the School occupied the buildings in Pembroke Place remained relatively unchanged until the mid-1960s. From 1965 to 1975, several modifications occurred. These reflected new priorities within the LSTM and a reorientation of existing patterns of teaching and research. Changes in the established departments were responses to internal staffing issues and new collaborative research programmes. The new departmental structure presented a statement by the LSTM on the discipline of tropical medicine it wished to promote.

With the retirement of Adams in 1966, the Sub-department of Clinical Tropical Medicine was discontinued. Maegraith succeeded him as Physician in Tropical Diseases at the LRI. Adams had cared for members of the Far Eastern Prisoners of War Association at the Mossley Hill Hospital. The LSTM assumed responsibility for these men, admitting them to the Tropical Ward at the LRI or to Tropical Diseases Centre at Sefton General Hospital. The President of the LSTM, Brigadier Philip Toosey, was also President of the FEPOW: both organisations welcomed the closer association. David Smith transferred from the Department of Tropical Hygiene to the post of senior lecturer in Tropical Medicine to take over Adams' teaching duties. The Tropical Ward at the LRI was shared for a few years with Dr David Weatherall whose work on thalassaemias and other inherited blood disorders was supported by an MOD grant of £5,000 over three years. The generosity of Lieutenant Colonel J R Danson, who provided £40,000 for the extension fund was recognised by naming the outpatient clinic in the new wing, the Danson Clinic.[22]

The Department of Tropical Hygiene under Professor Thomas Wilson continued on the same small scale. He and other members of staff maintained active research interests in filariasis in Southeast Asia, recognised at the international level. Wilson revised the teaching for the DTMH using small group tutorials and seminars. As a department, however, it remained the least focused and smallest unit in the School.

Kershaw resigned from the chair of Parasitology and Entomology in 1966. With his departure, the School returned to the pre-war pattern of separate departments, The Walter Myers Department of Parasitology and Everett Dutton

Sub-department of Entomology.[23] Within Parasitology, a Sub-department of Veterinary Parasitology concentrated on non-human parasites.[24] The opening of the University's Veterinary Field Station, at Leahurst on the Wirral in 1942, provided new opportunities for large animal parasitology. The LSTM had not enjoyed such facilities since it gave up the laboratory at Runcorn in 1914. The intellectual reason for fractionating a large unit into three smaller composite units, that the subject had become too unwieldy, is inadequate. The success of the host/parasite interaction studies need not necessarily have been affected by dividing the department, but the style of research in the new arrangement differed from the previous years. Rather than acting as a self-contained research group the parasitologists and vector biologists served as basic sciences underpinning tropical medicine rather than taking a strong leading role in the discipline: one that in future could dominate the LSTM.

Kershaw's move to a chair of biology at the Royal College of Advanced Technology at Salford, with several of his research staff, indicated his affinity for pure science and parasitology broadly conceived and not restricted to tropical problems. For Kershaw the necessary harnessing of his work to the politically complicated discipline of tropical medicine had become unattractive. In his place came Professor Wallace Peters.

Peters was a specialist in drug resistance, particularly malaria parasites. He joined the LSTM from the CIBA laboratories in Basel, Switzerland. The School enjoyed several useful links with CIBA. CIBA's new anti-schistosomiasis drug Ambilher, was used at the Tropical Diseases Centre and in the field; Gilles, Lucas and Bell in Nigeria reporting favourable results. Dr Rawewan Jarumilinta made brief visits for collaborative work on amoebiasis.[25] The links with CIBA staff and collaborations shows the opportunistic network that the School created, as and when it could. Scientific disciplines tend to function in networks and tropical medicine was therefore conforming to established practice. However, as the debate over the most suitable location for teaching and research – First or Third World – continued, linking networks were particularly valuable. The soliciting of Peters to join the staff at Liverpool was an added bonus from investing in such a network.

Confirmation of the reports of malaria parasites resistant to chloroquine in South America and Southeast Asia promoted a new research effort. This subject dominated the research of the Department of Parasitology under Peters. He was joined by Mr Robert E Howells, who transferred from the University Department of Pathology, and Dr A T C Bourke, who had recent field experience of drug resistant malaria in Thailand and Vietnam. Howells was one of three new University lecturers and Bourke joined as a Technical Assistance Lecturer. Peters continued to build up his research team. Discussions with the University resulted in a successful application to establish a MRC Research Group on the Chemotherapy of Protozoal Diseases and Drug Resistance in the School in 1968. This provided staff for a period of five years. Dr D C Warhurst moved to Liverpool from the NIMR at Mill Hill, becoming the first appointment under this scheme. Maegraith commented repeatedly on the lack of continuity in research staff. A new policy in the late 1960s, increasing the fees of overseas students to three times those of home students, thwarted the traditional reliance of the School on these PhD students as research workers.[26]

In April 1967, Peters was appointed to the WHO's Expert Advisory Panel on Malaria. He acted as a consultant on chemotherapy in Geneva. Therefore, the team in Liverpool enjoyed an international reputation in this important new research area. Besides Peters' links with CIBA he actively cultivated links with British pharmaceutical companies and spoke to the Association of Advisers to the Pharmaceutical Industry. This active promotion of the work of the department brought immediate rewards. To begin research on drug resistance, Peters brought his strains of rodent malaria with him from CIBA. Colonies of *Anopheles stephensi* were established as experimental vectors in new insectaries. Peters' team and this biological capital, strategically advertised, attracted new anti-malarial compounds for testing. The international significance of the problem and the provision of funds and equipment from outside were persuasive, but what had been unsuitable for the LSTM after the war was applauded in Peters' department.[27] It was also rewarded. In 1968, the WHO appointed the LSTM one of four Regional Malaria Reference Centres for Screening Potential Anti-malarial Compounds. The work complemented but did not compete with Maegraith's own research interests in this field.[28] Dr Nibhar Jaroonvesama joined the Department of Tropical Medicine from Bangkok in 1966 and her research investigated differences in the pathophysiology of drug resistant and drug sensitive malarias in rodents. Joint work on rodent malaria began to yield significant results in the early 1970s.[29] The designation of Liverpool as a centre for chemotherapy, drug action and drug resistance extended beyond the malaria work. In 1970, the Wellcome Trust awarded £20,000 over three years for the study of these problems in leishmaniasis and Chagas' disease.

Broadcasts for the BBC in 1967, on chloroquine resistant malaria, indicated a perception of the problem at the popular level. Publicity of this sort usefully reminded the public of the importance of the LSTM. The exotic diseases and destinations connected with the School made good listening. The potential for good publicity also came from the expertise of Alistair Reid on snake venom, anti-venom and its use in biological products and physiological research.[30] Reid's appointment as a senior lecturer (Technical Assistance) indicated the increasingly diverse activities of the LSTM and tropical medicine. In the Sub-department of Entomology, William W MacDonald continued his work on vectors' genetic susceptibility to carriage of parasites. In 1966 and 1967, he spent time in Bangkok establishing a research station for the study of *Aedes aegypti*. In the 1970s, the work of the two Sub-departments of Entomology and Veterinary Parasitology continued to develop strong research identities within international networks. This involved considerable time abroad on visits and consultancies. The difficulty was to hold together these disparate research interests in a unit short of funds and becoming administratively complex. However, the LSTM was not content to stay within the traditional boundaries of the discipline.

## TROPICAL PAEDIATRICS AND CHILD HEALTH

Child health was not a priority of tropical medicine when the School opened. Maternal and infant mortality among the wives of military officers and civil administrators was certainly higher in the tropics than at home, but the effects of the tropical climate could be mitigated by sending children home for schooling. As the twentieth century progressed, individual prophylaxis based upon medical knowledge and segregation policies alleviated the dramatic effects of tropical diseases. There is little evidence that the discovery era of tropical medicine paid attention to the expression of tropical diseases in children, except when they represented reservoirs of infection. The immediate concern was to find means of preventing the death of the colonisers and traders in the tropics, as far as children were concerned the policy was to keep away from them, particularly at night. The incidence of 'childhood' diseases (measles, mumps, and poliomyelitis) in indigenous children was either ignored or assumed by some to be non-existent. Historians consider the developing interest in the health of children relates to their function as a labour force, as future purchasers of British manufactures and as part of the hegemony of imperialism.[31] Early colonial initiatives to provide improved child health services, usually as an addition to basic infant and maternal welfare, often utilised the interest of individuals and non-government organisations such as missionary societies. In the inter-war years, the League of Nations Health Committee commissioned surveys revealing the scope for maternal and child health.[32] A practical interest in ameliorating the conditions of poverty and ignorance underlying these problems remained muted. The LSTM offered no appreciable exception at this time.

In the 1920s, working from the laboratory of the School in Freetown, the malariaologist George MacDonald, investigated the incidence and clinical expression of malaria in local children.[33] This epidemiological study coincided with the contemporary work of Blacklock and Gordon on malaria and pregnancy.[34] Despite considerable opportunities, there was no continuation of this line of research in either Liverpool or West Africa. It was not recognised as a concern at this time. Later, Gordon and Hicks used children in tests of anti-schistosomiasis

167

drugs.[35] These were opportunistic studies, there was no policy encouraging research on child health.

In the late 1950s the School expanded the scope of the DTMH course by asking invited guest lecturers to discuss subjects not otherwise included in the course. Outside expertise also relieved the pressure upon core staff to meet the demands of the teaching programme. Dr David Morley of the Western Guild, Western Nigeria spoke on 'The development of a paediatric service in a rural area of the tropics.' Besides the lectures, Dr A B Chrisitie gave practical demonstrations on poliomyelitis at Fazakerly Hospital. Christie was also lecturer in infectious diseases in the medical faculty. Professor John Hay, head of the University Department of Child Health and consultant paediatrician at Alder Hey, confirmed the tentative interest of the medical faculty in developing links with the LSTM. Hay asked the School to offer undergraduate lectures for the medical students' course on paediatrics from 1960 onwards.

The emphasis on non-tropical disease in the tropics, such as poliomyelitis, represented a significant reinterpretation of the diploma course and the remit of the School. Childhood infections in Britain progressed to a minimal incidence through immunisation programmes, improved nutrition and better general standards of living. In the developing world, they remained common causes of mortality and morbidity. At the turn of the century, such infections were central to undergraduate medical education. Practitioners who worked overseas would not have required further training but expressed little interest in these diseases. The incidence of tropical diseases was overwhelming and there was considerable confusion about the occurrence of many non-tropical diseases in the tropics.[36] Curricular developed for the tropics after the war reflected the diminishing importance of these diseases and the demonstrations at Fazakerly indicated that some students were not sufficiently well prepared before taking the diploma. If the LSTM was to live up to Maegraith's vision that the impact on the tropics was in the tropics, it was essential that more accurate epidemiology become a focus of the School. Equally, the selective care of particular groups according to race or status was no longer acceptable. Tropical medicine was obliged to include the whole population and concentrate on the most vulnerable.

## THE SENIOR LECTURESHIP

On the institutional side, Maegraith and Hay were responsible for developing tropical paediatrics in Liverpool. Gilles, who was involved with planning the intellectual side of this initiative, had already established his interest in certain aspects of child health before joining the School as Lecturer-at-Large. At the

MRC laboratories in The Gambia, he worked on immunity and infection studies of malaria in children.[37] In Nigeria, a survey of the status of child health was an important part of the Afuko village study.[38] Gilles also worked in collaboration with Ralph Hendrickse, professor of Paediatrics, head of the Department of Paediatrics and Director of Institute of Child Health, University of Ibadan, Nigeria.[39] Hay, Maegraith and Gilles considered Hendrickse had the ability and experience to develop tropical paediatrics as a sub-discipline of tropical medicine at Liverpool. They asked for his opinion in drafting the preliminary submissions to the University.[40]

Hendrickse was born and educated in apartheid South Africa. He worked at the McCord Zulu Hospital, Durban for six years developing an interest in paediatric medicine before taking post-graduate qualifications in Glasgow and Edinburgh in 1955. In October that year, having qualified MRCP in June (special subject paediatrics), he was appointed Senior Registrar in Paediatrics at University College Hospital, Ibadan. His own experience testified to the dearth of specific training in tropical paediatrics. Hendrickse relied upon marrying his clinical experience and an additional qualification of one of the professional colleges in order to gain a specialist appointment in the field of paediatrics.

In 1957, he became a consultant paediatrician in the hospital and lecturer in Paediatrics in the College. He was also gained his MD from the University of Cape Town that year. The thesis discussed sickle cell anaemia and related conditions in Nigerian children. In 1959, he became senior lecturer. In 1961, he visited Britain again as a holder of the Heinz Fellowship of the British Paediatric Association. He worked at Great Ormond Street Hospital in London and the Department of Paediatrics in the University of Birmingham, but visited neither School of Tropical Medicine. He returned to Ibadan in 1962 via various centres in America after gaining a Rockefeller Fellowship. On his return, the University offered him the chair of Tropical Paediatrics and leadership of the department. In 1964, he became Director of the Institute of Child Health in the University.

Hendrickse's personal and subsequent employment history represented a very different pattern to other members of staff at the LSTM. He was himself from a developing country and had held a professorial appointment at a University in a different developing country. In addition to his professional qualifications, Hendrickse had served on university and other committees. He was a founder member of the Paediatric Association of Nigeria. He acted as a consultant for the Nigerian Ministry of Health on projects such as the measles vaccination programme. His experience was therefore not just as a paediatrician, but as an administrator and organiser.

The School imported his expertise and outlook from the developing world, in order to transfer it back again to a wider audience. Over the next thirteen years, the School effected this transfer in four ways. First, the position of senior lecturer in Child Health and Tropical Paediatrics provided an example to similar institutes in the developed and developing world. Second, the diploma course established in collaboration with Hay and using the clinical facilities of local NHS hospitals, prepared paediatricians using a unique combination of clinical experience and dedicated teaching. Third, his research highlighted unresolved issues and provided publicity for the initiative of the LSTM. Four, in his role as editor of a new School journal launched in 1981, the *Annals of Tropical Paediatrics*, he could influence the agenda for the sub-discipline of tropical paediatrics. Hendrickse's expertise transformed the definition of tropical medicine adopted by the LSTM, a definition they wished to advertise around the world.

Plans for a senior lecturer and new diploma course in the School and University Department of Child Health were announced in the quinquennial estimates returned by Child Health for the period 1967–1972.[41] Despite the closeness of Hay and Maegraith, a formal association between the LSTM and the department waited until the School had completed its new wing and subsequent reorganisation of the buildings. In 1966, the DTMH curriculum was 'streamlined' to allow the same number of staff to cope with an increased number of students. Within this leaner course, there was a greater emphasis on the paediatric aspects of tropical diseases. The curriculum was reorientated not reduced. This reorientation began an epistemological shift from tropical medicine towards medicine in the tropics. Besides the direct teaching, the School envisaged that the promotion of child health within its curricula would serve two other primary functions. First, the School would become a clearing-house and repository for information on the incidence of childhood diseases, and current research in child health in the tropics. This would begin to assist in deconstructing the myths about such diseases in the tropics. Second, in collaboration with clinical colleagues in Liverpool and overseas the School would promote research in tropical paediatrics.

Besides revising the DTMH course, the ambitions of the LSTM were better served by the plans for recruiting an additional member of staff and mounting the new course, the Diploma in Child Health and Tropical Paediatrics. The rationale for introducing the diploma referred to a pattern whereby students would complete their DTMH and then seek clinical attachments in paediatrics. The DTMH could not provide sufficient specialist paediatric teaching and the clinical attachments carried no responsibility for children in hospital. After some modifications to the original proposal, the University acceded to the viability of the course with its acknowledged market. They stipulated that funding for the salary and other costs of the senior lecturer came from outside sources for the initial period of five years. The University also reserved the right to refuse to support the post at the end of this period.

The intention was to have the lecturer in post on 1 January 1968. It was not until early 1969 that the Leverhulme Trust confirmed a grant of £45,000 over six years for a senior lecturer, a senior technician and travelling expenses.[42] The Leverhulme Trust offered the money to the School not the University, although they recognised it was a joint application. The appointment, however, was a University lectureship. Hay was to take responsibility for the clinical side of the work and the limited teaching within the current Diploma of Child Health. Maegraith would be responsible for the teaching on the new course and research.[43] On a day-to-day level, the arrangements for the management of this post relied upon the trust and co-operation of Hay and Maegraith for its smooth operation. Hendrickse very sensibly insisted on knowing the details of these arrangements.

Hay and Maegraith corresponded with Hendrickse, inviting him to apply for the position. His name went forward with their support to a meeting of the Selection Committee on 21 April 1969. He received the unanimous support of the Committee. Gilles represented the School as Maegraith was away. A month later, on 22 May, a meeting of the University Council offered him the position of senior lecturer in Tropical Paediatrics and Child Health in the Department of Tropical Medicine on a five-year contract starting 1 October 1969. His contract stipulated that he would be able to spend two months each year in the tropics. He was also to have an Honorary Consultant contract with the Liverpool Regional Hospital Board including duties at the Alder Hey Children's Hospital and a neonatal unit at another hospital. The honorary post at Alder Hey represented the first formal link with other hospitals in the Merseyside region since the opening of the Tropical Diseases Centre at Smithdown Road Hospital (renamed Sefton General Hospital) during World War II. The first diploma course would begin in September 1970 and Hendrickse was therefore able to plan his research and teaching. Maegraith invited him to shadow the DTMH to further orientate the course towards paediatric medicine and assist with preparations for the DTCH.[44] Hendrickse offered ten illustrated lectures to the DTMH students on child health and taught the DCH and fifth-year medics at the University and in the clinic. This relieved Maegraith who had undertaken the teaching until his appointment.

On a practical level, the success of the application to Leverhulme and Hendrickse's appointment brought new burdens to the School. By 1969, there was little free space in the building. No suite of rooms lay vacant awaiting occupation by Tropical Paediatrics. Three and a half years after occupying the new wing, the School was planning a further extension to accommodate the new department in the near future.[45] In the first instance, however, Tropical Paediatrics functioned as a Sub-department of Tropical Medicine, physically accommodated within the existing departments. Outpatient work would use the Danson Clinic. Animals for experimental purposes were crowded into the existing animal houses. Hendrickse and his secretary, Miss M E McGrath, each had a 'chair and a desk in an office in the School of Tropical Medicine'.[46] The second extension of the LSTM was planned specifically for the new initiative taken by the School. The extent of even the initial plans indicates the commitment Maegraith made to Tropical Paediatrics.[47] His retention of the office of Dean until the organisation of the extension was complete reinforces this point.

The DTCH served as a mechanism to create the first new department in the School since the short-lived Department of Chemotherapy.[48] Unlike the DTMH, the DTCH was a unique course of study. It aimed to educate physicians to offer better care to neonates, infants and children up to five years of age in the difficult conditions that prevailed in developing countries. The acquisition of practical skills was doubly beneficial. When the paediatrician returned home, these skills were available to co-workers. As a course requirement each student researched and submitted a dissertation. Bound copies were available on open access in the library. The dissertations provided a unique resource: they were often the only literature on child health and/or paediatrics for certain countries. The dissertation also prepared the students for research when they returned home. Establishing a research culture was important.

The diploma also functioned by providing unexpected publicity for the LSTM. In June and July 1972, after the first eight students had successfully gained the DTCH, an editorial in the *Lancet* took the School to task. The short two paragraph article complained that the LSTM was again contributing to the attempt in Britain to 'patch up the gaps in the far-from-satisfactory undergraduate programme with a plethora of postgraduate diplomas...[in]...far-from-tropical Liverpool'.[49] The reply from Maegraith and Hay provided a cheap advertisement for the aims and structure of the course. Members of staff had long ago learned to dodge the accusation that tropical medicine could not be practised in temperate Liverpool. Maegraith and Hay referred, as had the editor, to the excellence of the staff and their extensive experience. Indeed, they considered it was exactly the experience of working outside of their home environment that most stimulated the students. The clinical work provided them with direct responsibility for patients and offered the opportunity to observe good practice, much of which might be adapted upon their return home. Maegraith and Hay denied the accusation that the course was an excuse for ambitious physicians to dress up their letterhead with an additional qualification. They argued that a clear out-put from the course was important for students and fund providers who at least required certificates of attendance.[50] Whether it was valid or not Maegraith missed the point that there was an alternate perception to acquiring a diploma, particularly one from Britain.[51] The diploma itself could transform a useful course of study into a mandatory qualification. If it became a necessity that paediatricians acquire a qualification such as the DTCH, taking the course continued the dependency of developing countries on the developed world. Maegraith acknowledged that 'it is beyond the present capabilities of many tropical countries to embark on formal postgraduate medical education'.[52] He stressed the importance of the transfer of knowledge, but refrained from commenting on the ideology of the inherent dependency culture. Hendrickse did not engage in the debate.

## RESEARCH

In the borrowed accommodation at the LSTM and a small teaching and research laboratory at Alder Hey Children's Hospital, some research began. Hendrickse indicated to Maegraith before his arrival his intention to analyse data collected over many years in Ibadan. His interests included malaria in childhood and in collaboration with other colleagues including Gilles, included the relationship between nephrotic syndrome and quartan malaria. He continued this research after his arrival in Liverpool, maintaining close links with his former colleagues in Nigeria.[53] This relationship between specific tropical infections and pathological conditions in children was a hallmark of Hendrickse's style of research. He presented papers at scientific meetings around the world, providing excellent publicity for the LSTM.[54]

New research, fostering a profile for Liverpool, concentrated on gastroenteritis. A serious and common problem in the tropics, outbreaks of gastroenteritis, occurred among disadvantaged children in Britain. The incidence of fatal diarrhoea in hospitals also caused concern. This was later linked to problems with bottle washing and the use of strong detergents.[55] Hendrickse took charge of the gastroenteritis unit at Alder Hey and established a laboratory there for research and teaching. Some students had not enjoyed the facilities of such a laboratory before. The Leverhulme grant provided funds for a technician, Mrs J Morris, and laboratory equipment. Some research support on this disease, malabsorption and immunological derangements in children came from the Children's Research Fund. Teaching commitments and the need to find a further source of funding for the paediatrics initiative understandably checked research output.

The appointment of additional Technical Assistance staff eased the pressure on Hendrickse. A new project compared growth, development, illness profiles and immunological responses in bottle- and breast-fed infants. Dr Anthony J H Stephens also promoted breast-feeding in Liverpool. Studies in Liverpool complemented work in the tropics. Immunological studies in tuberculosis and coeliac disease were also started. As with the teaching much of the research was groundbreaking, not for its sophistication, but because this represented the interaction of the disciplines of tropical medicine, paediatric medicine, and nutrition studies that had not converged before in a formal arrangement.

## THE DEPARTMENT OF TROPICAL PAEDIATRICS AND CHILD HEALTH

The senior lectureship and diploma course launched tropical paediatrics in Liverpool. In practical terms, it would remain limited to Hendrickse plus support from the Department of Child Health and the Regional Hospital Board unless additional funding was forthcoming. Support from the University converted Hendrickse's post to a tenured position on 2 February 1973. In this year the School accorded Tropical Paediatrics departmental status, although the University did not recognise the Department of Tropical Paediatrics and Child Health as a separate department. Hendricke's appointment within the University released the Leverhulme grant for an additional member of staff, Stephens. There was no further University funding for additional staff or the capital expenditure for expansion of the department.

Estimates at the end of 1969 indicated a sum of £200,000.00 as a capital sum for construction and £30,000.00 per annum for recurrent expenditure for an additional wing to house Tropical Paediatrics. In the inflationary economy of the 1970s, these sums were too conservative. Moreover, in a climate when fund providers such as the Wellcome Trust and the Nuffield Foundation had shown themselves disinclined to give money for new buildings, raising this amount of money would be difficult. The Wolfson Foundation rejected an initial approach. The WHO supported the principle of the project, but would only offer their support for centres in the developing world. They already provided joint sponsorship with UNICEF for the teachers of paediatrics course from developing countries at the Institute of Child Health, London. Private philanthropy not forthcoming, an approach to the Treasury via the Minister for Overseas Development began in 1971. This started a long protracted process of determining what the ODA would support and tailoring what Liverpool offered accordingly.

The rationale for this application relied upon two basic concerns in international development. First, fear over the expanding population. Second, maximising the economic potential of the Third World. Support for tropical paediatrics and child health at Liverpool would engage with these concerns. Experience showed families naturally self-limited their size when children were likely to survive past five years of age. The debilitating effects of malnutrition and infectious diseases affected the physical and mental development of children, turning them from an asset to a burden on their community. The provision of funds for Liverpool would help shift the focus from 'remedial measures directed mainly at the older members of society...[and] produce the fundamental changes that may be expected from investment in the health of the very young'.[56]

The ODA accepted the principles on which their support had been requested and invited a formal submission justifying the establishment of a centre of tropical child health in Liverpool. In particular it was important to indicate the location of such a centre in Liverpool rather than overseas. Interaction with the local community, particularly ethnic and immigrant populations, was planned as paediatrics expanded. These populations provided interesting comparisons with the problems facing community health services in the tropics which Liverpool trained paediatricians would function within or indeed lead. The ODA encouraged the LSTM to consider the precedent of the Centre for Tropical Veterinary Medicine at Edinburgh established with ODA money as a basis for their submission.

In December 1973, sufficient clarity on the 'need for and structure of the course', its size, cost and the likely ODA contribution enabled an ODA advisory meeting to be held at the School. The ODA Advisory Committee represented a group of informed and influential individuals clearly kindly disposed to the aims of the LSTM.[57] The only significant difference between the proposed ODA supported course and the diploma currently in operation was the introduction of an overseas placement during the clinical year. This would widen the experience of the students and quieten the criticism of funding the teaching of tropical paediatrics in a developed country. It remained only a suggestion. At this meeting, the committee recommended support of £300,000.00 capital and £70,000.00 annually for seven years against recurrent expenditure.[58]

In August 1974, the MOD confirmed, subject to parliamentary approval, funding would be forthcoming to continue and expand the work of the department when the Leverhulme grant expired in September 1975. Provision for the capital costs of the new extension over a period of three years facilitated the expansion.[59] The MOD was apparently flexible about payments for the new building and the appointment of additional staff.[60] However, they refused to meet initial estimates of expenditure for extra support staff arguing that they would conduct work other than paediatrics while building was in progress. Hendrickse therefore urged the School to consider a grant of funds from the School recurrent budget.[61] Money was not forthcoming. Up until this time there had been no subvention from general funds, the activities of Tropical Paediatrics being met entirely from the Leverhulme grant. Despite the success of outside funding even on the scale offered by the MOD, the poor overall financial status of the LSTM handicapped the department.

## THE MAEGRAITH WING AND TROPICAL PAEDIATRICS

On 28 July 1975, work began on the 'Maegraith Wing' named by popular demand after the outgoing Dean of almost thirty years. The capital cost of the part of the four-storey extension of the right side of the LSTM not concerned with paediatrics, came from donations and School reserves. It housed the Community Health Department discussed in chapter 8. The successful application to the Ministry was essential to the future viability of the department. The MOD justified its decision because the programme at Liverpool was of direct benefit to the Third World, despite its location in the First World. This had a strategic significance for the School. MOD support for developments in Liverpool recognised the value of a British institution concerned with teaching and research in the developing world. It strengthened the argument that financial aid for development could be legitimately utilised in this way, and was not a misuse of aid funding. The School hoped that the grant of MOD money for a British- based project with recurrent elements would set a precedent for future funding policy.

Assistance with recurrent expenditure facilitated the basic projects discussed when the senior lectureship was planned. Much of the time under Leverhulme funding was used to establish the principles for training community orientated paediatricians for work in the developing world and begin research on problems of child health in developing countries. The idea of a data repository placing the School at the centre of tropical paediatric research now also came to fruition. To assist with data analysis for this purpose a lecturer in Statistics, Sarah J B Macfarlane, joined the department. Her arrival brought the first social scientist onto the staff. The appointment of an organic chemist had once seemed far removed from the discipline of tropical medicine. In contrast, Macfarlane's appointment indicated a new expansiveness of the discipline in Liverpool. Statistics and epidemiology had been an important part of the LSHTM since 1927, although the London School had not linked statistical work with paediatrics in particular. Her career had taken her into northern Europe but the LSTM provided a new range of opportunities. Her outlook opened a new professional vista for the LSTM. Only five years previously Hendrickse had to explain the purchase of a calculator capable of statistical analysis to the Leverhulme Trust.[62]

In the same year, Hendrickse became professor of Tropical Paediatrics and Child Health in the University. It was, however, a personal chair albeit the first appointment at this level in Britain. The University remained unwilling to recognise the separate academic status of the department. In the next two years, external approval for his position in Liverpool was manifest by appointment to four prestigious committees: Council on International Development, MOD; Tropical Medicine Panel, Wellcome Trust; Tropical Medicine Research Board, MRC; Council, RSTMH. Publicity for the work of the department, the DTCH course, support from the University and the successful bid for funding provided the opportunity to launch the department, not as an experiment, but an institutionalised force when the new wing opened. The fledging Department of Tropical Paediatrics would succeed, where Chemotherapy had failed after the war, as a significant new direction for the LSTM built upon a preceding interest. It succeeded because it had powerful support and because its supporters perceived a need in the developing world. Fortunately for the School, this need could be met within the 'enlightened self-interest' that still pervaded Britain's aid policies.

Dr Michael Chan joined the department in October 1976 as a further senior lecturer, with clinical responsibilities at Fazakerly Infectious Diseases Hospital. The statistical research team was strengthened by the appointment of Barry Moody, a computer programmer, under a grant from the Wellcome Trust. The appointment of Moody was part of a collaborative project with the Institute of Child Health in Ibadan. Data from a longitudinal growth and development study previously collected by Dr M D Janes was analysed in Liverpool during Janes' secondment. His temporary appointment became permanent through ODA assistance in 1978 when he joined Macfarlane to work on the data bank project.[62] The Statistical Unit (Macfarlane and Moody) developed teaching programmes, including the San Serriffe Game, which asked students to analyse the neonatal problems of an imaginary island. The Unit also supported other research projects in the department as these developed in the 1980s. Where possible they provided an advisory service for other departments and outside institutions.

The two departments occupied the Maegraith wing early in 1978. The official opening ceremony on 5 May 1978 was conducted by the Rt Hon Judith Hart, Minister for Overseas Development. The building provided Tropical Paediatrics with the first proper facilities since Hendrickse's appointment almost ten years before. From an adequate institutional base, the department successfully attracted research funding. The Wellcome Trust supported work on childhood anaemia in Papua New Guinea. Oxfam and the Canadian International Development Research Council funded work in the Sudan on mycotoxins and the pathogenesis of kwashiorkor. The Pilkington Will Trust funded a senior lecturer/registrar to work at Alder Hey on the ongoing gastroenteritis study.

In March 1981, a new quarterly journal, the *Annals of Tropical Paediatrics*, testified to the acceptance of the tropical paediatrics. As tropical medicine itself had created recognisable institutions, qualifications and dedicated literature, the sub-discipline of paediatric medicine as practised, taught and studied at the

LSTM was now identifiable. With a further year of ODA funding still in hand Tropical Paediatrics presented a short but successful history. However, the continuation of the department relied entirely upon the ability to attract funding of a scale sufficient to meet the running costs of the entire department.

As head of department, Hendrickse approached the ODA to seek continuation of funding for a further period. An ODA team visited the School, and linked hospitals in October 1981. They were interested to learn what efforts the department had made to find alternative funds. The early 1980s were difficult years for the higher education sector. The University's grant to the School in 1980/81 reflected a reduction of 1.85 per cent in the UGC grant to the University. Further cuts were likely. This strengthened the claim of the School on the ODA given its unique work on tropical paediatrics in the context of development overseas as opposed to higher education in Britain. The team recommended further support for three years although this was to diminish by ten per cent in each of the three years. Thereafter there would be no further central support for the LSTM.

In January 1982, the ODA confirmed their intention to offer support, on a tapering basis, until March 1985. The letter detailing the award referred the LSTM to their assurances during the visit in 1981 that in the next three years the department would become self-supporting. Should the ODA consider that appropriate steps to realise this goal were not instigated they would 'wish the School to initiate arrangements to wind up the department'.[64] The University and the LSTM provided the necessary assurances of future support. The University agreed to fund the recurrent expenses of the professor, one senior lecturer, one technician and one secretary. The LSTM launched a Tropical Paediatric Appeal Fund and agreed to meet any short fall from reserved funds, enabling the School to meet the remaining expenses of the department. On the strength of these efforts, the ODA continued provision of funds until 1985. The output of the department and its unique status in development medicine were apparently not to be lost. Without the ODA core funding, Tropical Paediatrics joined the other departments of the LSTM in the mid-1980s in an insecure future but with an equitable stake all the same.

On 1 January 1988, Hendrickse became professor of Tropical Paediatrics and International Child Health and head of the department of the same name at the LSTM. This was a University appointment and signalled recognition of the department. Hendrickse had worked hard to raise separate funds to endow the chair and thus help to commit the University to continuing the department.

## CONCLUSION

The opening ceremony of the Nuffield Wing was a moment for celebration. It provided the opportunity to extend the School and the type of kind of tropical medicine practised from Liverpool. Immediate benefits were evident in the increase in DTMH students, taught masters students and research facilities for staff and PhD students. External change provided a means for more radical internal reorganisation of the School. Maegraith changed the orientation of the School after 1945. He developed the focus of the LSTM as an academic research institution and took the School back into the tropics. With the completion of the new wing in the mid-1960s, he focused on the development of the home institution once more.

The increasing strength and independence of the Sub-departments of Parasitology, Medical Entomology and Veterinary Parasitology would see these evolve to full departments of the School and University. The greatly increased commitment of the WHO to research provided money for use within the School. Staff still served on commissions and expert committees overseas but increased the extent and sophistication of their work at Liverpool. These departments functioned increasingly as University departments. The Department of Tropical Medicine remained active in research and an intermediary between projects elsewhere in the School. Maegraith also used this department to launch his new initiative for the School, the academic discipline and the tropics. In 1969, the School appointed Ralph Hendrickse as senior lecturer in Tropical Paediatrics and Child Health. The position of senior lecturer serviced the DTCH, the first postgraduate course and qualification for paediatricians practising in the tropics.

Tropical paediatrics as it developed at Liverpool brought in methodologies employed elsewhere in the discipline, particularly the statistical analysis of epidemiological and other data. These methodologies were in no way unique. However, staff at Liverpool configured a departmental structure and curriculum that offered a unique training in paediatric medicine for the tropics. The School also served as a repository for data on child health and carried out an active research programme. The aflotoxin work in particular yielded controversial results and stimulated subsequent research.

Concerns over the expanding global population and the benefits of healthy children in the economic and social development of third world countries prompted the School to broaden its focus. The involvement in paediatric medicine and child health also represented an epistemological shift from tropical medicine towards medicine in the tropics. The creation of the Department questioned this divide. Tropical specialists resented the implication that health in the developing world was not their special preserve and that tropical medicine was nothing more than ordinary medicine in the tropics. However, paediatric practice highlighted the need to consider non-tropical conditions as they appeared in children in the tropics. Infectious diseases such as measles, diphtheria and polio needed consideration alongside malaria and the effects of malnutrition. The Department of Tropical Paediatrics therefore sought to unite aspects of tropical medicine and medicine in the tropics.

A large part of this chapter has looked at funding for the department. A grant from the Leverhulme Trust initially supported the post of senior lecturer. The ODA provided funding for a second extension to the School to house Tropical Paediatrics, which opened in 1978. In addition to the capital costs, they also provided recurrent funding for five years. This allowed the School to consolidate its work. The ODA recognised that paediatric medicine at the LSTM provided a resource for the developing world. They considered supporting this resource was an appropriate use of overseas development funding because Liverpool provided an apposite location for this initiative. The involvement of the ODA in providing support for tropical paediatrics illustrates how the priorities of development and the role of tropical medicine within development were subject to change. The notion of the LSTM acting as a resource in Britain for developing countries overseas fitted with Maegraith's plans for the School from the mid-1960s onwards.

Tropical Paediatrics successfully applied for subsequent funding from the ODA. They offered this grant on condition that the LSTM demonstrate that they could support the department before the period of the funding expired. The time involved in securing funds highlights contemporary difficulties associated with the need to function on soft money. In the early 1980s, the special nature of the LSTM as a resource for the developing world provided no immunity from the simultaneous reductions in higher education funding and the rising costs of an inflationary economy. Financial pressures increasingly caused the various departments at the School to justify their contribution to the discipline. This led to public divergence of opinion on the meaning of tropical medicine and its pursuit by the School. After reviewing the role of education at Liverpool in chapter 7, chapter 8 returns to the crucial debate on the future direction of the LSTM. In this debate Tropical Paediatrics had to argue its continued importance and could not rely upon its unique origin twenty years before.

NOTES

[1] The opening featured as a special article in *The Times*.

[2] D Kelves, *In the name of eugenics*, New York: Knopf, 1985.

[3] V Fildes, L Marks & H Marland, *Women and children first: international maternal welfare, 1870-1945*, London: Routledge, 1993.

[4] M Black, *The children and the nations: the story of UNICEF*, New York: UNICEF, 1986.

[5] D Dwork, *War is good for babies and other young children: a history of the infant and child welfare movement in England 1898–1918*, London: Tavistock, 1987.

[6] M Worboys, 'The discovery of colonial malnutrition between the wars', D Arnold (ed), *Imperial medicine and indigenous society*, Manchester: MUP, 1988, pp. 208–225.

[7] H Kamminga & A Cunningham (eds), *The science and culture of nutrition, 1840–1940*, Amsterdam: Rodopi, 1995.

[8] H L Moore & M Vaughan, *Cutting down trees: gender, nutrition and agricultural change in the Northern Province of Zambia 1890–1990*, London: James Currey, 1994.

[9] S Craddock, *Retired except on demand: the life of Dr Cicely Williams*, Oxford: Green College, 1983; A Dally, *Cicely: the story of a doctor*, London: Victor Gollancz, 1968.

[10] R G Whitehead, 'Kwashiorkor in Uganda', E M Widdowson & J A Mathers (eds), *The contribution of nutrition to human and animal health*, Cambridge: CUP, 1992, pp. 303–313.

[11] K A Dahlberg, *Beyond the green revolution: the ecology and politics of global agricultural development*, New York: Plenum, 1979.

[12] Interest in aspects of child health in relation to disease and nutrition in the tropics developed in the 1950s and 1960s. For instance, the MRC laboratories at Fajara in The Gambia studied malaria immunity in children. In the 1950s, the MRC (interestingly not the CMRC) established The Infantile Malnutrition Research Unit in Uganda and The Tropical Metabolism Research Unit in Jamaica. E M Widdowson, 'Protein-energy malnutrition', F E G Cox (ed), *Illustrated history of tropical diseases*, London: Wellcome Trust, 1996, pp. 370–377.

[13] The permanent members of staff were designated as editors in 1907. Thereafter senior members of staff joined the editorial 'team' as they were appointed to the School. After 1969, the journal was edited by a 'panel' and by a board from 1973 onwards. A year later the structure of the editorial board was formalised: the Dean acted as Chair, and the board consisted of heads of departments, a senior editor and assistant editor.

[14] From 1945, Gladys Phillips collated all papers published by staff on an annual basis and these were bound for the library.

[15] Obituary, *67th Annual Report of the LSTM, 1965–1966*, pp. 33–34. The attitude of the LSTM towards members of the support staff, a paternalistic appreciation of their loyalty similar to the hired staff of a family firm, was characterised by Dagnall's obituary.

[16] TM/3/1.17b, Council Meeting, 21 July 1969, Management of the Incorporated LSTM.

[17] Professional Standing Committee (constituted to deal with technical business); Library Committee; *ATMP*: Editorial Committee; Voluntary Funds Committee; Planning Committee.

[18] The Advisory Committee, which recommended funds of the new wing for Tropical Paediatrics in 1974, was chaired by J K Kilgour, and included Dr P W Dill-Russell: both were elected members of Council.

[19] *74th Annual Report of the LSTM, 1972–1973*, p. 23.

[20] The first Vice-Presidents: Lord Cohen of Birkenhead, Lord Cole, Lt-Col J R Danson, L O'B Harding, Sir Edward Reid, H Marston Riley. Lord Cole, 1967–1976, (Chairman of Unilever, Chairman of the Trustees, Leverhulme Trust, initial funding for the senior lectureship in Tropical Paediatrics and Child Health). Later notable Vice-Presidents: David Sainsbury (gift of £110,000 from his Charitable Trust for the Maegraith Wing); Rt Hon Selwyn Lloyd, Speaker of the House of Commons, President, (personal appeal on behalf of the LSTM raised £175,000 for the Maegraith Wing); Lord Howick of Glendale, Chairman Commonwealth Development Corporation; Sir Eric Griffiths-Jones, Chairman Commonwealth Development Corporation.

[21] R G Hendrickse, personal papers (hereafter RGH), Notes on matters discussed during the visit of the Vice Presidents to the LSTM, 3 December 1969.

[22] Obituary, *77th Annual Report of the LSTM, 1975–1976*, pp. 22–23.

[23] MacDonald was promoted to senior lecturer, and placed in charge of the Sub-department.

[24] Clarkson, senior lecturer in Veterinary Parasitology was placed in charge of the Sub-department.

[25] CIBA Horsham Ltd arranged for the issue of 16,000 copies of Maegraith's pamphlet, *Exotic diseases in practice*, to general practitioners.

[26] See for instance S N Ali, 'Studies on the metabolism of the malaria parasite and the action on antimalarial compounds', PhD thesis, University of Liverpool, 1969; R D G Theakston, 'An ultrastructural study of host-parasite relationships in malaria and related infections', PhD thesis, University of Liverpool, 1969; N Jaroonvesama, 'Pathophysiological phenomena in the host infected with normal and drug-resistant malaria parasites', PhD thesis, University of Liverpool, 1969.

[27] The research was supported by CIBA, Hoffmann-La Roche, ICI, MRC, WHO, R & D Branch of the US Army, Wellcome Trust. R D G Theakston was supported by a NIH grant.

[28] P Migasena & B G Maegraith, 'Pharmacological action of anti-malarial drugs: action of chloroquine and hydrocortisone on blood-brain barrier in *P. knowlesi* malaria', *TRSTMH*, 61, 1967, 6.

[29] R E Howells, W Peters, C A Homewood & D C Warhurst, 'Theory for the mechanism of chloroquine resistance in rodent malaria', *Nature*, 228, 1970, 625.

[30] H A Reid, 'Arvin – a new anticoagulant from viper', *Nursing Mirror*, 8 December 1968, 39–41; *idem*, 'Snake bite in the tropics', *BMJ*, ii, 1968, 359–362; *idem* & H M Gilles, 'Arvin treatment in sickle-cell crisis', *TRSTMH*, 63, 1969, 22–23.

[31] J Beinart, 'Darkly through a lens. Changing perceptions of the African child in sickness and health 1900–1945', R Cooter (ed), *In the name of the child: health and welfare, 1880–1940*, London: Routledge, 1992, pp. 220–243.

[32] Dr Mary Blacklock wife of D B Blacklock undertook commissions for the League of Nations Health Organisation.

[33] G MacDonald, 'Malaria in the children of Freetown, Sierra Leone', *ATMP*, 20, 1926, 239–262.

[34] D B Blacklock & R M Gordon, 'Malaria parasites in the placental blood', *ATMP*, 19, 1925, 37–45, *idem*, 'Malaria infection as it occurs in late pregnancy: its relationship to labour and early infancy', ibid., 327–363.

[35] R M Gordon, 'Emetine periodide in the treatment of *S. haematobium* infections among West African Children', *ATMP*, 20, 1926, 229–238; *idem* & E P Hicks, 'Fouadin and Auremetine in the treatment of *S. haematobium* infections among West African children; together with observations on the after-results of treatment with emetine periodide and emetine hydrochloride', ibid., 24, 1930, 443–447.

[36] See for instance L Rogers, *Pathological evidence bearing on disease incidence in Calcutta*, Glasgow: Alex MacDougall, 1925.

[37] H M Gilles, 'Effects of heavy and repeated malarial infections on Gambian infants and children. Effects on erythrocytic parasitisation', *BMJ*, ii, 1956, 686–692; *idem*, & I M McGregor, 'Studies on the significance of high serum gammaglobulin concentrations in Gambian Africans. I: Gamma-globlin concentrations of Gambian children in the first 2 years of life', *ATMP*, 53, 1959, 492–500; I M McGregor & H M Gilles, 'II: Gamma-globlin concentrations of Gambian children in the 4th, 5th and 6th years of life', ibid., 54, 1960, 275–280.

[38] H M Gilles, *Akufo – an environmental study of a Nigerian village community*, Ibadan: University Press, 1964.

[39] H M Gilles & R G Hendrickse, 'Possible aetiological role of *P. malariae* in 'Nephrotic syndrome' in Nigerian children', *Lancet*, i, 1960, 806–807.

[40] RGH, Maegraith to Hendrickse, 8 April 1969.

[41] RGH, Memorandum in support of recommendations that (a) a course in Child Health and Tropical Paediatrics be instituted, (b) a diploma in Child Health and Tropical Paediatrics be established, 10 October 1967.

[42] RGH, Leverhulme Trust Fund to Maegraith, 5 February 1969. The offer was reduced to five years if the post of senior lecturer was not filled by October 1969.

[43] RGH, Maegraith to Hendrickse, 18 June 1969.

[44] RGH, Hay to Hendrickse, 3 June 1969.

[45] RGH, Meeting, 29 April 1969, Proposed new wing.

[46] RGH, R G Hendrickse, The need for postgraduate training in tropical paediatrics, address to the Vice Presidents of the LSTM, 3 December 1969.

[47] RGH, Maegraith to Bates, 18 September 1969.

[48] The details of the DTCH are discussed in the following chapter as part of the changes in teaching in the School as a whole.

[49] 'The new DTCH course at Liverpool', *Lancet*, i, 1972, 1323.

[50] Letters, *Lancet*, ii, 1972, 40–41.

[51] Ibid., 226.

[52] Ibid., 41.

[53] R G Hendrickse, E F Glasgow, A Adeniyi, R H R White, G M Edington & V Houba, 'Quartan malarial nephrotic syndrome', *Lancet*, i, 1972, 1143–1148.

[54] A Adeniyi, R G Hendrickse & V Houba, 'Nephrotic syndrome (malarial) in Nigerian children – clinical and immunochemical correlative studies', *Proceedings of the second International Symposium of Paediatric Nephrology*, Paris, 1971.

[55] Hendrickse, personal communication.

[56] RGH, Minute of statement made to the Minister for Overseas Development on the subject of tropical child health, 20 December 1971.

[57] The ODA Advisory Committee: Dr J L Kilgour (Chair) Chief Medical Adviser ODA, Mr M G Bawden (Secretary), Science, Technology and Medical Department ODA, Dr P W Dill-Russell Chief Medical Adviser ODA (retired), J K G Webb, Professor Child Health Newcastle, D H Wolff, Nuffield Professor of Child Health, Institute of Child Health, London, Dr B A Whaton Secretary, Overseas committee British Paediatric Association, Dr J W Farquhar Reader in Child Life and Health and Maegraith.

[58] RGH, Record of a meeting at the LSTM to discuss proposals for a new Department of Tropical Child Health, 12 December 1973.

[59] RGH, Bawden, MOD to Maegraith, 2 August 1974. The capital grant was increased to £410,000.00 because of an increase in costs while the final agreement with the MOD was reached. The actual figure for recurrent expenditure was £65,400.00 per annum.

[60] RGH, Telephone conversation with Bawden, MOD, 17 October 1974.

[61] RGH, Memorandum, Department of Tropical Paediatrics and Child Health, 18 November 1974.

[62] RGH, Hendrickse to L Proctor, 9 December 1970.

[63] RGH, Hendrickse to Kilgour, 18 May 1978.

[64] RGH, I T Field, ODA to Hendrickse, 29 January 1982.

# 7

# TEACHING AND STUDENTS

## INTRODUCTION

The twin aims of teaching and research underscored the foundation of the LSTM. The preceding chapters have made only passing reference to the teaching activities of the School in Liverpool. Chapter 5 discussed the export of the School as a combined teaching and research model to Thailand and the example that Liverpool presented for British policies of overseas assistance through higher education in the 1950s and 1960s. This chapter reviews the early teaching in Liverpool, the special wartime courses and the additional technical teaching for nurses. After 1945, teaching had a greater impact on tropical medicine as practised from Liverpool.

Initially, teaching at the LSTM represented a tool to assist imperialist policies in the periphery. Later, medical education became a transfer of technology in the same way as medical practice itself. The emphasis on a monopoly of knowledge for European benefit changed to using education as a means of influencing the development of the Third World. The link with development was not politically neutral. In the 1970s, reaction in the medical press to new courses indicated a concern with the principles of creating further qualifications for, and filling gaps in the education of, overseas doctors. At the individual level, however, students greatly enjoyed their educational experience in Liverpool. Courses remained oversubscribed despite the increasing costs of studying in Britain.

The teaching function of the School provided a vital link with the University. The launch of the DTM as a University course brought the fledgling School into closer association with the new University. Later, teaching would facilitate financial negotiations between the School and University and add regular central government support to other sources of income. University responsibility for the salaries of recognised University Teachers assisted the School by increasing its establishment and providing an attractive career structure for home-based tropical experts. The University also provided an additional social environment for members of the School staff, who were eligible to join the clubs and sports facilities.

The creation of the basic DTM at both Schools of Tropical Medicine marked the foundation of the discipline, as discussed in chapter 1. Thereafter teaching at the School served a relatively utilitarian function until 1945. It did not change the direction of the School or the discipline until the School began to reassess its role after World War II. In re-evaluating the role of the School, the teaching function was scrutinised at several levels. First, changes in the working conditions of MOs in the colonies and the long-term future of the CMS necessitated consideration of the aims and content of the courses in Liverpool. Second, the expansion of higher education in the colonies and close links with the Faculty of Tropical Medicine in Bangkok reinforced the idea of the School in Liverpool as a working model for the developing world. Subject to public display, the School needed to consider if the teaching it offered served the needs of the colonies or the developing world. Third, the increasingly separate identity of the basic sciences within the discipline of tropical medicine promoted the separate provision of parasitology teaching in connection with other departments of the University. Fourth, the increasing re-conceptualisation of health within development programmes encouraged the LSTM to broaden its definition of tropical medicine and the scope of its activities. In the case of paediatric medicine, mounting a new course functioned to create a separate department within the School. With respect to International Community Health, new courses and teaching methods followed the reorganisation of the existing Department of Tropical Hygiene. However, this department presented a more radical challenge to teaching within the School through the promotion of multidisciplinary education and establishing courses for non-medics.

The School frequently acknowledged the contribution of its research students to scientific output. Although PhD students remained at Liverpool for only a finite period, they provided a cohort of researchers that the School would have been unable to fund in any other way. In the inter-war period some staff employed by the School for the Sierra Leone laboratory or for specific research such as chemotherapy completed PhD dissertations. However, these were not necessarily University of Liverpool degrees. After World War II, the number of available grants allowing foreign students to study overseas increased the number of PhD students (as opposed to members of staff who submitted a thesis). A special relationship developed with students from Thailand as discussed in chapter 5, but the School was happy to accept students from anywhere. In 1974, the Department of Tropical Community Health organised two 'International pot-luck suppers' celebrating the diversity of the students at the School. This has become an annual event.

Besides recognised University qualifications, the School introduced a range of short, non-University courses responding to perceived needs in health care and health care education. The role of teaching within the School changed from a utilitarian function to proactive out-reach policies. An emphasis on directly training people to work in the tropics shifted to teaching the teachers who would work overseas. The profile of the students changed as a function of the changing course objectives. The initial emphasis on training British practitioners for the CMS attracted a steady flow of male physicians from England, Scotland and Ireland. However, useful fee income resulted in a pragmatic admissions policy. The School was happy to welcome students from overseas, missionaries and others who desired an education in tropical medicine if they had appropriate qualifications. After World War II, the LSTM continued to provide education useful to CMS Officers, but looking to the future they also adapted the diploma course to meet the needs of locally educated doctors from the tropics. Besides these students, the other recognisable body consisted of the nurses taught at the Tropical Wards at the RSH and the LRI. In time, the nurses would move from this peripheral, segregated position to a central role in teaching and learning at the School itself.

The total number of students increased over time. For many students the length of time they registered with the School increased as the number of courses of twelve and eighteen-months duration developed. As the courses were all at the postgraduate level, students were often married with children. Students, admitted to the School for recognised University courses, were also registered students of the University. As such, they were able to make use of central library, sports, welfare and advisory services. However, an awareness of the additional needs of overseas students and the need to relieve pressure on the course secretaries prompted the School to employ an Accommodation and Welfare Officer in the mid-1980s. The transitory CMS officers sought a brief training in tropical medicine to qualify for overseas service. In time a disparate group of professionals mainly from developing countries who, through their own professional development, affected the delivery of health care in the Third World, replaced the European medical officers.

## THE DIPLOMA IN TROPICAL MEDICINE

Plans for the London School explicitly referred to the provision of additional training for men embarking on careers in the CMS. Manson had publicly advocated the 'necessity for special education in tropical medicine' during the 1890s.[1] Retrospectively aware of his own lack of knowledge when first posted overseas, he wanted to create a school where his accumulated knowledge and experience could be taught to men about to embark on their professional career in the tropics. The requirement from the CO that prospective medical officers must demonstrate their proficiency in tropical medicine by attending a course of instruction at the London School created a ready market when that School opened in October 1899.

As reviewed in chapter 1, the staff of the Royal Southern Hospital, and the Pathology Department of University College, Liverpool rose quickly to the suggestion that there was a pressing need for courses of instruction in tropical medicine. In May 1899, the first student, John W Hayward MD commenced what appeared to have been private studies in tropical medicine at Liverpool.[2] At a rate of one guinea per week, students could utilise the facilities of the Tropical Ward, laboratories, museum and library for private study. He was joined in June by the Reverend P Ollsen, a Missionary and in July, by P W O'Gorman, a Captain in the IMS. Ollsen stayed under a month and O'Gorman for two weeks, presumably refreshing his knowledge and learning new techniques. Students could also expect assistance from the teaching staff on an *ad hoc* basis.[3] In October 1898, six further students joined. Professor Ribbing of Lund University in Sweden took half the course. The Reverend K Smith remained until the end of the year with his four medical colleagues who took the full course.

Liverpool began its formal teaching with a course of instruction and examinations leading to Certificates of Proficiency in Tropical Medicine, and in Medical Parasitology, depending upon what syllabus students followed.[4] The course ran three times a year starting in January, April and October. This allowed the traditional academic break over the summer months. For three guineas, missionaries and planters were entitled to a special course of three lectures given by the lecturer in Tropical Medicine. These helped those 'who live in the tropics at a distance from medical men, and therefore wish to know something about tropical disease and hygiene for the advantage of themselves, their families and their dependants'.[5] The lectures provided simple information to assist in distinguishing between the tropical diseases of high incidence and advice on the treatment, including the treatment of indigenous people, including suggestions of what medicines to have to hand. The final lecture offered guidance on living in the tropics, including the care of children. In particular, the importance of observing a set of sanitary rules and ensuring that indigenous people observed a separate set of sanitary rules. For instance, the lectures advised that Europeans should live segregated from the local people, particularly native children. Observance of this rule was imperative at night when children represented a reservoir of disease, especially malaria. In this way the School propagated and reinforced contemporary scientific racism among the public.

The School offered a further special course for qualified nurses. Nurses received clinical instruction on the ward and attended the missionaries' and planters' lectures and an additional lecture on nursing in the tropics. Resident nurses were exempt from the course fee of two guineas. Those successfully completing the course and demonstrating their competence received a certificate. In 1904, the Colonial Nursing Association provided a grant of £30 per annum to train and maintain three nurses. The nurses received instruction while working for the Tropical Ward at the RSH. A further series of elementary lectures on tropical diseases and sanitation for employees of firms in Liverpool recognised the financial help the School received from commerce in the city. This teaching did not appear in the prospectus and the fee was nominal.[6]

This was an extensive range of courses for an institution still in its first years. However, this teaching was reactive rather than proactive. Initial appeals for funding reiterated Liverpool's unrivalled opportunities for teaching tropical medicine, but the suggestion to organise such courses had come from outside the city. Perhaps for this reason the Liverpool School failed initially to persuade the CO that they should recognise Liverpool's teaching and make attendance at either Liverpool or London mandatory rather than privileging the London School. The course leading to these School qualifications won belated recognition from the CO in 1900. In that year, the admissions more than doubled, however, of the twenty students at least nine took only a part of the course. Moreover, it is not clear whether any was a CMS officer. Of sixty-six students admitted between 1901 and the first diploma course, only seven were definitely attached to the CMS.

In 1904, the University received its charter and instituted a DTM, after the ten-week course. The School continued to offer the Certificate to those who had satisfactorily attended part of the course, as many did who were not embarking on careers in the CMS, but merely service or a career overseas. In 1909, the School realised that because of the success of the 'discovery era' it was obliged to squeeze an expanding syllabus into the period of the original course with diminishing success. An extra three weeks increased the course to thirteen weeks. A special summer school in Tropical Pathology and Medical Entomology replaced the normal third course, to allow for readjustment of the teaching calendar. Besides the increase in scientific facts, further pressure came from attempts to broaden the scope of the students' learning experience. During 1910, observation of the sanitary administration of the port and city was introduced, Professor Edward Hope, MOH, demonstrating the more important sanitary operations. This addition would prove useful to those students who held sanitary administrative appointments in tropical districts.[7] Over time, the length of the diploma course increased to accommodate further additions to the curriculum, as the available body of knowledge associated with the discipline increased. The content of the diploma course also reflected the close association with veterinary medicine in Liverpool. The Institute of Comparative Pathology, next door to the laboratories of the School in Runcorn, provided easy access to the tropical parasites of veterinary importance. The LSTM was involved with teaching in the new Veterinary School founded in 1904.[8]

In the analogous field of public health education, diploma level qualifications enjoyed widespread recognition.[9] In 1924, the CO decided to send out to the colonies only MOs who were also trained in public health. The LSHTM offered a new combined DTMH twice a year, each course lasting for five months. The LSTM retained the existing diploma course but added a further ten-week course leading to a DTH in 1926. This course took place immediately after the examinations for the DTM. Admission to the course was open only to those already holding the DTM. Thereafter the DTM ran twice a year in the autumn and lent terms, and the DTH followed in the lent and summer terms. As an independent course, the DTH was available to former students already in receipt of the DTM. This policy increased the economic viability of the new course. Besides new students, the DTH had a potential market among the four hundred and one students who had already qualified at Liverpool. However, hygiene remained segregated rather than integrated, and this retarded the development of preventative medicine within the broader scope of tropical medicine as practised from Liverpool.

Facilities for teaching improved after Blacklock's appointment to the chair of Tropical Hygiene. Blacklock translated his interest in rural life to teaching on the DTH. In 1936, he arranged to lease land from the Leeds and Liverpool Canal company near Melling and established an ideal 'native village'. The Practical Sanitation Station illustrated contemporary methods of sanitation and principles of healthy and economical native housing. This represented a greater commitment to teaching aspects of tropical hygiene. There were constant problems with vandalism at this site, and in 1939 the 'village' moved into the grounds of Fazakerly Isolation Hospital. The outbreak of war closed the site. After the war, changes in the teaching profile of the School and staff commitments rendered the project redundant.

In 1924, Danson, Chairman of the School, gave £500 to convert the laboratory attached to the Tropical Ward to additional private in-patient facilities. The laboratory was a dedicated teaching facility that accompanied the new ward at the LRI in 1914.[10] It became more convenient to concentrate teaching in the main laboratory at the School next door in Pembroke Place. Private beds provided a more cost-effective use of this space, after the gift of the capital required for conversion. It also represented the centralisation of the laboratories and teaching activities (ward rounds aside) in one building for the first time. Increased numbers of patients also offered new opportunities for nurse education. During World War II, with the involvement of the School with the hospitals of EMS and the establishment of the Tropical Diseases Centre, Adams initiated four courses of nurse training each year. Those who successfully completed the course, and the majority did, gained a Certificate.

In October 1935, the School formalised its teaching for non-medical personnel. This had been a feature of the very early years of the LSTM and related to its civic function in the city as well as the utilitarian need to raise funds from student fees. Initially, the new courses lasted for four days and ran three times a year. After review, it changed to a three-day course, three times a year and then to a two-day course, four times a year. These were not extensive courses, but they provided a useful service in educating the public in the basic principles of disease prevention in the tropics. The School also supported other less didactic methods of health education by the issue of leaflets and brochures from time to time, advertising the dangers of diseases in the tropics and simple tactics of avoidance.[11]

## SPECIAL COURSES

Besides the core courses reflecting the definition of tropical medicine at Liverpool, the School mounted a number of special courses. These were either on demand or in response to an emergency. They were often time-consuming, difficult to teach and unlikely to be cost effective if proper audits had been conducted. However, strategically mounting such courses created good publicity.

In 1909, in response to a letter from the CO, the LSTM mounted a special course of Instruction in Entomology.[12] This was not a particular honour. The CO also invited the London School, the British Museum and the Universities of Oxford and Cambridge to provide similar courses. The course equipped any interested CO staff in East and West Africa with a basic knowledge of the techniques of mounting, preparation and care of entomological specimens. For the price of a three-week course, at a guinea a week (the 'private study' fee) administrators, medics, and veterinarians could economically assist the Entomological Research Committee in its research.[13] A similar request from the Overseas Nursing Association in 1927 led to the provision of additional nurse training at the LRI with instruction from the staff of the School. The CO was prepared to pay the fees for nurses of the West African Nursing Staff to gain preliminary instruction before going overseas.[14] Alfred Holt and Company and the Liverpool Steam Ship Owners Association, from time to time, requested 'refresher courses' for their ships' surgeons. These men were usually qualified with the DTM from Liverpool or London, and found the normal classes incompatible with their work.[15] Besides special courses, the LSTM continued to receive requests from Britain and overseas for private study in the laboratories and observation of cases on the wards.[16] Many of these were from missionaries. However, in the 1950s, the School stopped providing courses of instruction for laymen.

World War II disrupted the normal teaching routine. The DTM and DTH courses began in September 1939 as normal, but lasted only five months including examination. This allowed commissioned MOs to obtain their qualifications in a single period of leave. Diploma teaching was then suspended. In the autumn of 1940, at the request of the CO, the London and Liverpool Schools agreed to teach their diploma courses in alternate years to make the best use of resources. In the first months of 1940, several RAMC officers approached the LSTM for instruction in tropical medicine and studied on an *ad hoc* basis. Yorke communicated with Lt General MacArthur at the WO, who suggested that the School could run intensive two-week courses for newly recruited RAMC officers who had a tropical posting and no experience of tropical medicine. The first course began in June 1940, and by the end of the year, one hundred and forty four army officers had learned the basics of parasitology, entomology and practical tropical hygiene at Liverpool. Edinburgh, the RAMC College at Milbank and the London School also offered similar courses. The teaching continued in 1941 with fifteen separate courses. The teaching for these courses alone amounted to thirty weeks in that year, imposing a heavy load on professional and non-professional staff. Naval MOs also attended on occasion.

In July 1941, the Director of Pathology at the WO approached the School and requested special courses in laboratory technique for army pathologists. Yorke arranged an additional week after the normal course for RAMC officers. The first course ran in August 1941, thereafter each alternate course (with a few exceptions) included an extra week for the pathologists until all those currently commissioned had been trained. The teaching and the cost of materials were initially borne by the LSTM. At the end of 1941, the School applied for a fee of a guinea per week for each officer on the course.[17] In return, the WO offered one guinea per man for the course. As courses lasted two or three weeks, this was barely half what the School asked for. Hobhouse commented tartly that the School ought to decline the offer 'if it is their estimate of the value of the School' but counselled acceptance.[18] Although no more courses ran for British officers after 1943, the American Army requested assistance in May 1945. The LSTM provided instruction for American MOs until August 1945.

*Table 3* Courses for RAMC officers, 1940–1943

| Year | Two-week courses | | Additional one-week course in laboratory technique | |
|------|------------------|------------------|-------------------|-------------------|
|      | No. of courses | No. of officers | No. of courses | No. of officers |
| 1940 | 5 | 144 | 0 | 0 |
| 1941 | 15 | 549 | 0 | 6 |
| 1942 | 15 | 657 | 9 | 41 |
| 1943 | 13 | 509 | 1 | 0 |
| Total | 48 | 1,859 | 10 | 47 |

After the war, higher education became one of a range of tools to hasten development and maintain peace. The reputation of the School for mounting dedicated short courses led the British Council to sponsor a 'refresher course' at Liverpool in the summer of 1948.[19] The aim was to recruit those already qualified and about to proceed overseas to the colonial territories of France, Belgium, Holland and Portugal. Doctors from Egypt, Iraq and Palestine would also be welcome. Seventeen attended the three-week course in July 1948, one each from Britain (the only woman), Denmark, Poland, Spain, Burma and West Africa, two from Mexico, three from France and five from Italy. The Europeans still outnumbered those from the tropics, but the mixture of nationalities indicated the future profile of students on this type of course.

The LSTM continued to receive requests from Britain and overseas for private study in the laboratories and observation of cases on the wards.[20] Many of these requests came from religious missions. However, in the 1950s the School stopped providing courses of instruction for laymen as it consolidated its image as a provider of higher qualifications for medical personnel in the developing world.[21] Participation in initiatives such as the WHO European Regional Office Training Course on Insect and Rodent Control confirmed this new status. The three-centre, two-country, course sponsored by the WHO, jointly organised with the Institute of Tropical Hygiene and Geographical Pathology in Amsterdam and the LSTM, included a visit to the Port of London and the Wellcome Museum.[22]

In addition to the development of the international links, the School was keen to promote an interest in technical education, using the resources of the School and good will of the staff. This initiative required a significant input from technicians. In 1966, the School offered a five-day course for members of the Public Health Laboratory Service, at the request of their Board.[23] Dr J A Boycott, who suggested the course to the Board, had spent a week at the LSTM as an RAMC officer during the war. The course provided instruction for young medical staff and qualified technicians. The need for accurate diagnosis of imported disease in travellers required extra training. The clinical staff – Adams, Bell, Seaton, Haddock, and Edeson and Wilson from Tropical Hygiene – provided summaries on the major diseases. The detailed work and selection of teaching material fell on Dagnall, the Chief Technician. In addition to parasites and helminths of the blood, intestines and body systems, the course covered genetic blood disorders, the eosinophilias, G6PD deficiency, and sickle cell. These were innovative additions as they were apparent in immigrants to Britain and required diagnosis. The content of courses such as this indicated the subtle changes in the scope of tropical medicine at Liverpool, although not advertised as such until the 1970s. The course became an annual event.

The training of technicians developed further when the Institute of Medical Laboratory Technicians recognised training in parasitology for their intermediate and final examinations from the mid 1960s to 1975. In the evenings, the scanning electron microscope at the School was used to prepare technicians for the vocational qualifications of the Royal Microscopical Society. In the late 1970s, this was the only course outside of London. Technical staff also taught at the Liverpool Polytechnic in the evenings, maintaining some connection with the city. These special courses were important to the School, building goodwill and providing useful publicity. As with the other kinds of special courses offered it is doubtful if many of the courses were cost effective. In response to many requests for assistance, the School waived the fees. In the 1980s, the School was forced to become more aware of the cost of materials and value of staff time.

## DIPLOMA IN TROPICAL MEDICINE AND HYGIENE

With the end of the war, the School began to re-establish some degree of order and return to its pre-war functions. The diploma courses recommenced in January 1946. This was the last session with the two diplomas. Davey, professor of Hygiene, reorganised the courses and in September 1946, the School offered a combined DTMH. The new course lasted for four months and ran twice a year beginning in September and January. The DTMH course integrated preventative and curative aspects of tropical medicine as taught in Liverpool. However, the hygiene component remained relatively unimaginative. Davey asked for comments from the first cohort of the DTMH students.[24] The School staff received universal praise, but some of the visiting lecturers did not fare so well. The students were aware of their complete lack of tropical experience. In general, the students were also pleased with the content of the course. More detailed comments revealed that the integration of the two previous courses was not entirely successful either operationally or intellectually.

The course was excessively detailed, related to conditions of good laboratory practice unobtainable in the tropics and unnecessarily scientific in its orientation. The increasing knowledge in the fields of parasitology and entomology had taken these subjects beyond their ready application for an average MO. Maegraith's detailed pathophysiological approach to tropical medicine was apparently inappropriate in the DTMH lecture theatre. In this way, the teaching did not relate to the realities of practising tropical medicine. The presentation of subjects was systematic, but lacked prioritisation of the most important problems. The School had lost its immediacy with the tropics, and now taught a practical course as an abstract academic subject. Post-war students apparently wanted a different kind of education from their pre-war counterparts. In the late 1940s, the CO stressed a new role for the MO:

> Research, preventative and social medicine, mass survey and treatment of community wide diseases, increased provision for medical treatment, intensified training of local staff for posts in all grades of the medical services and the fullest possible co-operation between neighbouring Colonies are the main lines on which further advances are going to be made.[25]

Although the School had readily admitted students from around the world, teaching had focused on the needs of preparing a CMS officer. In the post-war era, the School consciously catered for two groups of students. While serving the CO, the School also looked to the future, to tropical countries outside of the British Empire and gradually to the new countries of the Commonwealth, to fill the places on the diploma course. This created tensions in the type of course provided and assumptions about the educational background of such mixed groups.

The CMS had insisted on a specialist education since 1899, but it took until 1924 to provide dedicated training for the members of the other services. In 1943, this system came under review, following the issue of a Memorandum on Post-war Training for the Colonial Services. The Memorandum discussed the role for the colonial services in the social and economic development of the colonial territories. MOs faced the same general problems as the colonial administrative services.[26]

A further review of the role of the CO and Britain's relations with the colonial territories followed the end of World War II. The Labour Government, returned to power in the first post-war election, encouraged 'the progress of the peoples of the Colonies towards control of their own affairs'.[27] Rather than granting immediate freedom from British rule as many had expected they would, the Labour Party committed itself to policies that prepared the colonies for self-government.[28] This policy involved staffing the public services with local people. However, there was necessarily a delay while educational improvements could begin to produce adequately trained staff. The more specialised the education the greater the delay. Thus in the case of medicine it would be some time before sufficient numbers of local people could be trained as physicians and surgeons and be able to deal with the health needs of their countries:

> Every colony has its Department of Medical and Health services. In nearly all of them, there is still a serious shortage of medical staff both in the hospitals and in the field. The outflow of medical graduates from the colonial teaching hospitals cannot for many years to come be sufficient to make good this shortage and vacancies for Medical Officers from overseas exist in almost all Colonial Medical Departments, though mainly in West, East and Central Africa and Malaya.[29]

As the progress towards self-government proceeded, the British Government made contingency plans to ensure the continued availability of staff during the transfer of power and immediately afterwards by creating Her Majesty's Overseas Civil Service in 1954. This also protected the staff as far as pension rights were concerned. By 1960, the British Government guaranteed that where necessary they would pay for additional expenses, inducement pay and allowances, while the local governments would continue to be responsible for local rates of salary and other conditions of service.[30] This financial assistance would mean that newly independent governments would be able to retain the skills of ex-patriot staff formerly in the employ of the colonial services in order to preserve professional standards in the early years of self-government. This was considered essential in technical services such as medicine, which relied on hospital based care and laboratory medicine. Even in the absence of a formal CMS, the need for additional training in tropical medicine continued to support the DTMH.

The School continued to train CMS staff, but after World War II, the role of the LSTM changed. Its role as a support mechanism to the practice of colonialism was no longer desirable. Comments on the new diploma indicated that teaching at the School would need to be more responsive to the changing political climate than before. As the School listened to its gentle critics and observed the special role it might enjoy among the international organisations, its teaching role changed more quickly and perceptibly than its research interests.

Most significant in a sense, however, was a shift in the student cohort. From its inception, the School admitted foreign nationals. If they had the requisite qualifications necessary for registration on the Colonial Medical Register, they were eligible to enter for the University diploma examinations. However, there was a perceptible link between the course, the CMS and the CO. In the years after the war this link dissolved. The bulk of the students were now no longer white CMOs being trained to work overseas as part of the colonial regime. The new emphasis was to teach doctors of indigenous origin to the same level to replace the white medical officers of national medical services, and later to 'teach the teachers'. Thus, as the home candidates for the DTMH declined, they were replaced by foreign students in increasing numbers. Alarmed at the small number of candidates after the war, the School did not wait for this situation to improve but actively promoted itself overseas. With the unpopularity of colonialism and the belief in education as a means of advancement, the School received applications from an increasing number of overseas students. Funding for these students came from a variety of sources: scholarship schemes in their home countries, the British Council, the Commonwealth, and the WHO.

Besides these changes in the main teaching function of the School, the DTMH, the LSTM began to re-style itself as a centre for higher education in tropical medicine. In this sense, the School began to represent a resource useful within Britain rather than merely for those serving overseas. Yorke and Maegraith had drawn attention to the research resource that the School represented. In the 1960s, through the provision of higher degrees of the University of Liverpool, the School began to represent an educational resource in Britain.

## TAUGHT MASTERS DEGREES

The recognition that the DTMH represented a practical introduction to the tropical medicine for doctors intending to practise in the developing world, and not a scientific training, was realised in the creation of distinct postgraduate qualifications in the sub-disciplines. In 1963, in collaboration with the

197

University Departments of Botany and Zoology, the Department of Parasitology and Entomology introduced a taught masters degree in Parasitology. In 1970, this became the MSc in Applied Parasitology and in 1978 the MSc in Applied Parasitology and Medical Entomology. The first course looked broadly at the subject and contained aspects on parasites of man, animals, birds, freshwater fish, marine fish and plants. This reflected Kershaw's commitment to parasitology as an independent discipline, not merely a basic science serving tropical medicine. The aim was to provide a basic grounding in research techniques in this field. This was a significant University and School teaching programme. It indicated the increasing similarity of this department with comparable university departments devoted to the zoological and/or biological sciences. Students on the course were eligible for support from the Science Research Council, Advanced Course Studentship scheme.

While the course showed the academic standing of the LSTM, it also threatened to fragment the discipline into its composite parts. Revision of the course for the 1971/72 session brought new objectives and aims. The reshaped MSc operated from the School and not in conjunction with other University departments and aimed to produce:

> a graduate with a good grounding in the principles of parasitology, familiar with the most important parasites of man and animals; capable of applying a broad range of parasitological techniques to the solution of parasitological problems.[31]

Assessment comprised a practical research project defended by oral examination. The MSc in Applied Parasitology continued to provide a useful source of trained personnel for the LSTM either as research assistants or as PhD students. The intensive teaching and lack of bench space restricted the number of students accepted.

In the following session, the School offered a variation on this course to students with veterinary qualifications. In addition to the compulsory teaching for third-year veterinary undergraduates, the MVSc in Applied Parasitology, which started in 1973, continued to reinforce the links with the Veterinary Faculty of the University. The MSc in Applied Parasitology also offered entomology training as it related to control of parasites and later options in entomology resulted in a change of title to Applied Parasitology and Medical Entolomology from 1978. In the 1970s and 1980s, the School offered an increasingly diverse range of courses. Some of these initiatives were joint projects with the University while others were independent School activities. In the recent history the teaching served to direct the School.

## DIPLOMA IN TROPICAL CHILD HEALTH

Links with a University department and involvement with undergraduate teaching were characteristics shared with the first of these new teaching initiatives, the DTCH. The previous chapter discusses the creation of the senior lectureship and Department of Tropical Paediatrics and Child Health. This section focuses on the content of the course and the student profile. Previous concern that the teaching of separate parts of the discipline would lead to its fragmentation was not a consideration as the LSTM embarked upon its ambitious project to teach tropical paediatrics. Parasitology represented a biological science investigated independently from a connection with tropical medicine. On the other hand, tropical paediatrics at Liverpool reinforced the need for the School in Liverpool and for isolating medicine in the tropics as a distinct subject for study.

The DTCH course was an eighteen-month course in two parts. During the first twelve months, students undertook clinical attachments at Alder Hey Children's Hospital, Mill Road Maternity Hospital and Fazakerly Isolation Hospital. This period as a Senior House Officer equipped younger students with practical experience which was related to health problems in their country of origin by tutorials and seminars with departmental staff. A variety of clinics supported the diploma students including neonatal, ear, nose and throat, orthopaedics, ophthalmology and casualty. Students expressed some dissatisfaction with these clinics, apparently far removed from their experience of paediatric medicine in their own country. They preferred the general medical units. Hendrickse himself commented on the difficulty of integrating various elements of the course,

> The tropical medicine instruction is given by teachers, all of whom have had extensive experience of medicine in the tropics, but most of whom have had very limited experience of paediatric practice. Conversely, many, but by no means all, of those who offer instruction in Paediatrics and Child Health have had no experience in practice in tropical countries. A serious problem exists therefore in trying to achieve a reasonable synthesis of the 'tropical' and 'paediatric' aspects of the teaching programme.[32]

Aware of this problem from an early date, the School attempted successfully to bridge the gap. This awareness reinforced the epistemological break between tropical medicine as previously practised and the opportunity to widen the discipline towards the practice of medicine in the tropics. The laboratory at

Alder Hey provided instruction in bench techniques. Among other innovations, the Department of Tropical Paediatrics developed a manual to guide students in learning the necessary laboratory techniques. This helped to overcome one of the difficulties of the course, levelling the experience and abilities of the students.

In the final six months, students returned to the School for a period of intensive classroom teaching. Additional students who were already experienced clinicians joined the existing students at the School. The DTMH served as the basis for the first half of this period concerned with theoretical and laboratory studies. In time reliance on this course became more selective as additional staff with specialist skills joined the department. The second three months concentrated on tropical paediatrics with further clinical work and additional dedicated tutorial and seminar teaching.

The first examination consisted of three elements: a written paper on paediatrics and child health in the tropics; a clinical examination and viva voce in general paediatrics and neonatal paediatrics; and a viva voce on paediatrics and child health in the tropics. In the light of the external examiners' comments, continual assessment of the clinical work offered guidance in cases where the written performance of a student was weak. Students were also required to submit a dissertation.

If there was some dispute about the need for a formal diploma, in terms of student demand, the DTCH was a success. Hendrickse had travelled extensively in the year following his appointment at Liverpool, presenting the objectives of the new diploma course to audiences interested in paediatrics in the tropics. This was a conscious effort to generate endorsement of this unique initiative in postgraduate education in paediatrics. The diploma course received more suitable applications than there were available places. For the first course in September 1970, there were seventy enquiries and fourteen formal applications for the six places. Two additional students, who attended for the final six months teaching at the LSTM, joined these six students.

Figure 3 shows the country of origin of the DTCH students in the first ten years of the diploma. Besides other considerations, the department tried to achieve a balance among the students. When the ODA assessed their support for the new wing, they offered to fund a common-room providing students with the opportunity to learn from one another. In addition to improved facilities the new wing also increased the number of students admitted to the course. After the ODA continued their support for the course, the intake increased.

Of the one hundred and ten students who had completed the DTCH by 1981, the destinations of ninety-four were known.[33] Of the total student intake, only twenty-two were formally working in paediatrics before taking the course. Of the ninety-four students for which data exist, at least, fifty-five were now in

*Figure 3* DTCH Students, 1972–1982

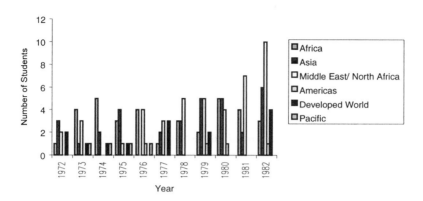

some form of paediatric practice. Others may have been in a situation where the luxury of practising as a paediatrician was unrealistic. Fourteen former students were involved in teaching paediatrics. Among those who were necessarily practising paediatric medicine, two were involved with PHC and the assessment of health needs in a community.

A handful of students had been particularly successful in developing paediatric medicine upon their return home. Dr H S Badrek led the organisation of a new hospital for mothers and babies in Jeddah, Saudi Arabia. Dr A A Nasher from Yemen inaugurated a new children's hospital in Mansoora, joined the WHO Regional Advisory Board on Health Service and Health Manpower Development and conducted research on oral rehydration, anaemias and malnutrition. Dr A Kurisaquila established paediatrics as an independent speciality in Fiji and encouraged social and preventative aspects of paediatric practice in the medical school curriculum. These examples illustrate the impact the School hoped the DTCH would have on paediatric medicine in the tropics. How much of this initiative stemmed from the acquisition of the Liverpool diploma and the period of study overseas is not quantifiable from the available data. The School was happy to make the correlation as justification for the teaching it offered and to win support from funding agencies.

## TEACHING HEALTH CARE TEAMS

The DTCH had strengthened the commitment of the School to concentrating their energy in the tropics. This course offered specialist training in contrast to the DTMH which the School had repackaged as a general introduction to tropical medicine. The DTCH recruited postgraduate doctors who would otherwise enter paediatric medicine in the tropics without appropriate dedicated training. It functioned to expand the discipline by focusing on tropical medicine among a particular, previously neglected, demographic group. The students and their future patients represented a new target group for the tropical medicine practised from Liverpool. The next innovation at the School was to open out the discipline turning away from the specialist to embrace the community health worker. The emphasis was not to teach tropical medicine, but rather to prepare others to teach PHC to community practitioners in whatever guise they appeared.[34]

Chapter 8 discusses the transformation of the Department of Tropical Hygiene via Tropical Community Health to the Department of International Community Health, the tensions this created within the School and the challenge to tropical medicine as a discipline. This chapter reviews the teaching initiatives generated by the new department in the context of other courses. In 1973, the LSTM introduced a new School course: the Certificate in Tropical Community Medicine and Health. This was not a University qualification. In the earliest years, the School had offered the option of taking part of the diploma course to those who were not qualified as doctors but planned to work in the tropics, often in inaccessible areas. They tended to be missionaries or other members of a religious order. Such people perceived themselves as providing the only medical care in an alien landscape. Anything they could learn would therefore be of benefit. The new CTCMH offered similar opportunities to a new professional group of non-medically qualified personnel interested in the delivery of formal health care overseas. This course offered an introduction to tropical medicine and its practice at the community level. Its students included nurses, sanitary engineers and those likely to lead a health care team overseas. The Certificate in Tropical Nursing courses ended in March 1973. Later the School offered additional training for nurses who were unable to spend enough time at the School for the Certificate course.

The Certificate course was the first significant attempt at multidisciplinary teaching. This was not a popular objective in the hierarchical medical profession of the developed world. Evidence from the analysis of health care delivery in the developing world indicated it was a necessity. Ten extra bench spaces on the DTMH course reserved places for the Certificate students without compromising the usual intake of those with medical qualifications. This quietened the opposition. Instead of clinical lectures, these students followed an elective in community medicine preparing them for work in the periphery of developing countries. This teaching emphasised the social and economic factors determining the status of individual and community levels of health. It challenged students to prioritise health planning within financial and manpower limits by teaching rationales for decision making. This relied upon appreciating the importance of an ecological approach and applying the basic principles of epidemiology as they affected the community. The inclusion of special lectures by colleagues in the University, such as Dr Mansell Prothero from the Department of Geography, heralded a less myopic vision of tropical medicine. Prothero lectured on 'social epidemiology', in particular the relationship between the spread of malaria by the movement of people in Africa. The new awareness by the School of the importance of teaching such subjects characterised the new and redefined departments created at Liverpool in the 1970s. The innovation was commendable, but could have come sooner. Prothero published his benchmark book *Migrants and Malaria* in 1965.[35] He had been writing on the subject since 1961.[36]

By the mid-1970s, students on the Certificate course learned aspects of parasitology, entomology and tropical medicine in tailored courses. They shared other parts of the course such as the outside visits with the diploma students. The interaction of physician and non-physician continued, but the certificate students prepared for future roles with a greater emphasis upon operational activities than their physician colleagues.

In 1975, the Department of Tropical Community Health in collaboration with the University Faculty of Medicine and the Board of Community Health launched a new degree, the Masters in Community Health (Developing countries). This was a development of the Diploma in Public Health, taught around the world, and the Certificate Course in Tropical Medicine and Hygiene. N Rex E Fendall of the Department of Tropical Community Health considered the DPH inappropriate to the health care needs of disadvantaged people in poor countries. The Certificate course did not have the academic standing of a higher degree. The new course targeted those qualified in medicine and other allied health professions. It offered the same ethos as the Certificate course to a higher professional group. Fendall hoped to recruit personnel from overseas with some experience in health care administration, disease control, operational research and teaching in the field of community health.

The twelve-month course included a guided three-month placement in a 'disadvantaged country'.[37] In this period, the students undertook independent operational research on aspects of the health care delivery system in addition to support tutorials. This was an ambitious undertaking. It avoided the criticism that students learned medicine in the tropics from the comfort of Liverpool. The course used the seconded Technical Assistance Lecturers and other staff overseas to locate the student places. The School of Public Health, Teheran, Iran also agreed to host students. Later links were established with the Reza Pahlavi University, Shiraz; the Hindu University of Banaras; Tribhuwan University,

Nepal; Hacettepe University, Ankara; the University of the West Indies, Jamaica, and Ife-Ife University, Nigeria. Links with host institutions for the MCommH students provided other useful contacts for the LSTM. An association with countries of the Middle East and Turkey served to broaden the range of influence of the School.

The first MCommH course began in January 1975 despite continued resistance to multidisciplinary teaching.[38] In the first term, students followed the DTMH course except for lectures in tropical medicine and clinical sessions. Instead, students took courses in epidemiology, statistics, sociology, psychology, organisation and management of the health services. The second term was devoted to fieldwork. The students conducted an operational research project and presented a thesis upon their return to Liverpool. During the period of study overseas staff from the department travelled with the students providing supervisory support. The remainder of the course offered further training in health and social services though elective choices. This allowed students to concentrate their education in areas related to future employment. In 1975, the intake was restricted to ten students. The number increased to sixteen the following year.

Although a worthy innovation and one necessary with the remainder of the course spent in Britain, the study visits required a great deal of time to arrange. They relied upon goodwill overseas and efficient organisation in Liverpool. The visa arrangements were particularly onerous and not always successful. External pressures, such as industrial action among airline staff and rapid increases in travel costs, created an additional burden for teaching and secretarial staff. Because of these operational difficulties, some students spent part of their fieldwork attached to local community-health projects. This proved surprisingly successful, reinforcing the commitment of the department to the health of disadvantaged communities regardless of their geographical location. Later the fieldwork was adapted, enabling students to work in teams conducting a systems analysis of an institute or current programme. By its redefined methodology, the fieldwork further reinforced the concept of teamwork the degree aimed to convey.

Students were funded by the WHO, the British Council, Commonwealth Foundation and Rockefeller Foundation; some were directly sponsored by their governments and others paid their own fees and living expenses. Despite some student criticism of the teaching, the funding organisations endorsed the initiative of LSTM in offering this kind of training. The large number of applicants (fifty for fifteen places on average) testified to the perceived desirability among practitioners and social scientists from overseas of taking the course and/or gaining the qualification from Liverpool.

As the departments diversified the curriculum for the DTMH became increasingly complex if not overloaded. By the mid 1970s Tropical Community Health organised the teaching of their component of the course around four central themes: environmental health and hygiene; population control and community action; organisation and management; epidemiology and international community control of disease. These themes prepared the heath professional to work largely unaided, with little technical support, in a rural setting. A central skill gained from the course would be the ability to organise community health services, PHC and environmental protection programmes. This pressure on the DTMH curriculum promoted other departments in the School to consider their input and whether all their teaching objectives were delivered efficiently by this one course. For instance, the higher degrees in parasitology and entomology aimed to produce researchers for fundamental laboratory based research. The dichotomy between research training degrees in fundamental science and applied qualifications with reference to either practice or operational research characterises the recent climate of the LSTM.

A new School course in Teaching Primary Health Care ran from April to July 1979. This was the first international course of its kind. It aimed to improve teaching skills for those already involved in training basic health workers. There were clear objectives: curriculum development, assessment/selection of students and the role of the teacher in policy formation. The fees for this four-month course were £2,000, but this did not deter the fourteen successful applicants. The School could not afford to subsidise its students and the fee had to be set at an 'economic level'. In 1987, because of the comments from the past students on the Teaching Primary Health Care course, the Department of International Community Health introduced a Management for Primary Health Care course. This targeted doctors appointed to management positions with no previous experience of management strategies. This situation apparently squandered the benefits from improved teaching of PHC. The teaching of the School represented a series of strategies for improving health care delivery at successive levels.

In conjunction with the Government of India and the British Council, the School organised a series of Maternal and Child Health courses. They also responded to the increasing use of personal computers in administration and research and ran two courses, Information Systems for PHC and Computing Skills for Health Workers, reflecting this trend. A room equipped with individual PCs in the refurbished Pilkington Wing was designated as the 'Microcomputer Laboratory'.

In September 1983, the School launched a Masters in Tropical Medicine course. This twelve-month course targeted physicians and emphasised training in research methodologies and the epidemiology of tropical diseases. Like the

MCommH, where possible students would spend three months overseas on a clinical/epidemiological assignment. It reconfirmed the commitment of the School to its historical role in providing education in tropical medicine at Liverpool. The MTropMed was linked with the MSc in Applied Parasitology and Medical Entomology and the MVSc as a modular joint masters programme. The modules on the course reflected current developments in the science of tropical medicine and the availability of staff. This allowed the course to continue with variable components in an uncertain institutional environment.

In the same year the MTropMed began, students in Freetown, Sierra Leone successfully completed the first course leading to a Certificate in Tropical Community Health and Medicine. The export of a packaged course provided a new output from the School. It formalised the educational transfer implicit in much of the teaching at the School after World War II.

Apart from some of the very recent innovations of the 1980s in science and health systems education, the DTMH represented the core of the teaching at Liverpool. Revision of this course was therefore an important exercise. In instances where departments had different views on the balance of the course, control of the reorganisation of the DTMH was crucial. The new courses preparing the health care team were innovative. However, they relied on the basic framework of the DTMH. This provided a hidden continuity in the teaching activities of the LSTM. The new courses were innovations as far as they responded to new definitions of health. The centrality of the DTMH ensured that the oldest course offered by the LSTM remained relevant to the perceived needs of the developing world. The acknowledgement of the changing curriculum of the DTMH tacitly acknowledged the changing definition of tropical medicine.

## STUDENTS

The student body of the LSTM represents a cohort of varied health care personnel who have practised, taught and conducted tropical medicine in the twentieth century. With the exception of former students who joined the staff or were involved with joint projects, there are no records of the destinations of this group of people. It is difficult to analyse over time the effects of studying at Liverpool in the absence of such data. The student register sometimes recorded the CMS officers' first overseas station after completion of the diploma course. The short duration of the diploma course and an atmosphere of intensive training rather than personal development may account for the lack of contact between the alumni and the institution. Only in the 1960s, in part to raise funds, did the LSTM form any kind of School association which provided information for people interested in the School and its former students. The Voluntary Funds Office began an annual newsletter in 1964, *Mid-Summer Notes*, which provided a point of contact.

However, in the case of overseas students the experience of studying in a foreign country had a more profound effect. This was not manifest by formal links with the School, but with the reverence in which students regarded members of staff. In the 1950s when individuals began to spend more time overseas on individual tours and consultancies, they often encountered past students of the School. Maegraith referred to the generous reception he enjoyed in China from a former student of the School's from 1909, Dr Fu-Chun Yen, Dean of the College of Medicine, Nanking. In 1949, Dr Neil Leitch wrote from Nigeria, 'I am looking forward very much to entertaining Professor Maegraith here towards the end of August, and hope that it will be my good fortune to entertain many other members of the staff, should they stray this way'.[39] In occasional correspondence about other matters, students expressed their satisfaction with the course and the experience of working overseas: 'the period spent in Liverpool has been the best one in my life'.[40] In addition to the academic staff, the overseas students remained in contact with the support staff of the School, course secretaries and technicians such as David Dagnall and Jeffrey Friend, and offered to send specimens to the School.[41]

Figure 4 shows the number of successful British and overseas DTMH students for the period 1930 to 1969.[42] In 1937, the number of overseas students exceeded the British as recruitment for the CMS declined. From 1951, there was some fluctuation in the total number of students but overseas students outnumbered British. From 1960, the size of the difference increased dramatically as the effects of decolonisation became evident. The popularity of the DTMH with overseas students continued to increase. In 1969, eighty-two per cent of the students were overseas, as opposed to fifty-six per cent in 1951 and sixty-eight per cent in 1961. The number of countries sending students to the School also increased. In 1951, overseas students came from five countries, in 1961 fifteen countries and in 1969 twenty-one countries. This reflected greater assistance with educational scholarships from funding agencies and the increased emphasis on training by developing countries. Increasing student applications for all School courses demanded better selection procedures for the limited number of places available. Staff in Tropical Community Health monitored students admitted for the Certificate course, and masters degree in their department and to the diploma course to achieve a balanced intake.

Overseas students often took the DTMH as part a longer period of study in Britain or in conjunction with study elsewhere in the developed world. Students registered for higher research degrees enjoyed an extended period of stay in Liverpool. In addition to their formal qualifications and academic work, these

*Figure 4* DTMH Students, 1930–1969

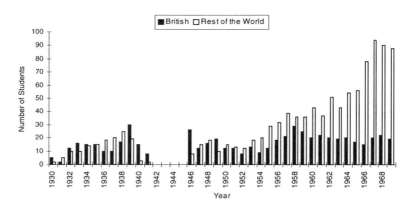

students also learned about life in an educational institution in Britain. Professor Santasiri Sornmani of the Faculty of Tropical Medicine in Bangkok explained with great pleasure his acculturation in Liverpool,

> I remember one thing, it impressed me so much, most of the Thai people keep to themselves...we had three [Thai students] in the School and so I said why not go and join the English people downstairs, the students...they have tea together at 11.00 am, so I said all right, I went down and asked may I join them for tea, ok they pay six pence or one shilling until it runs out and then we pay more, so they accepted the group so we tried to communicate with them and so I learned that the way to communicate with these people, you read the newspaper and what is the newspaper you also discuss in the morning, so I went back home and studied the Liverpool Echo and...we become very good friends, these three helping each other and then during Christmas time, we all went out across the road from the School there is a pub there and we had one round of beer, we enjoyed it so much we learned how to live in the English style in an English institution.[43]

Many of the Thais also referred to the value of studying abroad for the independence it engendered,

> the training in Liverpool was quite interesting because I had to develop the technique of the angiogram to do the caliometry to measure the blood flow in the liver and we had to prepare the instrument ourselves, so I used to go into the workshop downstairs to prepare all the things, fortunately I think that Dr Martin Skirrow who was before me was

good in this thing and he trained me to use the lathe and many things in the workshop downstairs and training there it gave me the confidence to tackle the problems, any problem we would just sit down to tackle the problem and that is very good, I mean when we come back, when we want to initiate anything we are not afraid, so we just tackle the problem and then do it step by step.[44]

The personal, social and professional skills learned by overseas students went some way towards preparing them for influential positions within the health services and medical education establishments in their own countries. Additional experience in understanding how organisations functioned and how scientific knowledge is generated were useful tools in an increasingly competitive environment of international funding of research and health and welfare projects. The preparation of research papers, which allowed overseas scientists and clinicians access to modern publishing outlets, was equally important. The planning, executing and writing of a research project were further transferable skills that could benefit a new generation of practitioners in the tropics, enabling them to apply independently for funds. It was of course an emulation of the style of first world medical research. The practice of high level science in developing countries, in the face of pressing immediate health needs, replicating tensions over teaching priorities at the LSTM.


## CONCLUSION

The DTMH continues as the most popular course at the School in terms of the numbers of students admitted each year. It represents continuity from the first DTM course in 1904 to the present multiplicity of teaching provided by the School for the developing world. Until 1945, teaching at the School, although obviously of a high standard, served a perfunctory role. The School pushed hard to gain recognition from the CO for its course of instruction. This was due to a mixture of pride and financial pragmatism, as the CO paid the fees of CMS officers. Not to gain recognition from the CO at this time would have created a hierarchy with the London School demonstrably at the top. Whatever other overlap may exist between the two Schools, there are only a few occasions, with extenuating circumstances, when there have been insufficient students for both Schools to mount a viable course.

After 1945, a more perceptible interest in the function of teaching at the School developed. Integration of the DTM and DTH offered a more useful course. Uncertainty over the future of the colonial services and the increased employment opportunities at home with the creation of the NHS were disincentives for doctors to consider overseas employment. While continuing to provide teaching for the declining number of CMS officers, the School marketed its teaching to the growing number of overseas doctors eligible for postgraduate study in the developed world. The DTMH thus served a dual function at this time.

The School exploited this new-found sensitivity and used teaching as means of responding more quickly to the problems of health care in the developing world. The division between research and application usually referred to laboratory research and public health measures. The development of teaching in the School represents a further application of tropical medicine as practised from Liverpool.

Higher degree courses in parasitology and later entomology represented the formalisation of research education at the LSTM. PhD students had worked at the School in increasing numbers since 1945. However, the School regarded these people as junior research staff rather than students. The taught higher degrees relieved the pressure on an increasingly congested DTMH curriculum. At the same time, this curriculum was under pressure from the desire to expand its focus on infant and child health and community health. The admission of non-medics to the diploma course acknowledged that the discipline of tropical medicine had moved beyond the medical profession and must include sanitary engineers, health inspectors and nurses for efficient use of limited health budgets. The developments in Thailand and the input of School staff into teaching programmes in various countries meant that the LSTM presented itself to the developing world as a model institution. In this role, the School was obliged to take a proactive stance with its range of courses and monitor their content.

The students provided much of the life of the School. Because the School remained committed to the tropics, the LSTM has welcomed students from the majority of the developing world. Before the end of empire, it was a popular destination for overseas doctors whose diverse qualifications were painstakingly scrutinised to allow eligible students to sit the diploma examinations. A comprehensive assessment of the effect of an LSTM education among the alumni is not possible. The experience of those who corresponded with the School, the DTCH students who remained in contact with the department, and Thai students who have a special affinity with Liverpool indicate the School was a special place. It welcomed those from overseas and provided them with a range of skills, many of which were unintended. The external support for students indicates the acceptance of the courses by sponsors of the education and development of the people of the developing world.

The new courses of the 1970s and 1980s provide evidence that teaching now functioned in a responsive manner. Tropical Paediatrics and International

Community Health used new courses to strengthen their departmental base within the School and attract external funding for their unique contributions to health care in the developing world. To an extent, they repeated at the departmental level what the School as an institution achieved with the first Certificate Course in Tropical Medicine. However, the effect of these new courses was to fragment tropical medicine as practised from Liverpool, compartmentalising the discipline into separate packages. The need to launch the Masters in Tropical Medicine representing the work of the Department of Tropical Medicine reinforces this point. The Joint Masters system provided a sensible economy of scale. However, the DTMH remained as a common link between departments. The final chapter reviews the issue of departmental identity.

NOTES

[1] P Manson, 'On the necessity for special education in tropical medicine', *Lancet*, ii, 1897, 842–845.

[2] TM/8/SX.1.1, LSTM register of students 1899–1923.

[3] TM/9/1.1, The Liverpool School of Tropical Diseases and Medical Parasitology, *Prospectus*, 1899.

[4] TM/9/1.1, *Prospectus*, 1899, p. 22.

[5] Ibid., p. 12.

[6] *4th Annual Report of the LSTM, 1902*, p. 7.

[7] *12th Annual Report of the LSTM, 1910*, p. 7.

[8] C E Savage, 'The beginnings of veterinary education at the University of Liverpool', Dissertation for Diploma Local History, University of Liverpool, 1992.

[9] R Acheson, 'The British Diploma in Public Health: birth and adolescence', E Fee & R M Acheson (eds), *A history of education in public health: health that mocks the doctors' rules*, Oxford: OUP, 1991, pp. 44–82.

[10] TM/11/0108/1, Opening of the Sir Alfred Jones Tropical Ward of the School, 23 July 1914.

[11] R Ross, *Malarial fever: its cause, prevention and treatment, containing full details for the use of travellers, sportsmen, soldiers and residents in malarious places, Memoir I*, 1903; 'Warning. Danger of mosquitoes. Notice to all who live in the tropics', LSTM, 1910.

[12] TM/8/CX.15.1, Entomology, Hopwood (CO) to Milne, 5 August 1909.

[13] TM/8/CX.15.1, Entomology, Hopwood to Milne, 8 February 1910.

[14] TM/8/CX.16, Nursing service, West African, 20 August 1927.

[15] TM/8/CX.18, Alfred Holt & Co, ship's Officers 1938–1939.

[16] TM/8/CX.20, Courses of instruction, Specials.

[17] TM/8/CX.14, Courses of instruction, Service, Hobhouse to WO, 7 January 1942.

[18] Ibid., Hobhouse to Yorke, 24 March 1942.

[19] TM/8/CX.21, British Council, Foreign Medical Officers 1948, 9 October 1947.

[20] TM/8/CX.20, Courses of instruction, Specials.

[21] TM/8/CX.22, Courses, 30 October 1951.

[22] TM/8/CX.23, WHO Course on Insect and Rodent Control 1959.

[23] TM/8/CX.24.1, PHLS Courses, 22 February 1966.

[24] TM/8/CX.6, Criticism by students.

[25] Colonial Office, *Appointments in His Majesty's Colonial Service*, London: HMSO, 1950, p. 54.

[26] Colonial Office, *Post-war training for the colonial service. Report of a committee appointed by the Secretary of State for the Colonies*, London: HMSO, 1946.

[27] Colonial Office, *Appointments*, p. 5.

[28] S A H Haqqi, *The colonial policy of the Labour Government (1945–51)*, Aligarh: Muslim University Press, 1960.

[29] Colonial Office, *Appointments*, p. 55.

[30] Colonial Office, *Service with overseas governments*, London: HMSO, 1960.

[31] *72nd Annual Report of the LSTM, 1970–1971*, p. 66.

[32] RGH, Hendrickse, 'The DTCH, University of Liverpool, progress report covering the period September 1970 to September 1972'.

[33] RGH, Information provided to the ODA in response to request, 8 September 1981.

[34] K Newell (ed), *Health by the people*, Geneva: WHO, 1975.

[35] M Prothero, *Migrants and Malaria*, London: Longmans Green, 1965.

[36] M Prothero, 'Population movements and problems of malaria eradication in Africa', *Bulletin of WHO*, 24, 1961, 405–425.

[37] *75th Annual Report, 1973–1974*, p. 21.

[38] TM/3/1.17b, Council minutes, 19 May 1975.

[39] TM/8/SX.2 L, Dr Neil Leitch to Miss E Yorke, 5 July 1949.

[40] TM/8/SX.2 L, Dr Adelio Lanzo to LSTM, 29 December 1956.

[41] TM/8/SX.2 L, G D Lehmann to Yorke, January 1934.

[42] Reliable data are not available for the period before 1930, after 1969 the greater diversity of courses makes the DTMH less representative of students at the LSTM.

[43] Interview with Professor Santasiri Sornmani, 13 January 1995, recorded by H J Power.

[44] Interview with Professor Tan Chongsuphajaisddhi, 9 January 1995, recorded by H J Power.

# 8

# INTERNATIONAL HEALTH AND FUNDAMENTAL SCIENCE: OUT-REACH POLICIES AND LABORATORY RESEARCH

## INTRODUCTION

The second new wing of the LSTM opened on 5 May 1978. The Maegraith Wing housed the Departments of Tropical Paediatrics and International Community Health. These departments represented the new vanguard of the School. In particular, International Community Health stretched the scope of tropical medicine, as practised from Liverpool, and ultimately challenged the legitimacy of the title 'tropical medicine' for the School and the discipline. The developments in the School since 1966 broadened the definition of tropical medicine and acknowledged that the practice of medicine in the tropics was of necessity part of its remit. In operational terms, the tropical paediatrics initiative reinforced the geographical definition of the activities of the School. International Community Health sought to define the activities of the LSTM not by geography but by socio-economic status. Within the context of the School, the meaning of the words 'tropical medicine' and 'international health' slid loosely into each other in the 1970s. By the 1980s, international health had become distinguishable from tropical medicine in its aims and objectives.

The wing honoured Brian Maegraith, who stood down as Dean in 1975 but accepted election as a Vice President the same year. He remained closely involved with the School until his death in 1989. He had served as Dean for three years after his retirement from the chair of Tropical Medicine, purportedly providing continuity during the planning and fund raising for the new wing and the future intellectual development of the School. Maegraith was a powerful and influential man who had steered the LSTM in a particular direction. This mantle now passed to a group of senior members of staff who in turn served as Dean until the external appointment of Professor David Molyneux as Director in July 1991.[1]

Higher education as whole was subject to greater measures of accountability and productivity assessments in the 1980s. Insufficient core funding for the LSTM, which for example threatened to close paediatrics in the mid-1980s, challenged the future viability of the LSTM as an independent institution. From the opening of the Maegraith Wing to the submission of the Report to Council by an Academic Review Working Party in 1990, the efficient internal organisation of the School became increasingly important. The LSTM would be challenged not only to justify its continued existence, but also to account for how it would function should it remain an independent institution dedicated to health in the tropics.

The original plan of rotating the office of dean resumed after Maegraith's retirement. For continuity and support, the Dean's office relied on a series of advisory committees, the first of which were the Fabric Committee and Safety Committee. These subjects indicated how the LSTM was balancing essential infrastructure maintenance with plans for expansion. The appointment of committees represented moves towards more democratic and transparent procedures in what was becoming a large institution. Often the only result of these committees was the generation of a large amount of paper and some feeling of representation among the staff. The Heads of Departments, Staff Academic and Chief Technicians Committees continued to meet and discuss policy. They were able to suggest changes but had no executive powers. These remained vested in the senior members of staff and lay members of Council serving on that body and the Executive Management Committee. Dissent over the role of Council in managing a modern teaching and research institution akin and in some respects analogous to a university faculty eventually found a voice.[2] In late 1970s and early 1980s, there was no open discussion of such questions. To rationalise this situation the School implemented the recommendations of the Academic Review Committee.

In spite of the grave financial situation, caused by reductions in higher education funding and provision for overseas aid, and inflationary pressure in the British economy, the academic output of the individual departments continued to increase. The fundamental research in the traditional departments continued to enjoy success in the competitive market of research funding applications. Equally, the overtly interdisciplinary approach to health adopted and developed by the Department of International Community Health found sponsorship and support for projects that redefined health care and analysed its most effective delivery. In the 1980s, within a physically and financially restricted environment, the juxtaposition of departmental interests resulted in a polarisation of the School.

The techniques used in the Departments of Tropical Medicine, Tropical Paediatrics, Parasitology, Medical Entomology and Veterinary Parasitology reflected the status of biomedical science in the last quarter of the twentieth century. The ability to visualise finer structures within the cell benefited from the techniques of electron microscopy and sophisticated histology. The deconstruction of the processes of life in various states of infection and immunity in the body were available to the clinical disciplines. The same basic sciences of biochemistry, immunology and molecular biology were applied with increasing frequency to protozoa, helminths, bacteria and viruses and the arthropods and freshwater molluscs acting as vectors. As a whole, the conglomeration of subjects brought together at the turn of the twentieth century for political and economic reasons as tropical medicine remained rather remote from other basic sciences and scientific clinical medicine for many years. By the 1970s aspects of the discipline were at the forefront of many fields of research and continued to embrace and lead developments into the 1990s. This represented successive refinements of the attempt to understand disease-causing organisms and latterly their interaction with the host. These were essentially the same questions, raised in the first decade of the School, particularly at the laboratories in Runcorn, somewhat intermittently thereafter, and at a consistent rate in the last thirty years.

Tropical medicine at Liverpool demonstrated an increasing sophistication in its research techniques. However, there is a continuity of purpose from the initial identification of parasites and vectors to the precise identification of the strains of parasites and vectors using the techniques of immunology and molecular biology. Research would indicate that it is possible to identify the particular genes of insects controlling transference. Theoretically, it is possible to re-engineer the genetics of the mosquito responsible for carrying malaria or filariasis, interrupting transmission at this point in the life cycle. It may not be possible to eradicate malaria-carrying mosquitoes as has been tried at various times, but it may be possible to interfere sufficiently in their genes to prevent transmission of the disease. The methodology is different but the principle, established after the work of Ross and the Italian malariologists, is essentially the same. The disease, defined by its causative organism and means of transmission, is tackled as an isolated entity. Its social meaning as an indicator of poverty and inequality remains outside of this definition. The scientific basis of tropical medicine in the colonial period with its overtly racial policies and role in the subjugation of indigenous people has developed in terms of its techniques and research methodology. The basic problems of poverty and inequality, obvious in the colonial period and since, remain untouched by this scientific sophistication. There is still a belief that science will ultimately triumph and combat the tropical diseases. Whether anyone will be able to afford the results of this science remains uncertain.

Some of the initiatives in Tropical Paediatrics and many of those in International Community Health do not have the same sense of continuity with the tropical medicine of the turn of the century. Their legacy is not colonial medicine dominated by the medical model and concerned with specific diseases but with a definition of health derived from the social sciences as well as the biomedical sciences. The determination of the Department of International Community Health to incorporate a strong non-medical approach to health and the interrelationship of this approach with the biomedical model characterised the School in the 1980s. Tensions around this dichotomy affect the operation of the LSTM, its relations with outside bodies, and the discipline of tropical medicine as it moves toward the centenary in 1998.

The intellectual direction of the LSTM was thus the second major issue in the Academic Review. For the first time, a distinct policy for research was established. Within a broad mission statement, viable and non-viable research projects were outlined. This presented a new platform for the School to move towards the next century. It is therefore important to understand the internal structure of the LSTM in the 1980s and the polarisation of interests that along with financial pressures necessitated its redirection.

## TROPICAL MEDICINE AS INTERNATIONAL HEALTH

The School extended its scope after the end of the formal colonial empire but maintained a geographical definition of tropical medicine. The School developed profitable links with countries in the Far and Middle East and North Africa (Libya). Equally, innovations such as the new Department of Tropical Paediatrics showed that the LSTM was expanding its focus within these geographical boundaries. As discussed in the previous chapter the impetus for the new department acknowledged the importance of practising medicine in the tropics as well as considering the specific diseases traditionally associated with the discipline. On the other hand, the School described as examples of 'international health' its work in Liverpool on clinical tropical medicine and advice on travellers' health. It used 'tropical medicine' and 'international health' interchangeably, before a more specific definition evolved for the latter term.

In November and December1970, Maegraith delivered the Heath Clark Lectures at the University of London, under the title 'One world' and subsequently published the lectures as a book of the same name.[3] He argued that the problems of health in the tropics were equally the problems of the developed world. He did not rely upon an appeal to humanitarianism, but referred to practical issues such as imported disease.

In 1971, Maegraith realised a nine-year struggle to have the wording on the Yellow Card issued by the Council of Europe altered. Passengers arriving in Britain from beyond Europe received a card as they passed through immigration. Information on the card advised anyone who had travelled or who lived in the same household as the traveller to show the card to a doctor if they become ill within twenty-one days of their return. The aim of the card was to guard against the spread of smallpox, because the disease represented a public health threat beyond the immediate consequences to the individual. Malaria presented no associated risk to the health of the population. For the individual, *falciparum* malaria in particular was potentially lethal if left undiagnosed and untreated. Clinical reports from the School referred repeatedly to the admission of semi-comatose patients with this disease. After 1971, the card reminded people who had been in a malarious region that they should bring this to the attention of their doctor should they subsequently become ill. Adequate preparation to deal with imported diseases was as much a part of Maegraith's vision of international health as the spread of European science and medical practice to the developing countries.[4] The question, 'Unde Vendis?' (From where) had already become synonymous with his views.

The awareness of imported diseases improved, but disease prevention among travellers remained poor. The DHSS issued their own advisory booklet, but the travel industry and the medical profession wrangled over who had responsibility. Maegraith entered the fray with a letter to the editor of the *BMJ*.[5] This internal debate within the profession did not reach the public who travelled to malarious destinations, at risk of infection and without good advice. Maegraith was delighted therefore when the LSTM advised on several episodes of the television serial 'Crossroads'. Nineteen million viewers watched 'Amy' as she blithely travelled to East Africa without taking any anti-malarials and promptly contracted the disease. Her GP, who had a friend at the LSTM, correctly diagnosed her condition upon her return. Amy recovered and proclaimed her anger at the travel agents that had sold her the ticket but failed to mention the necessary medical precautions.

Besides the long struggle over the wording of the advice on the Yellow Card warning, the School introduced improvements for dealing with imported diseases in collaboration with the Liverpool Regional Hospital Board. From 1972, a new diagnostic laboratory at the School provided an advisory service for northern Britain. Peters, as the Honorary Director and Consultant of the Regional Diagnostic Laboratory for Parasitic Diseases used immunological techniques for diagnosis for the first time in Liverpool. The laboratory offered routine serological tests for antibodies against four species of *Plasmodium*, several species of *Schistosoma, Entamoeba histolytica, Leishmania, Trypanosoma cruzi, Wuchereria* and *Strongyloides*. Later Dr M J Clarkson acceded to the request of the Regional Health Authority to provide a similar service for *Toxocara canis* in human serum. Edinburgh had ended its long tradition of teaching and practice with the closure of the Department of Tropical Medicine in April 1972, leaving Liverpool as the most northerly point in Britain for expertise in this field. As the diagnostic service of the School became better known and the amount of foreign travel escalated, the number of specimens increased. The clinic also continued to provide immunisations and introduced a telephone information service to individual travellers and GPs who appropriately sought expert advice.

## TROPICAL MEDICINE AS COMMUNITY HEALTH

In 1972, Gilles became Alfred Lewis Jones and Warrington Yorke Professor of Tropical Medicine. Gilles maintained the department's interest in basic biomedical research in the laboratory and commenced new programmes complementing work in other departments. In 1973, for instance, a new project, in collaboration with pharmacologists in the University, investigated the pharmacogenetics of drugs used commonly in parasitic diseases, extending the focus on chemotherapy. A new commitment to practising and researching tropical medicine at the community level was also apparent. In the same way that paediatric aspects of tropical medicine predated the creation of a separate department, Gilles' existing interest in community medicine highlighted this approach before the Department of Tropical Community Health was fully functional.

The appointment of the Baring Senior Lecturer in Tropical Community Medicine, Dr Shunmugan Reddy, to the Department of Tropical Medicine in April 1971 offered Gilles an excellent opportunity to oversee research in the community.[6] This five-year position was similar to that of Lecturer-at-Large created in 1958. Reddy was immediately seconded to the new Department of Community Medicine in the Amadu Bello University, Zaria, northern Nigeria. He became professor of Community Medicine in 1973. Reddy was the second non-white member of the teaching staff at the LSTM. He worked under Gilles, building up the department in Zaria and researching at the village level as Gilles had done in Afuko. Teaching programmes similar to those instituted at Ibarapa were envisaged. The successful solicitation of private funds indicated the commitment of the LSTM to the principles of technical assistance, the early problems of the government programme notwithstanding. When the MRC Tropical Medicine Research Board granted £85,000 over five years in 1973 for the Malumfashi Project, Reddy, now professor of Community Medicine, and Gilles found themselves with the means of conducting an 'ecological health programme' of research. Additional funding from other sources enlarged the scope of the project.

The proposed project was a large undertaking. The Malumfashi Project would observe the changes associated with damming and irrigating previously dry land in northern Nigeria and modernising the system of agriculture by mechanisation, pesticide and fertiliser use. The survey would look not just at the medical impact of this programme but its effects in terms of social and economic impacts on the local population. The study would inform the teaching of community medicine and provide data for understanding the natural history of disease and health in a community.

In 1974, the MOD voted an additional Technical Assistance Lecturer in the field of Medical Geography/Demography. Mr Andrew Bradley joined Reddy at the University of Zaria. Bradley was a useful addition to the team working in Nigeria and he represented an area of expertise in which the LSTM was weak. Before going overseas, Bradley undertook preliminary training at the LSHTM in epidemiology, statistics and demography. These disciplines were strengths of the London School, developed since the 1920s. He spent a month in the field with David Smith, seconded to the MRC unit at Kisumu, Kenya: other Technical Assistance Lecturers ensured that on-the-job training was still possible for new staff. The project continued to expand intellectually and in terms of the number of personnel attached to its various programmes. Where Tropical Medicine provided synthesis, Tropical Community Health proved to be at the vanguard of the discipline. Its evolution challenged the form and function of the LSTM.

## TROPICAL HYGIENE BECOMES TROPICAL COMMUNITY HEALTH

Unlike the London School, Liverpool did not prioritise hygiene. The sanitation era of Ross and possibly Boyce coincided with the discovery era. Without the energy of these two men, discovery dominated sanitation. The School had no Department of Tropical Hygiene until 1929. In 1934, Blacklock became the first holder of the Middlemass Hunt Chair of Tropical Hygiene. On his retirement, Davey replaced him as professor. The department remained the smallest in the School. After World War II, when the research output of other departments increased, Davey explained his position,

> Owing to the small staff in the department, the heavy burden of committee work, and the demands on the services of the staff in a consultative capacity abroad, it has not been possible to carry out in Liverpool any programme of research in tropical hygiene. The department is, however, keenly interested in problems of immunity to

malaria, the growth of populations in the tropics, medical education in colonial university colleges, and other subjects of which it is consulted by visitors from overseas with a view to field research. It is believed that the department is thus fulfilling its function more satisfactorily than if it were tied to research projects in Liverpool.[7]

In the absence of a regular research output, Davey made three major contributions. First, he united the DTM and DTH into a single course dealing with the cure and prevention of tropical diseases. Second, he represented the LSTM as spokesperson on the interrelation of population growth and medical aid, maintaining a profile in an important area of the social sciences and development studies. Third, his input to the Inter-University Council for Higher Education Overseas made a valuable contribution to the School's own involvement with higher education overseas. Davey attributed his own skills in these three areas to his initial education as a philosophy undergraduate, a background few could match. Wilson, whose rather different expertise in filariasis would see him regularly serving overseas as a consultant for WHO, replaced him. From Blacklock to Wilson, there was a steady accumulation of knowledge passed to the students via the teaching material for the DTMH. Each incumbent of the chair added a different perspective to the museum and other teaching aids but did not seek fundamentally to redevelop the department. Tropical Hygiene was the last department in the School to be overhauled and therefore suffered the most radical of changes. After the retirement of Wilson in 1971, the department and chair were renamed Tropical Community Health. N Rex E Fendall replaced Wilson and the mould was broken.

Fendall's expertise lay in training medical auxiliaries and advising on the problems associated with increasing population in the Third World; a description of the developing world used for the first time in the LSTM in 1970.[8] The new title for the department also indicated a major conceptual shift. The title represented the first use of the word 'health' in the LSTM in this way. The titles of other departments either signified their association with scientific disciplines or with medicine and medical practice. Tropical hygiene was obviously concerned with prevention and had traditionally prepared students for work as a District MO who was otherwise concerned primarily with curative medicine. This meant giving specific instruction in the provision of clean water, sewage disposal and avoidance of vectors of disease. The MO then applied this knowledge within the limited medical and sanitary infrastructure of the colonial departments. In its preventative aspects, the diploma remained overtly medical in its orientation. The promotion of health via implementation of social science research was lacking.

Fendall came to the School with practical experience as a policy adviser. He worked for the Rockefeller Foundation on a programme examining health care systems around the world. When this was complete, he transferred to the Population Council in New York. He had also undertaken pre-investment survey work for the World Bank. His portfolio of skills and experience therefore gave him a different outlook from his predecessors. Although he had worked for the CMS in Kenya, during the 1960s his work had been in the economics and policy of health care systems in the Third World.

Fendall was therefore experienced in working with those who determined medical policy as part of socio-economic development. As the International Bank for Reconstruction and Development increasing planned development in the Third World, it was imperative that the LSTM communicate its message, about the importance of medical aid and the best methods of spending what was available, to such an audience. Reports of this kind used different criteria for assessment and sought to realise different objectives to the British based organisations the LSTM had relied upon previously. The emphasis was not on the general improvements in life quality but rather on short term measurable improvements in health directly translatable into economic performance. As third world debt spiralled in the 1980s, links with WHO would prove insufficient to guarantee that the voice of the School continued to be heard unless it spoke to the economists. Policy generation would become an increasingly important part of the research work of the School. The LSTM had previously transferred medicine, practice and education systems overseas. Policy at the level of health care delivery systems added a new item to the list of School transfers.

## DEPARTMENT OF TROPICAL COMMUNITY HEALTH

The Department of Tropical Hygiene was obviously responsible for teaching the 'hygiene' components of the DTMH. Before his unexpected death in 1972, Edward Ensor began considerable alterations to the teaching methods in the department. Reconfiguration of the museum changed this facility from a passive element into a more dynamic 'Learning Laboratory'.[9] The changes were not merely cosmetic, they were underscored by re-evaluation of the role of the diploma course. These physical and ideological changes accelerated after the arrival of Fendall. New equipment for self-teaching using audio-visual (tape-slide) equipment helped to relieve the shortage of staff and create greater independence and self-reliance among the students. Fendall also asked for the purchase of video equipment for both recording and playback. Debates on controversial topics introduced the students to advocacy at a practical level. A mock-up of a village dispensary aimed to present students with an understanding of the physical circumstances in which they would work. The DTMH curriculum also changed. The difference between the practice of medicine in developing and developed societies was emphasised by invited guest lecturers. The students were consciously prepared for aspects of health beyond medicine. New topics included population dynamics, family planning, managerial medicine, international health, statistics, epidemiology, communicable diseases (as opposed to tropical diseases) and environmental health. The syllabus was large, matching the demands placed upon community practitioners in the developing countries. The aim was to prepare students to work as efficiently as possible within the limited infrastructure of support services, staff and resources. Fendall's other immediate innovation was to admit three nurses to the DTMH beginning in January 1972 alongside their medical colleagues, although they did not sit for the diploma. This caused some concern that nurses would take the places of physicians and create difficulties because of the diversity of backgrounds among the students.[10]

The Certificate Course in Tropical Nursing ended in 1973.[11] This had relied upon Adams. After his retirement, the course lacked an overall co-ordinator. More effective use of teaching time would result from increasing interdisciplinary teaching. The intention was to take this integration much further and admit other non-medical personnel to the DTMH. The practical need to create teams of health workers replaced the emphasis on the individual. Fendall therefore followed up the introduction of nurses as students with a request for a Public Health Nurse Tutor.[12] The final product was the range of dedicated courses for non-medics discussed in chapter 7.

Fendall presented the library with a collection of forty-eight books on population and family planning. The librarian commented that his generosity upgraded the holdings on population issues. His books were the first on family planning held by the library.[13] Subsequent purchases of books selectively improved library resources for this subject. More than the name of the department needed overhauling. The increasing breadth of literature required by the new courses and methods of teaching brought the library to capacity once more. The Library Committee was obliged to consider ways to share existing material with the University in order to accommodate new books and periodicals for the expansion in community health literature.

The changes in teaching were contemporaneous with operational research projects. Active programmes of research combining epidemiology and the social sciences commenced. In combination with the teaching innovations, this research changed the face of the LSTM. It added considerably to the portfolio of expertise offered to students and outside bodies interested in using the intellectual capital of the School. Fendall restructured the new department to this end. Strategic staff appointments enhanced the image projected outwards from Liverpool. In research and teaching, Tropical Community Health promoted community development in the Third World. The focus of the department related not to geographical or climatic boundaries, but to socio-economic status: it was not in the tropics but among the underprivileged Fendall wanted the LSTM to make its impact. In August 1971, he visited Alaska to assess the implementation of a scheme for introducing medical auxiliaries known as Village Physician Assistants. He was equipped to advise on this scheme because the auxiliaries purportedly faced similar basic problems of poverty and ignorance that faced colleagues in the underdeveloped tropics. The overlap of conditions caused by a low socio-economic status with the former tropical colonies ensured that the tropics represented a major focus for Tropical Community Health. However, there was a clear intellectual commitment to an economic rather than a geographical definition of health.

The sudden death of Ensor left George Pringle as the remaining member of the old Department of Tropical Hygiene. He left at the end of 1973 when his research was completed. Dr Anthony J Radford, an Australian with considerable experience of primary health care in Papua New Guinea, replaced him as senior lecturer. Radford and Dr David J D Stevenson, Senior Lecturer (Technical Assistance), drafted a new syllabus for the DTMH and the electives for non-medics. Radford and Stevenson shared Fendall's research interest in population dynamics.[14] Radford's experiences in Australasia complemented Stevenson's knowledge of Africa and Dr Francis M Shattock's background in central Africa, Korea and Indonesia. The initial team of Tropical Community Health benefited from additional appointments under the Technical Assistance programme. When Radford returned to his native Australia, Dr Derek Robinson assumed his role in overall co-ordination of teaching. As the DTMH represented the unifying experience for all departments of the School, Robinson's co-ordination of the diploma and its review placed him in a strong functional position.

## MEDICAL AUXILIARIES

The School had followed and promoted the idea of the centres of excellence in the Third World. This model aimed to teach and train teachers to the highest possible level: a level compatible with universities or centres of excellence in the First World. The aim was to accelerate the development process of the third world countries by transferring first world practices. The School had a successful history of such out-reach policies though its links with Thailand, Ghana and Nigeria, the Lecturer-at-Large scheme and Technical Assistance.

While the LSTM still taught and examined at this level, Fendall led attempts to promote, monitor and improve teaching of medical auxiliaries at the local level. This implied no diminution in the standard of teaching. The LSTM still acted as a centre of excellence but the output was radically different. Tropical Community Health participated in local initiatives, such as the Canadian Development Association sponsored meeting in Anglophone West Africa in 1973 and the preparation of advisory documents for policy formation.[15] Without the resources at this time to implement demonstration schemes overseas, the LSTM relied upon the staff making personal contacts. The recognition of the School staff as leading authorities was therefore essential. Fendall spent a considerable amount of time travelling. His role as visiting lecturer in Tropical Public Health at the Harvard Medical School connected the LSTM with a prestigious teaching institute in America where their activities were less well known. Links with the BMA panel of health care teams, Church Mission Group on planning rural health centres, Heads of Departments Group and Social and Preventative Medicine Group of the Commonwealth Secretariat, the Commonwealth Human Ecology Council, WHO, Josiah Macy Jr Foundation, Rockefeller Foundation and UNICEF provided contact and opportunities for advertising the LSTM among non-governmental organisations with interests in medical education and in the Third World.[16] In 1975, Dr P Bradley spent two months in Bangladesh helping the charity, Save the Children Fund, establish a new maternal and child health project. The ability to respond to such requests would be increasingly important as NGOs became more powerful in the 1980s. Not dominated by medics, and the biomedical model of effective community health care, development charities such as Save the Children were able to appreciate the value of auxiliaries.

Study of the 'implementation gap' between gaining knowledge and its successful application in practice followed the department's introduction of teaching innovations. Secondments of the Technical Assistance Lecturers to Nepal and Nigeria facilitated this work. There was a double interest in assessing the effects of training health auxiliaries on the health of the population and its social development. Long-term policies were informed by this research and immediate changes in teaching implemented. The long-term goal implied establishing flexible principles for PHC in areas of poor socio-economic status. As with tropical paediatrics and tropical medicine the emphasis converged with the WHO ideal of strengthening health services on a global scale. In the mid-1970s, the term 'Primary Health Care' appeared with increasing frequency in this respect. The emphasis of the Department of Tropical Community Health on developing mechanisms for implementing PHC where it was most needed had brought the School to the forefront of an area in which it had taken little initiative in the past.

Besides research conducted by members of staff, the department accepted students registered for higher degrees. Dr Alberto Viau worked in Liverpool and for periods at home towards his thesis: 'Cost-effectiveness analysis of the use of paramedical personnel within a National Health Service system in Guatemala'. The cost/benefit analysis of health care delivery systems became increasingly important as accountability to the World Bank replaced general notions of welfare improvement in developing countries. Health was a basic right in the developing world only in so far as there were funds for its delivery. Efficiency gains in health care delivery systems were therefore of substantial benefit to developing countries with limited budgets. Quantitative evidence of the value of specific health care projects rendered them more likely to be funded.

In addition to the aspects relating to the training of medical auxiliaries, the department was also involved with policies to ensure that acceptance of suitably trained medical auxiliaries by the communities in which they worked. Fendall acted as a consultant for WHO and relied upon his knowledge of existing schemes such as the Ahmadu Bello University at Zaria.[17] In 1977, the British Council and the MOD supported a collaborative project with the Banaras Hindu University. Staff from India would receive training in social and community medicine and MCommH students from the School would spend their three months fieldwork attached to the University.

## FAMILY PLANNING

Many of the organisations keen to promote basic health care systems were also interested in promoting limitation of family size as a means of improving health and social welfare. Davey had spoken often on the need for integration of medical relief programmes with social and economic development producing balanced development. In particular Fendall acted as a consultant for the United Nations Family Planning Association, advising on the appropriateness of projects submitted for funding by the UNFPA and the success of their implementation. He translated the same considerations into research papers and then into policy documents.[18] In this way the LSTM became not just a laboratory and teaching resource, but also a policy 'think tank' on issues requiring the social as well as the medical sciences.

Internal integration and reorganisation occurred simultaneously with external approval for the work at Liverpool. In addition to frequent consultancies, an EEC grant of £7,830 per annum began in November 1976. The department was to initiate links with other centres of International and Community Health. The award of this grant to the department placed Liverpool at the centre of an international network. In April 1977, the department organised the Association of Schools of Public Health in the European Region meeting. The title of the meeting, 'Applicability of European postgraduate health care training programmes and technical services for the developing countries', reflected a primary concern of the department. The School hosting the first meeting of a series designed to examine the role of Europe in the training and assistance of the developing world, reinforced external perceptions of the LSTM as a significant force in the generation of health care policies. The original plan was for thirty delegates, seventy attended. The School offered £300 in support for this meeting, but otherwise it was self-funding. Sponsorship for delegates without means of support came from a variety of agencies including the MOD.

In March 1973, Fendall submitted a proposal that the title of his chair become International Community Health rather than Tropical Community Health.[19] This accompanied the development of the DTMH as a multidisciplinary course open to non-medics. In addition to funds from the Gatsby Foundation to support the Nurse Tutor, Fendall had secured support to enable non-physicians from Trinidad and Jamaica to attend the Certificate Course in Tropical Community Health. The decision to change the name of the department was shelved, apparently because of complications with the University's Masters in Public Health course.[20] In April 1975, Fendall raised the matter again, on the understanding that the Dean of the Medical Faculty would have no objection.[21] Maegraith supported the suggestions arguing that the title Department of International Health would prevent confusion with Tropical Child Health.[22] There was some concern that this might cause difficulty with the ODM who attached a specific meaning to 'international health'.[23] Given the amount of ODM support for the Department of Tropical Community Heath, it was unlikely that there would be any implications. As the plans for the opening of the Maegraith Wing were finalised, the School acceded to a change in title for the department. The tone of the official minute implied it was a pragmatic decision, in light of the role the department was playing. Concern that the definition of health, used and promoted by the department, would complicate the message the School wished to send was more likely to have caused the reticence. Permission to change the title of the department carried a clear proviso, 'that there would be no implications for the titles of other departments within the School nor for the title of the School'.[24]

## FUNDAMENTAL SCIENCE AT THE LSTM

Rapid inflation in the 1970s affected all the activities of the School. In 1974, heads of departments agreed to a ten per cent cut in recurrent expenditure. University posts planned for the next quinquennium were frozen. Still reliant upon the UGC for a third of its income, the School suffered from cuts in the central provision for education, like any other institute of higher education. Further cuts in the higher education budget in the 1980s were transferred again to the School via the University block grant. In 1986, the University created budget centres with specified savings targets. The LSTM, as a budget centre, formed two working groups to find economies in the administrative and academic relationship with the University. In periods of financial stringency basic research of the 'undirected' or 'curiosity driven' kind is often hard to justify. It promises no immediate application and is generally expensive as it applies diverse technologies and methodologies in new areas. Such research also tends to be the least accessible to those outside of the field. The increasingly technical nature of the *Annual Report* prompted a change in format in 1986 for this very reason.

Each generation of professional staff charged with the management of the School via the lay Council has been aware of this gulf. The Director of the Alfred Lewis Jones Laboratory in Sierra Leone was obliged to provide a six-monthly report on research progress. Blacklock earned the praise of the Professional Committee in Liverpool for his ability to produce text intelligible to the lay members of Council. Over the last twenty years, the problem was exacerbated, financial constraints had increased and the LSTM again became unsure of its structure and function, in particular the relationship with the University and the balancing of operational research with laboratory research. The broader the discipline and the larger the School, the more internal communication became perfunctory. Those working within the LSTM and the discipline at times were unable to perceive or understand how the sum of the parts formed the whole. From the outside, it is not clear that the parts could or should necessarily be united. Contemporary comment indicated this was a live issue.

The appointment of Wallace Peters as Dean in 1975 transferred leadership of the LSTM from the Department of Tropical Medicine. Maegraith made unique use of the office of Dean, but the chair of Tropical Medicine had effectively been the power-base of the LSTM since its foundation. The Dean was very much the public face of the LSTM and Peters represented fundamental laboratory science rather more than he did operational research and PHC.

The expansion of Tropical Paediatrics and Child Health and Tropical Community Health, with a new definition of health, was matched by re-establishing the pre-eminence of the scientific research at the LSTM. In 1975, WHO increased its support for basic scientific research in tropical medicine with the creation in Geneva of a new division: Tropical Disease Research and Training. The TDR project hoped to tackle selected diseases in an intensive period of research.[25] This initiative relied upon several principles. First, the parasitic diseases of the developing world had proven difficult to eradicate. The failure of the global malaria eradication programme served as a bitter reminder of the intractability of such diseases. Second, the pharmaceutical industry, with a few exceptions, declined to commit research and development funding for new products primarily for use in the tropics. Millions might suffer, but the majority were too poor to pay for expensive drugs. The WHO considered investment in immunology and chemotherapy to be essential in the absence of commercial interest in these technologies. Third, existing facilities for training indigenous researchers were still too limited and this programme offered an additional means to enhance such provision.

Invited groups of experts, 'Task Forces', reviewed the contemporary situation and decided priorities for the TDR projects.[26] Peters chaired the Task Force responsible for malaria chemotherapy and Howells joined as a member. Already in 1975, Peters had served as a Temporary Adviser to the United Nations Development Programme-World Bank-WHO Intercountry Onchocerciasis Control Programme. This twenty-year project to eradicate the disease had no effective drug with which to treat the infected population. The School hoped to contribute by establishing a research programme on the chemotherapy of filariasis. The Tropical Medicine Research Board funded this project. In November 1975, WHO invited Harold Townson to collaborate on a project to differentiate species of the vector of onchocerciasis, *Simulium damnosum*, using the technique of enzyme electrophoresis.[27] Dr David Molyneux was Project Leader designate for a related project to control trypanosomiasis in the same geographical areas as the Onchocerciasis Control Programme. International attention focused and directed fundamental disease-orientated research at the LSTM.

The study of parasites was not exclusive to the LSTM or the London School. Kershaw had continued working on parasitology after his move to the biology laboratories at Salford. Universities such as Keele, Brunel, Glasgow, Edinburgh, London and Nottingham all conducted basic biomedical research on parasites of medical and veterinary importance.[28] The training offered by the MSc and MVSc (Applied Parasitology) produced more graduates than were kept on at the LSTM either as PhD students or research assistants. Similarly, entomology and freshwater biology as zoological sciences rather than subjects connected with the topics were pursued elsewhere. In 1976, Molyneux left Liverpool to succeed Kershaw in the chair of Biology at Salford. The science of parasitology presented career opportunities beyond the two Schools of Tropical Medicine.

The LSTM still had certain valuable assets. It was recognised as a centre of excellence. Its laboratories were renowned for generating new parasitological techniques. This reflected the quality of the technical personnel as well as the academic staff. Instruction for the IMLT, the special courses for the Public

Health Laboratory Service and RAMC illustrate the special facilities at Liverpool. Dr Michael Chance, with MRC support, continued working on the interrelationships of the various species, subspecies and strains of rodent malarias (*P. berghei*) by hybridising their nuclear DNA complex.[29] In addition to *in vivo* strains, by 1975, the strains of *Leishmania* stored in liquid nitrogen at the LSTM totalled three hundred and eighty seven. There were also fifty-four strains of malaria parasites (drug-sensitive and drug-resistant), *Babesia* and trypanosomes *in vivo* or in liquid nitrogen. This 'protozoal bank' was an additional result of the range of projects funded among others by the Wellcome Trust, MRC, WHO, US Army Research and Development Command, CIBA, Hoffman La Roche and Abbott Laboratories. The work of PhD students sponsored by various organisations and governments also brought valuable material to the School. Replication of such a collection was not easy. The number of isolates increased as staff continued to bring in new material from overseas for analysis.[30] In 1978, the LSTM was appointed a WHO collaborating centre for the biochemical identification of *Leishmania*.

The interrelation of the Department of Parasitology with that of Veterinary Parasitology and Medical Entomology was a further asset. The work of MacDonald and Townson on the genetics of vector susceptibility to parasites suggested the mechanisms for manipulating species to favour non-transmitters. After the Department of Parasitology and Entomology split, joint research decreased until the rise of molecular biology in the 1980s.

The LSTM also had its historic connections with the tropics. Recognition of the expertise of the School underlay relationships with the different agencies involved with the developing world. The staff at the School and the zoological specimens offered a particularly refined resource for basic science research. Alistair Reid's work on snake-bite and venom research received external recognition. In 1977, the LSTM became a WHO Collaborating Centre for the Control of Antivenom. The Centre prepared the WHO Manual on Snake-Bite and developed the ELISA technique to screen antivenom for its neutralising ability.[31] As with pharmaceuticals it was essential to control the quality and consistency of biological products such as antivenoms. National recognition followed. In 1978, the NHS designated London and Liverpool as the two centres for keeping antivenoms and offering a service for bites of indigenous and imported snakes.[32]

What the School lacked were facilities and financial support other than specific research grants. This kind of funding was unreliable and intellectual continuity difficult to maintain. Careful auditing revealed the deficit between actual expenditure and overhead costs in those grants which made payments in this way. The School pushed for sources of funding to support general research rather than specific projects, but this was extremely difficult. A lack of central funding for maintenance of the human capital and raw materials threatened to squander these resources as well as wasting the time of senior staff as they repeatedly considered proposals for economies.

In the 1980s, within the parts of the School devoted to fundamental research greater co-operation occurred. A substantial grant from the Wolfson Foundation, one and a half million pounds over five years beginning in 1983, gave the LSTM the opportunity to expand its molecular biology work.[33] The award of the grant carried the proviso that the money could not relieve the University or government of the commitments to the School: sponsoring new units in molecular biology clearly utilised the funds in a suitable manner. The LSTM was initially slow to appreciate immunology as a research methodology, but it was determined not to do this in the case of molecular biology.[34] This new composite of methods, techniques, apparatus, language and applications was to become a significant part of the basic science research carried out by the LSTM. It provided a methodology useful to tropical medicine, paediatrics, vector biology or parasite biology. In this respect, the division of the School into the traditional departments began to look unnecessary and artificial. The Wolfson Molecular Genetics Unit for instance was located in the Department of Medical Entomology under Dr Julian Crampton. The collaboration of Crampton and Marcel Hommel (Molecular Immunology) on a successful WHO grant application resulted in the appointment of Dr M Hughes jointly in Medical Entomology and Tropical Medicine and Infectious Diseases for three years in the mid-1980s. Hughes used a technique developed by Crampton and Miss P Bond to work on antigenic variation of *Plasmodium falciparum*.

From a methodological standpoint, parasites and their relations with hosts and vectors became the raw materials for research into the molecular understanding of living systems and systems compromised by infectious agents and death. The laboratories of the LSTM, whether they used vectors or parasites as the starting point, employed these methodologies. This was not a discreet event at Liverpool. It functioned as part of the development of the biological sciences in the second half of the twentieth century.

In the 1980s, the phenomena of emerging and re-emerging infectious diseases revitalised an interest in infection and immunity around the world. The LSTM had sustained an interest in infection and latterly developed immunity studies. In 1986 after the retirement of Gilles and appointment of Marcel Hommel as professor of Tropical Medicine, the title of the department changed to Tropical Medicine and Infectious Diseases. This recognised the formal merger of the Department of Infectious Diseases of the University with its unit at Fazakerley Hospital and the Department of Tropical Medicine of the School in October 1985. Hommel was previously head of The Wolfson Tropical Immunology Unit in the Department of Parasitology. The Unit moved with

Hommel to Tropical Medicine and Infectious Diseases. The strength and success of these ventures was polarised with the equally successful developments in International Community Health. The Department of Veterinary Parasitology moved towards closer links with the University Department of Veterinary Preventative Medicine at the field station. This new association bought Clarkson's skills in parasite immunology back to the School.

In 1976, Peters presented his first *Annual Report* as Dean. He referred explicitly to its new format. This represented 'an evolution towards a School approach to our problems rather than the Old Departmental approach'.[35] The difficulty would be reuniting into one body disparate elements which had attained an identity by branching out successfully on their own, seeking alternative sources of funding and presenting different kinds of solutions to health problems in the tropics. The greatest dichotomy was between Tropical Community Health and the fundamental laboratory research conducted in the other departments of the School.

Tropical Community Health was distinct from the other departments in its definition of health from a social science perspective as well as a biomedical perspective. The department's primary commitment was to health. Disease was located among a range of factors affecting health. The infectious diseases were obviously important in departmental teaching. The department considered the investigation of consumer attitudes, staff attitudes, community attitudes and utilisation patterns of health as abstract issues not related necessarily to diseases such as malaria, schistosomiasis or tuberculosis. Moreover, operational research in the Department of Community Health had different objectives and audiences when compared to the output of the other departments. It is noticeable that the composite *Annual Report* introduced by Peters contained extracts from departmental submissions. The language of these extracts indicates the dissatisfaction with inadequate facilities which many members of staff endured and the internal tensions between Tropical Community Health and other departments. The substance of these extracts is interesting, albeit a replication of issues in internal School correspondence and committee minutes. Their significance lies in the public presentation of a troubled School.

The experience of teaching community health as part of the DTMH shaped the perception of the staff in this department. They found themselves confronted with physicians who thought in terms of individual patients in a hospital environment. The challenge was to convey the importance of the community in their everyday environment.[36] This rehearsed many of the arguments that advisers faced when confronted with physicians in government health departments in the developing world. The generation that had been brought up to strive for academic equivalence in the university setting were now confronted with aid agencies and international organisations prioritising low-cost providers of PHC. Practising advocacy skills in a debate obviously did not impress those within the LSTM who adhered to producing technically competent clinicians with parasitological and entomological knowledge. The tensions of the LSTM's role mirrored discussions over the proper content of the diploma course. The evidence of the DTMH was, however, more effectively marshalled by the Department of Tropical Community Health.

The time dedicated to teaching by staff in the Department of Tropical Community Health and demand for their expertise as consultants further supported their demands for increased facilities and recognition within the LSTM. The change of name, dropping 'tropical' and replacing it with 'international', publicly acknowledged interest in the health of disadvantaged communities anywhere as opposed to those living within arbitrary geographical boundaries that the School had difficulty in maintaining in any case. This had been tacitly acknowledged by innovations within the School and by much of Maegraith's rhetoric. However, his motto – the impact of the School on the tropics must be in the tropics – indicated a deep commitment to the traditional perception of the role of the School. Fendall wanted this radically modified, not subtly adjusted. Despite the change of name, it proved easier to create physical space for the department than intellectual space.

## THE MAEGRAITH WING AND INTERNATIONAL COMMUNITY HEALTH

MOD support for the Maegraith Wing only related to the parts of the building devoted to Tropical Paediatrics. They did include a student common room in their estimates recognising that interchange with other students was a valuable part of the learning experience in Liverpool. The remainder of the money came from donations and the appeal launched by the Rt Hon Selwyn Lloyd. The School was obliged to use reserve funds because of the nature of the building contract and the effects of inflation on material and labour costs. The Danson clinic of the Department of Tropical Medicine occupied the ground floor transferring from the Nuffield Wing. The third floor, paid for by the generosity of the Gatsby Foundation, became the Robert and Lisa Sainsbury International Community Health Department. The new accommodation for these departments released the existing buildings for other users. Hendrickse chaired a Space Allocation Committee. The Committee not only organised the immediate redistribution of rooms, but also established recommendations for future policies on space allocation within the School.[37] This was a real issue because the year after the Maegraith Wing opened the School completed the purchase of the building next door. Conversion of the former Salvation Army Hall waited until the immediate pressure on funds eased, but the School had not lost its resolve to continue expanding.

The International Community Health Department was now able to promote its concern with health in relation to socio-economic status – poverty – rather than a geographical location. This was a particularly appropriate time to make such a change. WHO launched its PHC programme after the Alma Ata meeting in the Soviet Union in September 1978. In advance of this meeting, the Regional Offices of the WHO each held preliminary meetings. Fendall attended the meeting in New Delhi in November 1977 and the Expert Committee meeting at Geneva in December 1977 before serving as a member of the British delegation at Alma Ata. The principles and objectives of the PHC encapsulated many of those promoted by International Community Health at Liverpool on training of basic health care providers. It was most appropriate therefore, that upon Fendall's retirement in December 1981, his replacement was one of the architects of PHC at the WHO, Kenneth Newell. In ten years the ideology of the department had changed considerably and affected the identity of the School.

Newall arrived at the School in January 1984. Shattock served as acting head of department in the intervening period when the post was frozen and negotiations with the University over their grant to the School continued. The department was severely affected by the decision of the ODA to curtail their Technical Co-operation (Technical Assistance) Medical Lecturers scheme. Newell therefore inherited a department with strong objectives but a diminishing staff. He sought to strengthen the basic components of the department: community medicine, nursing, education, environmental health, epidemiology and statistics. To these should be added health economics and management. The Gatsby Foundation provided funding, repeating the generosity that paid for the accommodation in the Maegraith Wing. Among the range of courses run by the department, Newell prioritised the MCommH. He indicated a commitment to increase the number of PhD students in the department. These students would, as elsewhere in the School, provide income and valuable assistance with research.

An ODA consultancy (administered with Tropical Paediatrics) developing training programmes for PHC in the Indian State of Orissa and strengthened the research potential of the department at the end of 1984. Three new members of staff joined the department specifically for the project, Timothy Martineau, an educator, Andrew Cassels, a community health physician specialising in management, and Charles Sayers, a health educator. Newell, Frederick Abbatt and David Nabarro administered the project from Liverpool. In 1985, the department established the Hearing Impairment and Deafness Research Group. The project was recognised by the WHO and funded by Leverhulme and Gatsby grants. The initial work concentrated on children and used an internationally recognised specification for a simple and cheap audiometer to determine the distribution and causes of impaired hearing in the developing world. These projects illustrated Newell's commitment to broadening the department Fendall had created.

Newell's early success in marrying departmental expertise and research interests with the benefits of contract resources in Orissa spurred the LSTM to establish an independent company within the School in 1986. LATH, Liverpool Associates in Tropical Health, undertook overseas consultancies and contracts on a commercial basis. Income generated from successful consultancies might replace the government grant funding from the ODA. If successful, LATH was not restricted to government projects. The diversity of expertise could directly benefit the School when intellectual output was subject to increasing exercises in accountancy. The same flexibility of approach that supported projects such as the hearing group within the LSTM also saw the potential of commercially marketing what the School had provided free or at cost price to overseas countries for many years. In the climate of the mid-1980s, it was no longer considered inappropriate to charge for health expertise in the developing world.

## ACADEMIC REVIEW WORKING PARTY: SYNTHESIS OR FRAGMENTATION?

The School has never been a rich institution. In the early years of World War II the Chairman of Council returned money from the University grant. He felt it was inappropriate to accept the money when the normal teaching programme of the School was suspended. This was the one and only time, because of exceptional circumstances, that the School had extra money at its disposal. On the contrary, there has been an abundance of projects looking for funding. At various times the competing interests of School staff have resulted in discernible attempts to deploy funding to suit individual needs. At no time, however, had the School, as opposed to individuals, drawn up a policy to direct research. After ninety years, the School took the decision to implement such a policy by commissioning the Academic Review Working Party. The University required an Academic Development Plan relating to reduction of the dependence of the School on the block grant. A working group produced an Interim Report suggesting an increase in fee income to the University through School courses rather than the loss of staff or replacement of senior with junior staff. Efficient generation of the Interim Report permitted the School time to prepare a long-term academic review.[38] In addition to financial difficulties, the School had also been involved in unpleasant allegations of racial prejudice. The allegations were not substantiated but promoted vigilance in operating non-discriminatory policies at all levels within the School.[39]

This chapter has reviewed the development of the Department of International Community Health under two influential individuals and their departmental staff from 1971 to the mid-1980s. As with other departments in the LSTM, International Community Health had gained from working hard to create a separate identity. In the case of this department, however, the separateness was more pronounced and challenged, rather than complemented, other aspects of the LSTM. In the same period, aspects of the fundamental research, while attracting substantial outside sponsorship and using a methodology that bridged departmental divides, became increasingly remote from immediate application. The socio-economic model of health relied upon aid for health or welfare projects. Fundamental research required a supportive academic environment. After ten years of struggling in a situation that could not satisfactorily provide either requirement, the School decided to rationalise.

The remit of the ARWP was to review and make recommendations on the administrative, financial and academic machinery of the School. In effect, the Working Party for the first time established parameters for the discipline of tropical medicine as practised at Liverpool by drawing up a 'Mission Statement'.[40] The importance of the Mission Statement lay in its applicability to all departments of the School. The expansion programme begun with the Nuffield Wing in 1966 was not curtailed, but it would be focused. Forthwith expansion would apply to the direction of the LSTM within the discipline. Innovations in application, in teaching and in research had expanded the meaning of tropical medicine. External circumstances provided the School with the opportunity to rationalise while accepting the broadest possible definition.

Council commissioned the ARWP in 1989. After several refusals, with apologies, Sir Arnold Burgen, Master of Darwin College, Cambridge agreed to chair the Working Party.[41] There was some discussion over the need for an external report and the constitution of School staff involved directly with its preparation.[42] Attempts to produce a representative balance among the members of the Working Party resulted in the solicitation of Sir Peter Froggatt, ex-Vice Chancellor of the University of Belfast to act as Vice Chairman.[43] The internal members were Dr David Smith, Dr Harold Townson and Dr Alexander J Trees.

There were three central recommendations of the Report, presented in February 1990. First, a Mission Statement would focus the function and ethos of the School. Second, the 'chief administrative, academic and executive officer of School' would be a full-time Director after open advertisement of the post. Third, the Director would take charge of a single unit. Interdisciplinary groups more appropriately reflecting the strengths of the School would replace the departments. Other recommendations detailed the administrative structure of the School below the Director and the functional relationship with the University as a single unit. Modifications of course management and research agendas were established. New and strengthened research areas were listed as AIDS, nutrition, epidemiology and statistics, and molecular genetics. AIDS and nutrition were commended for their interdisciplinary nature. Epidemiology, statistics and molecular genetics represented methodologies useful to teaching and research projects within the School. Molecular genetics represented a scientific basis for the School and is currently perceived as a dynamic branch of basic research beyond the LSTM.

In this research plan, the LSTM acknowledged the need for tropical medicine to recognise strategically its position within the medical science of the late twentieth century. At the turn of the twentieth century it was necessary for tropical medicine to set itself apart from bacteriology and immunology in order to secure the political support necessary to justify a special institution. At the turn of the twenty-first century, it was more useful to indicate the interrelatedness of the basic science at the School with other disciplines. The emphasis on epidemiology and statistics was welcome. The Department of International Community Health had commented on the constitution of the Working Party. They considered it failed to reflect their interests. Their concern was apparently well founded. No specific recommendation related to health-systems, although the term 'essential' described this research in the text. An interest in health economics as a function of development received commendation. If this became the focus of the School, the LSTM as the LSTM would cease to exist. Equally, reliance upon long-term fundamental research would be incompatible with the ethos at Liverpool, but several policies of basic science research were recommended in the proposals for a balanced institution. The Report reinforced the commitment of the School to improving health in the less developed countries of the tropics and subtropics. In November 1990, a Selection Committee offered the post of Director of the LSTM to the parasitologist, Professor David Molyneux.

## CONCLUSION

'Problems of health and attitudes in the tropics are different from what they were even a decade ago and the pace of development faster. The School's aim to raise the standard of health of the Third World does not change but its approach must be flexible and broad if it is to succeed.'[44] Gilles stood down as Dean in 1983. He closed his final *Annual Report* with what he described as 'personal words' although they were particularly apt for the period 1970 to 1990.

International Community Health moved away more quickly from health as freedom from disease towards the WHO definition of health 'as a complete mental and physical state of well-being'. Their interest in preventative medicine obviously included reference to specific diseases. The prevention of common infectious diseases prevailing in conditions of poverty, filth and ignorance was vital to any programme of health administration. Similarly, skills in organisation and management were important to those intending to run health care delivery systems. Accurate cost/benefit analyses were vital where the limitation of funds was acute. Interest in the education of women and in reproductive health, where a woman is neither sick nor a patient but benefits from good anti-natal care, skilled and hygienic midwives and post-natal help and advice, typifies this argument.

An interest in ethnic communities in Britain notwithstanding, Tropical Paediatrics at Liverpool reinforced a commitment to the tropics when compared with the stance of International Community Health.[45] The department took a deliberate stance, with projects such as PHC and health systems analysis, to ignore geography. The Working Party acknowledged the dichotomy between fundamental research and operational research. Plans for multidisciplinary projects recognised the acceptable breadth of activities of the School included both. The commitment to the tropics (assumed to include sub-tropics) remained unchallenged. The false geography of colonial science remained intact. This chapter reviewed the pre-history of the International Community Health by suggesting that elements in the Department of Tropical Medicine bridged the transition to International Community Health. International Community Health established an identity beyond tropical medicine in the field of development studies of which health is an important element. Development and internationalism presented a challenge for the future.

NOTES

[1] Wallace Peters 1975–1978, Herbert Gilles 1978–1983, William MacDonald 1983–1988, Ralph Hendrickse 1988–1991.

[2] TM/3/0111/1, Report to the Chairman of the Council of the Working Group into the role of Council members and the working of the Council, February 1992.

[3] B G Maegraith, *One world*, London: Athlone, 1973.

[4] In 1971, his booklet, *Imported diseases in Europe*, was reissued along with a German translation.

[5] B G Maegraith, 'Malaria risk to travellers', Letter to the editor, *BMJ*, i, 1973, 175.

[6] The Merchant Bank of Baring Brothers gave £40,000 over five years.

[7] *51st Annual Report of the LSTM, 1949–1950*, p. 13.

[8] N R E Fendall, 'The medical assistant in Africa, *Journal of Tropical Medicine and Hygiene*', LXXI, 1968, 83–95.

[9] Dr Edward Ensor of the Department of Tropical Community Health died unexpectedly. The School moaned his loss. He was the last of the staff of the School to carry a military rank. As far as staffing of the LSTM was concerned, the once close association of tropical medicine with the armed forces was over. The frequent occurrence of RAMC (retired) or IMS (retired) after the names at the front of the *Annual Report* had passed into history. The same would eventually be the case with respect to ex-CMS officers.

[10] TM/4/2/15.B, Executive Management Committee, 6 December 1971.

[11] In 1974, Gilles and the Department of Tropical Medicine ran a new short course in tropical medicine for nurses unable to study for the CTCMH.

[12] TM/4/2/15.B, Executive Management Committee, 18 September 1972.

[13] *73rd Annual Report of the LSTM, 1971–1972*, p. 85.

[14] A J Radford, 'Family planning and population policy in Papua New Guinea', *Papua New Guinea Medical Journal*, 15, 1972, 131–135.

[15] N R E Fendall, 'The use of medical assistants for improving health services Document 1, suggested guidelines for promoting the use of medical assistants', WHO working paper WHO/EDUC/73.163; *idem*, 'The use of medical assistants for improving health services Document 2, suggested guidelines for planning, implementation and evaluating a programme for the training and use of medical assistants', WHO working paper WHO/EDUC/73.164.

[16] Fendall was appointed a government representative to the UNICEF Executive Board meeting, May 1975.

[17] TM/4/2/15.B, Executive Management Committee, 15 May 1972, Fendall: Report on a visit to Nigeria and Geneva, 15–29 April 1972.

[18] N R E Fendall, 'Concepts in organisation of family planning programmes in developing countries', *ATMP*, 67, 1973, 251–259; TM4/2/15.B, Executive Management Committee, 19 September 1977, *idem*, Report on a consultancy for UNFPA in Pakistan, TM4/2/15.B, Executive Management Committee, 19 September 1977.

[19] TM4/2/15.B, Executive Management Committee, 19 March 1973.

[20] TM3/1.17b, Council, 18 June 1973.

[21] TM4/2/15.B, Executive Management Committee, 21 April 1975.

[22] TM3/1.17b, Council, 19 May 1975.

[23] TM4/2/15.B, Executive Management Committee, 20 June 1977

[24] TM4/2/15.B, Executive Management Committee, 21 November 1977.

[25] The diseases were malaria, onchocerciasis, trypanosomiasis, schistosomiasis, filariasis, leishmaniasis and leprosy. They were chosen as those most likely to respond to immunological techniques being applied with new vigour to tropical diseases, interview with Dr Louis Molineaux, 21 July 1998, recorded by H J Power.

[26] The name changed quickly to the less militaristic 'Scientific Working Groups'.

[27] H Townson, 'Studies of enzymes in the *Simulium damnosum* complex and *Aedes scutellaris* group', Working paper for WHO species complexes in vectors of disease with special reference on *Simulium damnosum* and malaria vectors, Geneva: 1976. *WHO Cyclostyled Report* VBC/SC/76.21; *idem*, S E O Meredith & K Thomas, 'Studies of enzymes in the *Aedes scutellaris* group', *TRSTMH*, 71, 1977, 110; *idem*, 'Enzyme differences between species of the *Simulium damnosum* complex', ibid., 111.

[28] R Hankins, 'Between tropical disease and veterinary medicine: the development of immunological studies of parasitism, 1900–1970', PhD thesis, University of Manchester, 1998.

[29] *75th Annual Report of the LSTM, 1973–1974*, p. 97.

[30] W Peters, M L Chance, M J Mutinga, J M Ngoka & L F Schnur, 'The identification of human *Leishmania* from Kenya', *ATMP*, 71, 1977, 501–502.

[31] ELISA, enzyme-linked immunosorbent assay.

[32] In 1983, following the death of Reid the name of the unit was changed to the Alistair Reid Venom Research Unit in his memory.

[33] The application was co-ordinated with the LSHTM, which received an equal sum.

[34] Personal Communication, Sir Ian MacGregor, 1992.

[35] *77th Annual Report of the LSTM, 1975–1976*, p. 28.

[36] A J Radford, 'Community health training for medical students and interns in Papua New Guinea: wards without walls', *Proceedings of a symposium on health services in developing countries*, 1974.

[37] TM/8/C.12, Space Committee.

[38] TM4/0026/1, Professional Committee, 23 March 1988.

[39] TM4/0026/1, Professional Committee, 4 December 1990.

[40] 'As a centre of excellence, the LSTM, through the creation of effective links with governments, organisations and institutions and by responding to the health needs of communities aims to promote improved health, particularly for peoples of the less developed countries in the tropics and sub-tropics by 1. Providing and promoting high-quality education and training; 2. Conducting first-class research and disseminating the results of that research; 3. Developing systems and technologies for health care and assisting in their transfer and management; 4. Providing appropriate consulting services. In fulfilling this mission the School also provides a clinical service of acknowledged excellence.'

[41] TM4/0058/, Executive Management Committee, 8 November 1988.

[42] TM4/0026/1, Professional Committee, 7 March 1988.

[43] TM4/0026/1, Professional Committee, 14 November 1988.

[44] *84th Annual Report of the LSTM, 1982–1983*, p. 23.

[45] For instance, Dr Michael Chan was appointed Honorary Consultant to the Chinese Community Services in the late 1970s.

# CONCLUSION: THE PAST AND FUTURE OF TROPICAL MEDICINE AT LIVERPOOL

Tropical medicine at Liverpool will endure into the next century. The institution founded in 1898 continues its teaching and research activities and the staff continue advising governments, national and international agencies and individual travellers about health and disease in the tropics. Increasingly the collective expertise at the School applies to disadvantaged people around the world whose need for basic health care relates to their low socio-economic status and marginal position in society. The tenacity of the School, its adaptability, albeit reluctantly on occasion, have held together a disparate set of applied and fundamental subjects under the title of tropical medicine. The School has retained its position as a premier institution in this field and performed this role responsibly. The Academic Review established transparent policies for the future management of the School and its intellectual direction. Future historians will decide upon the success or otherwise of this decision.

The foundation of the two Schools largely created the academic discipline of tropical medicine in Britain. As others have shown, the discipline was a combination of basic science and an enthusiasm to apply medicine overseas to assist development of the tropical colonies. Funds for the Liverpool School came from the self-interested commercial community, which had a tradition of supporting civic projects. In its early years, the Liverpool School lacked a clear direction. The teaching served an important role in winning recognition from the CO, but thereafter it was a perfunctory exercise. There were some demands from the sponsors, particularly Alfred Lewis Jones, but many of his ideas for the School did not mature. Although highly skilled, many of the early staff were not experts in the field. However, they were an innovative and excited group, dedicated to generating new knowledge. Private funding and personal ambition involved the School in various levels of practical sanitary work overseas, but this was only one facet of the potential output from Liverpool. The expeditions, laboratory research and sanitation reinforced the commitment of the discipline to the parasite-vector model. The adoption of this model served to distinguish tropical medicine from other disciplines concerned with micro-organisms or their effects on the body. Yet, the laboratory research also indicated that in reality, there were similarities of approach, particularly with respect to research on the host-parasite relationship.

Continuity of research was difficult in the first ten years at Liverpool. The utility of the expeditions interrupted work at home. Financial constraints on the physical establishment of the School were a hindrance. Access to clinical material was fraught because of the tensions between the RSH and the LSTM. The hurried foundation of the School required a longer period of consolidation to determine priorities and policies. The first period of the School, to the outbreak of World War I, showed how a subject in the service of empire also established its own internal priorities in addition to meeting the immediate economic development of the colonial territories.

The School reopened after the war in new laboratories. Clinical facilities were conveniently located in the LRI next door. Work on the parasite-vector model consolidated existing knowledge of tropical medicine. However, prioritising the array of activities from the pre-war period strengthened the identity of the discipline at Liverpool. In Manáos, Brazil and Freetown, Sierra Leone, the School established research laboratories. The fortunes of the Freetown laboratory were intimately associated with the difficulties facing the School during the depression. The laboratory institutionalised the functions of the research expeditions. It addition to research on the parasite-vector model it also developed fundamental research on the host-parasite relationship. The laboratory suffered from core underfunding, the vagaries of the inter-war colonial economy and the constraints of the racist policies of the WAMS. However, it highlighted the need for the LTSM to be involved with wider networks to function effectively. The need for funding dominated the research profile. The staff showed innovation and dedication, but projects such as the immunity investigation could only function with outside assistance. The experience of the laboratory broadened the interests of the LSTM, but it could not capitalise upon the results.

In Liverpool, the leadership of Warrington Yorke presented the first clear policy for the LSTM. The interest of the MRC rewarded his determination to link the School to current aspects of medical science beyond tropical medicine. The production of British drugs for use in the tropics was of considerable medical and economic significance. Yorke tempered the utilitarian function of testing chemical compounds with funding and facilities for basic research. The period to the end of World War II harked back to the days of the expeditions, although permanent laboratories proved more difficult to control and maintain. It also looked forward to a clear direction for the School in the field of basic science research. The experience of the laboratories in Freetown and Liverpool indicated the School could work more efficiently in a network of other interested parties. If the School remained committed to work overseas, connections with the colonial governments and the CO were imperative while Britain retained the empire. Equally, the LSTM had to engage with trends in current medical science to stay at the forefront of the discipline. The School had become a research institution, strengthening its academic standing but effectively abandoning its own attempts to apply research in the tropics.

The School emerged from World War II under new leadership. Brian Maegraith's impact on the School lasted for forty-four years. His distinctive views and enormous energy overturned Yorke's slow orientation of the LSTM. Maegraith had a particular methodology for his own research. He was equally clear on the functions of the various subjects within the discipline. In addition to the internal reorganisation of the School and hence the discipline, he perceived a need to change the external image of the School. Maegraith's arrival coincided with a particularly difficult period at Liverpool. A new Labour Government committed Britain to decolonisation. New international organisations concerned with health and welfare dwarfed the LSTM. Maegraith acknowledged the necessity to continue an association with colonial medical policies and the training of CMS officers, but considered it equally essential that the School function as an independent institution.

Maegraith discontinued the pursuit of chemotherapy. He considered the routine testing of drugs an inappropriate objective for a school of tropical medicine. He concentrated the efforts of the Department of Tropical Medicine on fundamental research in the pathophysiology of tropical diseases, particularly malaria. He created a research school, staffed by research students including a number of Thais in the 1950s, 1960s and 1970s. Staff working in parasitology and entomology also concentrated on fundamental research. Parastiology in particular developed a strong identity under William Kershaw. He did not share Maegraith's view that this subject should be constrained to concentrate on issues relevant to tropical medicine. This prioritisation of research illustrates the desire to impose a clear definition on the function of the School and the content of the academic discipline of tropical medicine.

The concentration on research had changed the identity of the School. Maegraith next sought to revitalise the application of the work of the LSTM. In the absence of opportunities to work continually overseas, the School found alternatives means. International organisations such as the WHO and national governments chose to assist developing countries by providing experts for specific time-limited projects. Initially, the LSTM provided expertise for the CO. However, by the 1950s the WHO regularly requested members of staff for their commissions and projects. Consultancies provided valuable opportunities for School staff to travel and make contacts with health professionals in a number of developing countries. These formal and informal contacts served to inform the School on the health needs of the developing countries. The School considered how it could best meet these needs on an independent basis.

In contrast to the period before World War II, after 1945, teaching at the LSTM influenced the shape of the School and the discipline of tropical medicine. In 1946, an integrated DTMH replaced the DTM and DTH. The School actively encouraged overseas students to take the DTMH. It repackaged the course as a reorientation for doctors wishing to practice in the tropics, including those born and educated there, rather than as a specific training for CMS officers. The international alumni applied tropical medicine as practised from Liverpool. Education now served to increase the presence of the School overseas.

In addition to teaching in Liverpool, the School became involved with developing medical education in the tropics. Their involvement took a number of different forms. At the LSTM, they created a special post of Lecturer-at-Large and immediately seconded Herbert Gilles to the University of Ibadan, Nigeria. In Ghana, they offered expert advice and training programmes at the School for Ghanaian technical and professional staff. The Faculty of Tropical Medicine at the Mahidol University, Bangkok recreated the School in Thailand. These three initiatives reproduced overseas the style and function of tropical medicine in Liverpool. The School could not directly influence the practice of tropical medicine overseas, but it could shape the development of curricula and institutions. In the early 1960s, the Ministry of Overseas Development adopted a policy Maegraith had helped to formulate to provide Technical Assistance Lecturers in tropical medicine resembling the Lecturer-at-Large. The experience of the School in education overseas informed the creation of these appointments. The academic functions of the School increasingly resembled those of ordinary university departments. The overseas interests provided a separate identity. The discipline encompassed academic research pursued for its own sake and out-reach policies with a more direct and practical application.

Out-reach policies in the 1950s confirmed the commitment of the LSTM to the tropics. This should not appear particularly surprising given the title 'tropical medicine'. However, with the breakdown of empire, the redesignation of the world as developed and developing relied upon socio-economic distinctions that replaced the former geo-political boundaries. In this context the title looked anachronistic and required active defence. In 1969, the School appointed a senior lecturer in Tropical Paediatrics and Child Health. A full department followed the successful launch of the DTCH. The interest in infant and child health, later extended to include maternal welfare, broadened the scope of tropical medicine at Liverpool. Colonial health policies characteristically neglected child health, particularly in relation to common infectious diseases and malnutrition. The School sought to redress this omission within the discipline and improve paediatric practice in the tropics. The use of local Liverpool hospitals for in-service training took advantage of a general interest among paediatricians in the practice of medicine in the tropics. An interest in common problems associated with bottle rather than breast-feeding and diseases such as measles provided a common link between the practice of medicine in and out of tropics. Nevertheless, paediatrics at the LSTM maintained the characteristics of the discipline. A focus on the effects of environmental factors associated with developing countries, such as the lack of adequate and appropriate nutrition augmented investigations of the host-parasite relationship. The DTCH served the same function as other teaching programmes, strengthening the virtual presence of the School in the tropics and subtropics when students returned home and applied their training.

Despite the innovations in paediatrics, the socio-economic definition of health issued a renewed challenge to tropical medicine. In the early 1970s, this model questioned the approach of the discipline as the best means for teaching and advising on the health of disadvantaged people. In microcosm in the later 1970s and 1980s, the teaching and operational research of the Department of International Community Health challenged other departments in the School to consider their function. In 1989, pressurised by successive reductions in the higher education budget and cuts in funding for overseas aid, the LSTM instigated a thorough review process. This investigated a disadvantageous relationship with the University and the internal organisation of the School. It assessed the administrative infrastructure and the future intellectual direction at Liverpool. This first comprehensive review looked at the School as a whole and rationalised its programme towards specific goals rather than merely commending a disparity of interests as a virtue. Accepting the need to consider the health of disadvantaged people in the developed world, the School has chosen not to discard its legacy and remains committed to the developing countries of the tropics.

The final innovation of the School has been the acceptance that the discipline of tropical medicine was beyond the scope of one institution. Previously the School accepted limits in its ability to apply tropical medicine. However, circumscribing its activities but admitting they still formed part of the discipline proved unacceptable. With this change of attitude, the School acknowledged the inherent interdisciplinary nature of tropical medicine. As the composite elements of tropical medicine had developed and a new socio-economic definition of health evolved, the artificial discipline became unbounded and hence unmanageable. There is room for two Schools of Tropical Medicine in Britain because they have different interests and offer different facilities. The field is so vast, in the disciplines it must encompass and the extent of the problems it faces, that both Schools are only a contribution to a much larger whole.

The academic discipline of tropical medicine at Liverpool has changed because the School has realised the vastness of the problem lies not in practitioner/patient ratios, hospital beds or the annual number of scientific publications. An understanding of the inextricable links between the interdisciplinary nature of the research and practice of medicine among disadvantaged people in the tropics and the international politics of social and economic development dwarfs these otherwise important criteria. Tropical medicine is not a neutral activity but functions as part of the troubled agenda of international development policy. The LSTM has realised this over the period of a hundred years of colonial and post-colonial history. With this knowledge it should be considerably better equipped for the next one hundred years.

# APPENDIX

The following tables present the general details, finance, motivation and output of the thirty-two School expeditions and six additional commissioned expeditions in terms of associated laboratory research and publications in the School's own series. The following abbreviations apply to the tables below.

| | |
|---|---|
| *ATMP* | *Annals of Tropical Medicine and Parasitology* |
| BCA | British Central Africa |
| *BER* | *Bulletin of Entomological Research* |
| BWF | Blackwater Fever |
| CO | Colonial Office (UK) |
| Tryps | Trypanosomiasis |
| *TYLR* | *Thompson Yates Laboratory Reports* |
| WAYFC | West Africa Yellow Fever Commission |
| Y Fever | Yellow Fever |
| *YFBB* | *Yellow Fever Bureau Bulletin* |

LSTM Expeditions, 1899–1904, General.

| | *Out* | *Return* | *Destination* | *Title* | *Parties* |
|---|---|---|---|---|---|
| 1 | 07/99 | 12/99 | Sierra Leone | Malarial | R Ross, H Annett |
| | | | | | E Austen, Van Neck |
| 2 | 1899 | 12/01 | Gold Coast | Malarial | R Fielding-Ould |
| 3 | 03/00 | 12/01 | Nigeria | Malarial | H Annett, J Dutton, |
| | | | | | J Elliot |
| 4 | 06/00 | 06/01 | Cuba & | Y Fever | H Durham, |
| | | | Brazil | | W Myers |
| 5 | 15/06/01 | 11/10/02 | Sierra Leone | Sanitation | R Ross, M Taylor |
| 6 | 21/09/01 | | Gambia | Tryps | J Dutton |
| 7 | 12/11/01 | | Gold Coast | Malarial | C Balfour Stewart |
| 8 | 22/02/02 | | Sierra Leone | Sanitation | R Ross |
| 9 | 11/09/02 | | Ismailia | Malarial | R Ross, |
| | | | | | Sir W MacGregor |
| 10 | 21/09/02 | | Gambia & | Tryps | J Dutton, |
| | | | Senegal | | J Todd |
| 11 | 11/10/02 | 03/03 | Gold Coast | Sanitation | M Taylor |
| 12 | 23/09/03 | | Congo | Tryps | J Dutton, J Todd, |
| | | | | | C Christy |
| *1 | 07/02/04 | | Ismailia | | R Boyce |
| *2 | 09/04 | | Panama Canal | | R Ross |
| 13 | 14/11/04 | | Gambia & | | R Boyce, A Evans, |
| | | | Sierra Leone | | H Clarke |
| 14 | 31/12/04 | | Gold Coast | | G Giles, |
| | | | | | R McConnell |

* Refers to special, commissioned expeditions.

LSTM Expeditions, 1899–1904, Finance and Motives.

| | Sponsored | Self-funded | Outside-funded | Motivation |
|---|---|---|---|---|
| 1 | Jones & BMA | | | Ross |
| 2 | Free passages | ✓ | | 1 continued |
| 3 | Free passages | ✓ | | |
| 4 | Free passages | ✓ | | |
| 5 | Private donation | ✓ | | |
| 6 | | ✓ | | |
| 7 | | ✓ | | |
| 8 | | ✓ | | |
| 9 | Suez Canal Co. | ✓ | | Request Suez Canal Co. |
| 10 | | ✓ | | |
| 11 | | ✓ | | 5 continued |
| 12 | Congo Free State | ✓ | | Request King of the Belgians |
| *1 | Suez Canal Co. | ✓ | | Request Suez Canal Co |
| *2 | Panama Canal Co. | | | Request Panama Canal Co. |
| 13 | Subscriptions | | ✓ | Sir W Macgregor Fund |
| 14 | Subscriptions | | ✓ | Sir W Macgregor Fund |

* Refers to special, commissioned expeditions.

LSTM Expeditions, 1899–1904, Output.

|  | Subjects studied | Linked research | School publications |
|---|---|---|---|
| **1** | Malaria | | *Memoir* 1, 2, Instructions |
| **2** | Malaria | | *Memoir* 2 |
| **3** | Malaria | | *Memoir* 3 Part 1 |
| **4** | Y Fever | | *Memoir* 7 |
| **5** | Malaria | | *Memoir* 5, 6 |
| **6** | Malaria, Tryps | ✓ | *Memoir* 10, *TYLR* 4 (2) |
| **7** | Malaria | | |
| **8** | Malaria | | |
| **9** | Malaria | | *Memoir* 9 |
| **10** | Tryps | ✓ | *Memoir* 11, *ATMP* 1 |
| **11** | Sanitation | | *Memoir* 8 |
| **12** | Tryps | ✓ | *Memoir* 8, 13, 16, 18, 20, 21 |
| ***1** | Malaria | | *Memoir* 12, *ATMP* 5 |
| ***2** | Entomology | | *BER* 2 |
| **13** | Malaria | | *Memoir* 14 |
| **14** | Malaria | | *Memoir* 15 |

* Refers to special, commissioned expeditions.

LSTM Expeditions, 1905–1914, General.

| | *Out* | *Return* | *Destination* | *Title* | *Parties* |
|---|---|---|---|---|---|
| **15** | 04/05 | 03/09 | Amazon | Y Fever | H Thomas |
| | | | | | A Breinl |
| **16** | 08/05 | | New Orleans | Y Fever | R Boyce |
| | | | & Honduras | | |
| **17** | 20/05/05 | | Greece | Malarial | R Ross |
| **18** | 05/05/07 | | Rhodesia & | Sleeping | A Kinghorn |
| | | | BCA | sickness | R Montgomery |
| **19** | 14/08/07 | | Nyasaland | BWF | J Barratt |
| | | | | | W Yorke |
| **20** | 10/07 | | Mauritius | | R Ross |
| **21** | 14/11/08 | | Jamaica | | R Newstead, W |
| | | | | | Prout, A Hanley |
| **22** | 03/09 | | Barbados | | R Boyce |
| **23** | 11/09 | | Egypt | | J Stephens |
| **24** | 25/06/10 | | Malta | | R Newstead |
| **25** | 06/10 | 09/10 | Sierra Leone | | R Boyce |
| | | | & Gold | | |
| | | | Coast | | |
| **26** | 05/10 | | Brazil | | H Thomas |
| **27** | 21/01/11 | 06/11 | Gambia | Sanitation | J Todd |
| | | | | | S Wolbach |
| **\*3** | 09/06/11 | 11/11/11 | Nyasaland | | R Newstead |
| **\*4** | 08/11 | 10/12 | Rhodesia | | W Yorke |
| **28** | 12/11 | | Yucatan | Y Fever | H Seidelin |
| **29** | 26/09/12 | | Panama | | D Thomson |
| **30** | 18/12/12 | | Jamaica | Vomiting | H Seidelin |
| | | | | sickness | |
| **\*5** | 01/13 | 04/13 | Cyprus | | R Ross |
| **31** | 07/13 | | Khartoum | | H Fantham |
| **\*6** | 10/13 | | West Africa | | H Seidelin |
| **32** | 11/14 | | Sierra Leone | | W Yorke |
| | | | | | D Blacklock |

\* Refers to special, commissioned expeditions.

LSTM Expeditions, 1905–1914, Finance and Motives.

| | Sponsored | Self-funded | Outside-funded | Motivation |
|---|---|---|---|---|
| 15 | Subscriptions | | | |
| 16 | | | | CO & US Medical authorities |
| 17 | | ✓ | | Lake Copais Co. |
| 18 | | | | |
| 19 | Subscriptions | | | |
| 20 | | | | Request CO |
| 21 | Subscriptions | | | |
| 22 | | | | |
| 23 | | | | |
| 24 | Government grant | | | |
| 25 | | | | |
| 26 | | | | |
| 27 | | | | |
| *3 | Colonial Office | ✓ | | Request CO |
| *4 | | | | Request British South Africa Co. |
| 28 | Subscriptions | | ✓ | Y Fever Bureau |
| 29 | | | | |
| 30 | | ✓ | | |
| *5 | | | | Request CO |
| 31 | | ✓ | | |
| *6 | | | | West African Y Fever Commission |
| 32 | | ✓ | | |

* Refers to special, commissioned expeditions.

LSTM Expeditions, 1905–1914, Output.

| | Subjects studied | Linked research | School publications |
|---|---|---|---|
| **15** | Y Fever | | *ATMP* 4 |
| **16** | Y Fever | | *Memoir* 19 |
| **17** | Malaria | | *JTMH, Lancet* |
| **18** | Sleeping sickness | | *ATMP* 2, 3 |
| **19** | Blackwater fever | ✓ | *ATMP* 3 |
| **20** | Malaria | | Report |
| **21** | Entomology | | *ATMP* 3 |
| **22** | Mosquito sanitation | | *Health Progress in the West Indies* |
| **23** | Helminthology | | *ATMP* 2 |
| **24** | Phlebotomus | | *ATMP* 5 |
| **25** | Y Fever | | *ATMP* 5 |
| **26** | | | |
| **27** | Sleeping sickness | | *ATMP* 5, 8 |
| ***3** | Sleeping sickness | | *ATMP* 6 |
| ***4** | Sleeping sickness | ✓ | *ATMP* 6, 7 |
| **28** | Y Fever | ✓ | *ATMP* 6, *YFBB* 2 |
| **29** | Malaria | | *ATMP* 7 |
| **30** | Vomiting sickness | | *ATMP* 7, *YFBB* 2,3 |
| ***5** | Malaria | | *PRSM* 7 |
| **31** | | | |
| ***6** | Y Fever | ✓ | *YFBB* Sup 2, *YFBB* 3 |
| **32** | Sleeping sickness, ankylostomiasis | | *ATMP* 9, 11 |

\* Refers to special, commissioned expeditions.

# NOTE ON SOURCES

The archives of the LSTM (prefix TM/), housed in the Sydney Jones Library of the University of Liverpool, have been the major source for this history. The collection is a rich combination of administrative, biographical, and scientific papers. There is an extensive newspaper cutting collection and a large amount of photographic material. The former librarian, Miss Gladys Phillips, amassed much of the collection during her period of office. She produced an unpublished typescript history, which continued the *Historical Record* up to World War II. In the preparation of this, and in response to enquiries, she corresponded with various former members of staff and their families to increase the scope of the collection. She also collected material on the history of the School. Unfortunately her fascination with famous names rather skewed her retention policies and broke up valuable complete collections. The majority of the material in the collection has remained unused following its inclusion in the archives, until the preparation of this history. The Library of the LSTM has an extensive journal and monograph collection dating from the late nineteenth century onwards.

Other related records such as the papers of the Royal Southern Hospital (prefix LRO 614 SOU) and Liverpool Royal Infirmary (prefix LRO 614 INF) are housed at the Liverpool Record Office.

The papers of the MRC (now transferred to the Public Record Office at Kew, although originally consulted at the MRC in Portland Place) were valuable, particularly with reference to chemotherapy.

Formal and informal oral histories with former members of staff and their families; students, particularly the Thai students, many of whom were later connected with the Faculty of Tropical Medicine in Bangkok; and others, who presented external views of the LSTM, have supplemented the existing archival sources.

Professor Ralph Hendrickse kindly gave me access to his personal papers relating to the  senior lectureship and Department of Tropical Paediatrics and Child Health (prefix RGH).

## INTERVIEWEES

Professor Nath Bhamaraprarati, 25 January 1995

Dr Prakob Boonthai, 23 January 1995

Mr Joseph Brady, 11 April 1994

Dr Robin Broadhead, 22 September 1994

Dr Panorchit Chariya, 17 January 1995

Professor Tan Chongsuphajaisddhi, 9 & 10 January 1995

Professor Herbert Gilles, 14 November 1994

Professor Chamlong Harinasuta, 17 January 1995

Professor Kunying Tranakchit Harinasuta, 9 & 10 January 1995

Dr Nibha Jaroonvesama, 20 January 1995

Professor Migasena, 13 January 1995

Dr Sricharoen Migasena, 11 January 1995

Dr Louis Molineaux, 21 July 1998

Dr Walter Ormerod, 22 April 1993

Dr Katcharinee Paramand, 31 January 1995

Professor Santasiri Sornmani, 13 January 1995

Dr Pratin Visniyourith, 17 January 1995

Dr George Watt, 18 January 1995

Dr Nicholas White, 11 & 26 January 1995

## BIBLIOGRAPHY

Acheson R, 'The British Diploma in Public Health: birth and adolescence', E Fee & R M Acheson (eds), *A history of education in public health: health that mocks the doctors' rules*, Oxford: OUP, 1991, pp. 44–82.

Adebayo A G, 'The production and export of hides and skins in colonial northern Nigeria, 1900–1945', *Journal of African History*, 33, 1992, 273–300.

Adeniyi A, Hendrickse R G & Houba V, 'Nephrotic syndrome (malarial) in Nigerian children – clinical and immunochemical correlative studies', *Proceedings of the second International Symposium of Paediatric Nephrology*, Paris, 1971.

Adler S, 'The trypanocidal effect of phenylglycine amido arsenate of sodium on *T. brucei* in rats and *T. rhodesiense* in mice', *ATMP*, 15, 1921, 427–432.

—— 'Note on bismuth as a trypanocide', *ATMP*, 15, 1921, 433.

—— 'Malaria in a chimpanzee in Sierra Leone', *ATMP*, 17, 1923, 13–18.

Ali S N, 'Studies on the metabolism of the malaria parasite and the action on antimalarial compounds', PhD thesis, University of Liverpool, 1969.

Allen T & Thomas A (eds), *Poverty and development in the 1990s*, Oxford: OUP, 1992.

Allmand D, 'LSTM scientific record', *ATMP*, 15, 1921, 1–48.

AMRU, 'Determination of plasma mepacrine: a note on the anticoagulant', *Lancet*, 249, 1945, 144–145.

—— 'Factors affecting the excretion of mepacrine in the urine', *ATMP*, 39, 1945, 53–60.

—— 'Mepacrine in animal tissues', *ATMP*, 40, 1946, 174–180.

Anderson W, 'Immunities of empire: race, disease and the new tropical medicine 1900-1920', *BHM*, 70, 1996, 94–118.

Annett H E & Breinl A, 'Short note on the mechanism of haemolysis in *Piroplasmosis canis*', *ATMP*, 2, 1909, 383–385.

*Annual Reports of the LSTM* (1899–1997).

*Annual Reports of the MRC*, London: HMSO (1926–1937).

Arnold D (ed), *Imperial medicine and indigenous societies*, Manchester: MUP, 1988.

—— *Colonising the body: state medicine and epidemic disease in nineteenth-century India*, Berkeley: University of California Press, 1993.

—— (ed), *Warm climates and Western medicine: the emergence of tropical medicine 1500–1900*, Amsterdam: Rodopi, 1996.

Beer J J, 'Coal-tar dye manufacture and the origins of the modern industrial research lab', *Isis*, 49, 1958, 123–131.

Bell H, 'Medical research and medical practice in the Anglo-Egyptian Sudan', DPhil thesis, University of Oxford, 1996.

Beinart J, 'The inner world of imperial sickness: the MRC and research in tropical medicine', J Austoker & L Bryder (eds), *Historical perspectives on the role of the MRC*, Oxford: OUP, 1989, pp. 109–136.

—— 'Darkly through a lens. Changing perceptions of the African child in sickness and health 1900-1945', R Cooter (ed), *In the name of the child: health and welfare, 1880-1940*, London: Routledge, 1992, pp. 220–243.

Besredka A, *Local immunization: specific dressings*, London, 1927.

Black M, *The children and the nations: the story of UNICEF*, New York: UNICEF, 1986.

Blacklock D B, 'Report of an investigation into the prevalence and transmission of human schistosomiasis in Sierra Leone', *Annual Report of the Medical Department of Sierra Leone*, 1923.

—— & Adler S, 'A malaria parasite of the chimpanzee', *ATMP*, 18, 1924, 1–2.

Blacklock D B & Thompson M G, 'A study of the Tumbu fly *Cordylobia anthropophaga* Grunberg in Sierra Leone', *ATMP*, 1923, 17, 444–501.

Blacklock D B, 'Report on the effects of bush clearance in reducing *G. palpalis* in the Cape Lighthouse Peninsula', *Annual Report of the Medical Department of Sierra Leone*, 1923.

Blacklock D B & Gordon R M, 'Malaria parasites in the placental blood', *ATMP*, 19, 1925, 37–45.

—— 'Malaria infection as it occurs in late pregnancy: its relationship to labour and early infancy', *ATMP*, 19, 1925, 327–363.

Blacklock D B, 'The development of *Onchocerca volvulus*, in *Simulium damnosum*', *ATMP*, 20, 1926, 1–48.

—— & Evans A M, 'Breeding places of Anopheline mosquitoes in and around Freetown, Sierra Leone', *ATMP*, 20, 1926, 59–84.

—— 'The further development of *Onchocerca volvulus* (Leuckart) (1892) in *Simulium damnosum* Theo', *ATMP*, 20, 1926, 203–218.

—— & Gordon R M, 'The experimental production of immunity against metazoan parasites and an investigation of its nature', *ATMP*, 21, 1927, 181–224.

—— 'The experimental production of immunity against metazoan parasites and an investigation of its nature', *Lancet*, i, 1927, 923–925.

Blacklock D B, *An empire problem: the house and the village in the tropics*, Liverpool: LUP, 1932.

Boyce R, Ross R & Sherrington C, 'The history of the discovery of trypanosomes in man', *Lancet*, i, 1903, 509–513.

Boyce R, *Mosquito or man? The conquest of the tropical world*, London: Murray, 1909.

—— *Health progress and administration in the West Indies*, London: Murray, 1910.

—— *Yellow fever and its prevention: a manual for medical students and practitioners*, London: Murray, 1911.

Breinl A & Kinghorn A, 'Note on a new *Spirochaeta* found in a mouse', *Memoir*, 21, 1906, 1–52.

Brown C W, 'Historical notes on Freetown Harbour', *Sierra Leone Studies*, 20, 1936, 96–122.

Bulmer M, 'Mobilising social knowledge for social welfare: intermediary institutions in the political systems of the United States and Great Britain between the First and Second World Wars', P Weindling (ed), *International health organizations and movements, 1918–1939*, Cambridge: CUP, 1995, pp. 305–325.

Butler S V F, 'A transformation in training: the formation of University medical faculties in Manchester, Leeds and Liverpool, 1870–84', *Medical History*, 30, 1986, 115–132.

Bynum W F, 'Chemical structure and pharmacological action: a chapter in the history of nineteenth-century molecular pharmacology', *BHM*, 44, 1970, 518–538.

—— 'An experiment that failed: malaria control at Mian Mir', W F Bynum & B Fantini (eds), *Malaria and ecosystems: historical aspects, Parassitologia*, 36, 1994, 107–120.

Carter H F, 'Remarks on the spirocheates occurring in the faeces of dysenteric patients', *ATMP*, 10, 1916–1917, 391–396.

Carter H F, Mackinnon D L, Matthews M A & Malins Smith A, 'The protozoal findings in 910 cases of dysentery examined at the LSTM from May to September 1916', *ATMP*, 10, 1916–1917, 411–426.

Carter H F & Matthews R J, 'The value of concentrating the cysts of protozoal parasites in examining the stools of dysenteric patients for pathogenic entamoebae', *ATMP*, 11, 1917, 195–204.

—— & Stephens J W W, 'Protozoal investigation of cases of dysentery conducted at the LSTM, Second report', *ATMP*, 11, 1917, 27–68.

Chernin E, 'Sir Ronald Ross, malaria and the rewards of research', *Medical History*, 32, 1988, 119–141.

—— 'The early British and American journals of tropical medicine and hygiene: an informal survey', *Medical History*, 36, 1992, 70–83.

—— 'Sir Patrick Manson: physician to the Colonial Office, 1897-1992', *Medical History*, 36, 1992, 320–331.

Christophers S R & Newstead R, 'On a new pathogenic louse which acts as the intermediary host of a new haemogregarine in the blood of an Indian field-rat (*Jerbellus indicus*)', *Thompson Yates Laboratory Reports*, 7, 1906, 1–6.

Cohen of Birkenhead, 'The Liverpool Medical School and its physicians 1642–1934', *Medical History*, 16, 1972, 310–320.

Colombo Plan, *Colombo plan for co-operative economic development in South and South-East Asia*, London: HMSO, 1950.

—— *The Colombo technical co-operation scheme*, London: HMSO, 1954.

—— *Brain drain: country papers, the working paper and the report of the special topic committee of the Colombo Plan*, Colombo: The Colombo Plan, 1972.

Colonial Office, *Post-war training for the colonial service. Report of a committee appointed by the Secretary of State for the Colonies*, London: HMSO, 1946.

—— *Appointments in His Majesty's Colonial Service*, London: HMSO, 1950.

—— *Service with overseas governments*, London: HMSO, 1960.

Cook G C, *From the Greenwich hulks to old St Pancras: a history of tropical disease in London*, London: Athlone, 1992.

—— 'Tropical sprue', F E G Cox (ed), *The Wellcome Trust illustrated history of tropical diseases*, London: Wellcome Trust, 1996, pp. 356–369.

—— 'Dr Patrick Manson's leading opposition in the establishment of the LSTM: Curnow, Anderson and Turner', *Journal of Medical Biography*, 3, 1995, 170–177.

—— (ed), *Manson's Tropical Diseases*, London: W B Saunders, 1996.

Cox F E G (ed), *Illustrated history of tropical diseases*, London: Wellcome Trust, 1996.

Craddock S, *Retired except on demand: the life of Dr Cicely Williams*, Oxford: Green College, 1983.

Creech Jones A, *Labour's colonial policy*, London, 1947.

Cueto M (ed), *Missionaries of science: the Rockefeller Foundation and Latin America*, Bloomington: Indiana University Press, 1994.

Cunningham A & Andrews B (eds), *Western medicine as contested knowledge*, Manchester: MUP, 1997.

Curtin, P, 'Medical knowledge and urban planning in tropical Africa', *American Historical Review*, 90, 1985, 594–613.

—— *Death by migration: Europe's encounter with the tropical world in the nineteenth century*, New York: CUP, 1989.

Dahlberg K A, *Beyond the green revolution: the ecology and politics of global agricultural development*, New York: Plenum, 1979.

Dally A, *Cicely: the story of a doctor*, London: Victor Gollancz, 1968.

Davey T H, 'Population growths in the tropics', *Health Education Journal* 6, 1948, 150–154.

Davies P N, *Trading in West Africa 1840-1920*, London: Croom Helm, 1976.

___ *Sir Alfred Jones, shipping entrepreneur par excellence*, London: Europa, 1978.

Department of Technical Co-operation, *Medical aid to the developing countries. Observations by HM Government on the report of a working party under the chairmanship of Sir Arthur Porritt*, London: HMSO, 1963.

Dobson M, 'Bitter-sweet solutions for malaria: exploring natural remedies from the past', W F Bynum & B Fantini (eds), *Strategies against malaria eradication or control?, Parassitologia*, 40, 1998, 69–83.

Donaldson F, *The British Council: the first fifty years*, London: Cape, 1984.

Dumett R S, 'The campaign against malaria and the expansion of scientific medical and sanitary services in British West Africa, 1898–1910', *African Historical Studies*, 1, 1968, 153–197.

Dutton J E, 'Preliminary note upon a trypanosome occurring in the blood of man', *Thompson Yates Laboratory Reports*, 4, 1902, 455–469.

—— & Todd J L, 'The nature of human tick fever in the eastern part of the Congo Free State', *Memoir*, 17, 1905, 1–18.

Dwork D, *War is good for babies and other young children: a history of the infant and child welfare movement in England 1898–1918*, London: Tavistock, 1987.

Easmon M C F, 'Sierra Leone doctors', *Sierra Leone Studies* (n.s.), 6, 1956, 81–86.

Eicher C K, 'African universities: overcoming intellectual dependency', T M Yesufu (ed), *Creating the African university*, Ibadan: OUP, 1973, pp. 27–36.

Fendall N R E, 'The medical assistant in Africa, *Journal of Tropical Medicine and Hygiene*', LXXI, 1968, 83–95.

—— 'The use of medical assistants for improving health services Document 1, suggested guidelines for promoting the use of medical assistants', WHO working paper WHO/EDUC/73.163.

—— 'The use of medical assistants for improving health services Document 2, suggested guidelines for planning, implementation and evaluating a programme for the training and use of medical assistants', WHO working paper WHO/EDUC/73.164.

—— 'Concepts in organisation of family planning programmes in developing countries', *ATMP*, 67, 1973, 251–259.

Fieldhouse D K, *Unilever overseas: the anatomy of a multinational, 1895-1965*, London: Croom Helm, 1978.

Fildes V, Marks L & Marland H, *Women and children first: international maternal welfare, 1870-1945*, London: Routledge, 1993.

Frazer W M, *Duncan of Liverpool: being the work of Dr W H Duncan, Medical Officer of Health, 1847-63*, Preston: Carnegie, 1997.

Gale T S, 'Official medical policy in British West Africa, 1870–1930', PhD thesis, University of London, 1973.

Garrett L, *The coming plague: newly emerging diseases in a world out of balance*, London: Virago, 1995.

Gilles H M, 'Effects of heavy and repeated malarial infections on Gambian infants and children. Effects on erythrocytic parasitisation', *BMJ*, ii, 1956, 686–692.

—— & McGregor I M, 'Studies on the significance of high serum gammaglobulin concentrations in Gambian Africans. I: Gamma-globlin concentrations of Gambian children in the first 2 years of life', *ATMP*, 53, 1959, 492–500.

Gilles H M & Hendrickse R G, 'Possible aetiological role of *Plasmodium malariae* in "nephrotic syndrome" in Nigerian children', *Lancet*, i, 1960, 806–807.

Gilles H M, *Akufo – an environmental study of a Nigerian village community*, Ibadan: University Press, 1964.

Gordon R M & Young C J, 'The feeding habits of *Stegomyia calopus*, Moigen', *ATMP*, 15, 1921, 265–268.

Gordon R M, 'Ancylostomes recorded from 67 post-mortems performed in Amazonas', *ATMP*, 16, 1922, 223–228.

—— 'The susceptibility of the individual to the bites of *Stegomyia calopus*', *ATMP*, 16, 1922, 229–234.

—— 'The occurrence of ancylostomes resembling *Necator americanus* amongst domestic pigs in Amazonas', *ATMP*, 16, 1922, 295–296.

—— & Young C J, 'Parasites in dogs and cats in Amazonas', *ATMP*, 16, 1922, 297–300.

—— & Evans A M, 'Mosquitoes collected in the Manáos region of the Amazon', *ATMP*, 16, 1922, 315–338.

Gordon R M, 'Notes on the bionomics of *Stegomyia calopus*, Moigen, in Brazil, Part II', *ATMP*, 16, 1922, 425–439.

—— 'A further note on the occurrence of ancylostomes resembling *Necator americanus* amongst domestic pigs in Amazonas', *ATMP*, 17, 1923, 289–298.

—— 'Emetine periodide in the treatment of *S. haematobium* infections among West African Children', *ATMP*, 20, 1926, 229–238.

—— & Hicks E P, 'Fouadin and Auremetine in the treatment of *S. haematobium* infections among West African children; together with observations on the after-results of treatment with emetine periodide and emetine hydrochloride', *ATMP*, 24, 1930, 443–447.

Gordon R M, Hicks E P, Davey T H & Watson M, 'A study of the house-hunting *Culicidae* occurring in Freetown, Sierra Leone and of the part played by them in the transmission of certain tropical diseases, together with observation of the relationship of anophelines to housing and the effects of anti-larval measures in Freetown', *ATMP*, 26, 1932, 273–345.

Hailey W M, *An African survey: a study of the problems arising in Africa south of the Sahara*, London: OUP, 1938.

Hankins R, 'Medical science in a colonial context: the work of the Sir Alfred Lewis Jones Research Laboratory, Freetown, Sierra Leone, 1922 to 1940', MSc thesis, University of Manchester, 1985.

—— 'Between tropical disease and veterinary medicine: the development of immunological studies of parasitism 1900–1970', PhD thesis, University of Manchester, 1998.

Haqqi S A H, *The colonial policy of the Labour Government (1945–51)*, Aligarh: Muslim University Press, 1960.

Hardy A, 'Cholera, quarantine and the English preventative hospital system, 1850–1895', *Medical History*, 37, 1993, 250–269.

Harrison G, *Mosquitoes, malaria and man: a history of hostilities since 1880*, London: John Murrary, 1978.

Harrison, M, 'Tropical medicine in nineteenth century India', *British Journal History of Science*, 25, 1992, 299–318.

—— *Public health in British India: Anglo-Indian preventive medicine 1859–1914*, Cambridge: CUP, 1994.

—— 'Medicine and the culture of command: the case of malaria control in the British Army during the two world wars', *Medical History*, 40, 1996, 437–453.

—— & Worboys M, 'A disease of civilisation: TB in Britain, Africa and India', L Marks & M Worboys (eds), *Migrants, minorities and health: historical and contemporary studies*, London: Routledge, 1997, pp. 93–124.

Havinden M & Meredith D, *Colonialism and development: Britain and its tropical colonies 1850–1960*, London: Routledge, 1993.

Hayes P, *Industry and ideology: I G Farben in the Nazi era*, Cambridge: CUP, 1987.

Haynes D M, 'From the periphery to the centre: Patrick Manson and the development of tropical medicine in Great Britain, 1870–1900', PhD thesis, University of California, 1992.

Hendrickse R G, Glasgow E F, Adeniyi A, White R H R, Edington G M & Houba V, 'Quartan malarial nephrotic syndrome', *Lancet*, i, 1972, 1143–1148.

Howells R E, Peters W, Homewood C A & Warhurst D C, 'Theory for the mechanism of chloroquine resistance in rodent malaria', *Nature*, 228, 1970, 625.

Jaroonvesama N, 'Pathophysiological phenomena in the host infected with normal and drug-resistant malaria parasites', PhD thesis, University of Liverpool,1969.

Jones J, 'Science utility and the second city of empire: the sciences and especially the medical sciences at Liverpool University 1881–1925', PhD thesis, UMIST, Manchester, 1989.

Kamminga H & Cunningham A (eds), *The science and culture of nutrition, 1840–1940*, Amsterdam: Rodopi, 1995.

Kelves D, *In the name of eugenics*, New York: Knopf, 1985.

Kingsley M, *Travels in West Africa: Congo Français, Corisco and Cameroons*, London: Macmillan, 1897.

Lane T, *Liverpool: gateway of empire*, London: Lawrence & Wishart, 1987.

Lawrence J, 'The First World War and its aftermath', P Johnson (ed), *20th century Britain: economic, social and cultural change*, London: Longman, 1994, pp. 151–168.

Leake C D, *An historical account of pharmacology to the twentieth century*, Illinois: Charles C Thomas, 1975.

Lee S, 'WHO and the developing world: the contest for ideology', A Cunningham & B Andrews (eds), *Western medicine as contested knowledge*, Manchester: MUP, 1997, pp. 24–45.

Liebanau J, 'The MRC and the pharmaceutical industry: the model of insulin', J Austoker and L Bryder, *Historical perspectives on the role of the MRC*, Oxford: OUP, 1989, pp. 163–180.

Lourie E M, Collier H O J, Ross A O F, Robinson D T & Nelson R B, 'Ambulatory treatment of early syphilis with penicillin: rationale, experimental basis and preliminary results', *Lancet*, 249, 1945, 696–701.

LSTM, *Historical Record 1898-1920*, Liverpool: LUP, 1920.

Lyons M, *The colonial disease: a social history of sleeping sickness in Northern Zaire 1900–1940*, Cambridge: CUP, 1992.

MacDonald G, 'Malaria in the children of Freetown, Sierra Leone', *ATMP*, 20, 1926, 239–262.

—— 'Malaria in the children of Freetown, Sierra Leone and five other papers', MD thesis, University of Liverpool, 1932.

McGregor I M & Gilles H M, 'Studies on the significance of high serum gammaglobulin concentrations in Gambian Africans. II: Gamma-globlin concentrations of Gambian children in the $4^{th}$, $5^{th}$ and $6^{th}$ years of life', *ATMP*, 54, 1960, 275–280.

McGregor I, 'Patrick Manson, 1844–1922: the birth of the science of tropical medicine', *TRSTMH*, 89, 1995, 1–8.

Mackenzie J M, *Propaganda and empire: the manipulation of British public opinion 1880–1960*, Manchester: MUP, 1984.

Macleod R & Lewis M (eds), *Disease medicine and empire*, London: Routledge, 1988.

Macleod R & Kumar D, *Technology and the Raj: western technology and technical transfers to India, 1700–1947*, New Delhi: Sage, 1995.

Maegraith B G, Adams A R D, Havard R E, King J D & Millett R F, 'Carbohydrate absorption in sprue', *Lancet*, 249, 1945, 635.

Maegraith B G, Adams A R D, King J D, Tottey M M, Rigby D J & Sladden R A, 'Paludrine in the treatment of malaria', *BMJ*, i, 1946, 305–309.

Maegraith B G, 'The diagnosis and treatment of sprue and associated syndromes', *Medical Press*, 216, 1947, 297–305.

___ *Pathological processes in malaria and blackwater fever*, Oxford: OUP, 1948.

—— 'History of the Liverpool School of Tropical Medicine', *Medical History*, 16, 1972, 354–368.

—— *One world*, London: Athlone, 1973.

—— 'Malaria risk to travellers', Letter to the editor, *BMJ*, i, 1973, 175.

Malins Smith A & Matthews J R, 'The intestinal protozoa of non-dysenteric cases', *ATMP*, 10, 1916–17, 361–390.

—— 'Further records of the occurrence of intestinal protozoa in non-dysenteric cases', *ATMP*, 11, 1917, 183–194.

Malins Smith A, 'A contribution to the question of the number of races in the species *E. histolytica*', *ATMP*, 13, 1919–1920, 1–16.

Manderson L, *Sickness and the state, health and illness in Colonial Malaya, 1870–1940*, Cambridge: CUP, 1996.

Manson, P, 'The necessity of special education in tropical medicine', *Lancet*, ii, 1897, 842–845.

—— *Tropical diseases: a manual of the diseases of warm climates*, London: Cassell, 1898.

—— 'The need for special training in tropical diseases', *Journal of Tropical Medicine*, 2, 1899, 57–62.

Manson-Bahr P & Alcock A, *The life of Sir Patrick Manson*, London: Cassell, 1927.

Marriner S, *The economic and social development of Merseyside*, London: Croom Helm, 1982.

Matthews J R, 'Observations on the cysts of the common intestinal protozoa of man', *ATMP*, 12, 1918–1919, 17–26.

—— 'A mensurative study of the cysts of *E. coli*', *ATMP*, 12, 1918–1919, 259–272.

—— 'The course and duration of an infection with *E. coli*', *ATMP*, 13, 1919–1920, 17–22.

—— 'The spread and incidence of intestinal protozoal infections in the population of Great Britain. I Civilians in Liverpool Royal Infirmary. II Army Recruits', *ATMP*, 12, 1918–1919, 349–360.

—— 'The spread and incidence of intestinal protozoal infections in the population of Great Britain. III Children', *ATMP*, 12, 1918–1919, 361–370.

Matthews J R & Malins Smith A, 'The intestinal protozoal infections among convalescent dysenterics examined at the LSTM, Third report', *ATMP*, 13, 1919–1920, 83–90.

—— 'The spread and incidence of protozoal infections in the population of Great Britain. IV Asylum patients. V University & school cadets', *ATMP*, 13, 1919–1920, 91–94.

May T, *An economic and social history of Britain 1760–1970*, London: Longman, 1987.

Migasena P & Maegraith B G, 'Pharmacological action of anti-malarial drugs: action of chloroquine and hydrocortisone on blood-brain barrier in *P. knowlesi* malaria', *TRSTMH*, 61, 1967, 6.

Moore B, Nierenstein M & Todd J L, 'A note on the therapeutics of trypanosomiasis', *ATMP*, 1, 1907, 161–162.

—— 'Concerning the treatment of experimental trypanosomiasis', *ATMP*, 1, 1907, 273–284.

—— 'Notes on the effects of therapeutic agents on trypanosomes', *ATMP*, 2, 1908, 221–226.

Moore H L & Vaughan M, *Cutting down trees: gender, nutrition and agricultural change in the Northern Province of Zambia 1890-1990*, London: James Currey, 1994.

Morgan D J, *The official history of colonial development 3: A reassessment of British aid policy, 1951–1965*, Basingstoke: Macmillan, 1980, pp. 236–270.

Moulin A M, 'The Pasteur Institutes between the two world wars. The transformation of the international sanitary order', P Weindling (ed), *International health organizations and movements 1918–1939*, Cambridge: CUP, 1995, pp. 244–265.

Neushul P, 'Science, Government and the mass production of penicillin', *JHMAS*, 48, 1993, 371–395.

Newell K (ed), *Health by the people*, Geneva: WHO, 1975.

Newstead R, 'On a new *Dermanyssid acarid* found living in the lungs of monkeys (*Cercopithecus schmitdi*) from the Upper Congo', *Memoir* 18, 1906, 41–45.

—— 'On another new *Dermanyssid acarid* parasitic in the lungs of the Rhesus monkey', *Memoir* 18, 1906, 47–50.

—— 'Descriptions of a new genus and three new species of Anopheline mosquitoes', *ATMP*, 4, 1910, 377–383.

—— 'On an new genus of *Psyllidae* from Nyasaland', *Bulletin of Entomological Research*, 2, 1911, 85–104.

—— 'On some new species of African mosquitoes (*Culicidae*)', *ATMP*, 5, 1911, 233–244.

—— & Carter H F, 'On a new genus of *Culicidae* from the Amazon region', *ATMP*, 4, 1911, 553–556.

Newstead R, 'A new tsetse fly from British East Africa', *ATMP*, 6, 1912, 129–130.

Nye E & Gibson M, *Ronald Ross: malariologist and polymath*, Basingstoke: Macmillan, 1997.

Okafor N, *The development of universities in Nigeria*, Longman: London, 1971.

Parascandola J & Jasensky R, 'Origins of the receptor theory of drug action', *BHM*, 48, 1974, 199–220.

Parascandola J, 'Carl Voegltin and the arsenic receptor in chemotherapy', *JHMAS*, 32, 1977, 151–171.

—— 'The theoretical basis of Paul Ehrlich's chemotherapy', *JHMAS*, 36, 1981, 19–43.

Pedler F, *The lion and the unicorn in Africa: a history of the origins of the United Africa Company, 1787-1931*, London: Heinemann, 1974.

Peters W, Chance M L, Mutinga M J, Ngoka J M & Schnur L F, 'The identification of human *Leishmania* from Kenya', *ATMP*, 71, 1977, 501–502.

Phillips A, *The enigma of colonialism: British policy in West Africa*, London: James Currey, 1988.

Phillips D R & Verhasselt Y, *Health and development*, London: Routledge, 1994.

Porter A N & Stockwell A J, *British imperial policy and decolonization, 1938–1964*, Basingstoke: Macmillan, 1987.

Power H J, 'Malaria, drugs and World War II: the role of the LSTM in the development of Paludrine', paper presented at Symposium, Malaria & War, Wellcome Institute for the History of Medicine, London, 6 May 1994.

—— 'Keeping the Strains alive and more: Trypanosomiasis research at the LSTM's laboratory in Runcorn', paper given at the Oxford Wellcome Unit, 22 February 1996.

—— ' "Bringing the horse to water": Leonard Rogers' research on amoebic dysentery and its reception in Britain, 1902 to 1908', W F Bynum (ed), *Gastroenterology in Britain: Historical essays*, London: WIHM, 1997, pp. 81–95.

—— 'Drug resistant malaria: a global problem and the Thai response', A Cunningham & B Andrews (eds), *Western medicine as contested knowledge*, Manchester: MUP, 1997, pp. 262–286.

—— 'The role of chemotherapy in early malaria control and eradication programmes in Thailand', W F Bynum & B Fantini (eds), *Strategies against malaria, eradication or control, Parassitologia*, 40, 1998, 47–53.

Procopio J, 'Harold Wolferstan Thomas: Cientista canadense a servicia da medicina no Amazonas' *Revista Brasiliera de Medicina*, 10, 1953, 371–373.

Prothero M, 'Population movements and problems of malaria eradication in Africa', *Bulletin of WHO*, 24, 1961, 405–425.

—— *Migrants and Malaria*, London: Longmans Green, 1965.

Radford A J, 'Family planning and population policy in Papua New Guinea', *Papua New Guinea Medical Journal*, 15, 1972, 131–135.

—— 'Community health training for medical students and interns in Papua New Guinea: wards without walls', *Proceedings of a symposium on health services in developing countries*, 1974.

Reid H A, 'Arvin – a new anticoagulant from viper', *Nursing Mirror*, 8 December 1968, 39–41.

—— 'Snake bite in the tropics', *BMJ*, ii, 1968, 359–362.

—— & Gilles H M, 'Arvin treatment in sickle-cell crisis', *TRSTMH*, 63, 1969, 22–23.

*Report of the Commission on Higher Education in the Colonies*, London: HMSO, 1945.

Rogers L, *Pathological evidence bearing on disease incidence in Calcutta*, Glasgow: Alex MacDougall, 1925.

Ross, R 'The possibility of extirpating malaria from certain localities by a new method' *BMJ*, ii, 1899, 1–4.

Ross A O F, Nelson R B, Lourie E M & Collier H O J, 'Treatment of early syphilis with penicillin', *Lancet*, 247, 1944, 845–848.

Savage C E, 'The beginnings of veterinary education at the University of Liverpool', Dissertation for Diploma Local History, University of Liverpool, 1992.

Schreuder D M, 'The cultural factor in Victorian imperialism: a case study of the British "civilizing mission" ', *Journal Imperial Commonwealth History*, 4, 1976, 283–317.

Scott H H, *A history of tropical medicine*, 2 vols, London: Edward Arnold, 1939.

Service M W, 'A short history of early medical entomology', *Journal of Medical Entomology*, 14, 1978, 603–626.

Siddiqi J, *World health and world politics, the WHO and the UN system*, London: Hurst & Co, 1995.

Spinks A, Tottey M M & Maegraith B G, 'The pharmacology of Paludrine and some other new antimalarials', *Proceedings of the Biochemical Society*, 40, 1946, i–ii.

Spitzer L, 'The mosquito and segregation in Sierra Leone', *Canadian Journal of African Studies*, 2, 1968, 49–61.

—— *The creoles of Sierra Leone: responses to colonialism, 1870–1945*, Madison: University of Wisconsin Press, 1974.

Stephens J W W & Christophers S R, 'The native as the prime agent in the malaria infection of Europeans', *Reports of the Malaria Commission of the Royal Society*, Series 2, 1900, 3–19.

—— 'The malarial infection of native children', *Reports of the Malaria Commission of the Royal Society*, Series 3, 1900, 2–13.

—— 'The segregation of Europeans', *Reports of the Malaria Commission of the Royal Society*, Series 3, 1900, 21–24.

—— 'Proposed site for European residences in the Freetown Hills', *Reports of the Malaria Commission of the Royal Society*, Series 5, 1901, 1–4.

Stephens J W W, 'Two new human cestodes and a new linguatulid', *ATMP*, 1, 1907–1908, 549–556.

—— 'A new human nematode, *Strongylus gibsoni*', *ATMP*, 2, 1908–1909, 315–316.

—— 'A new malaria parasite of man', *ATMP*, 1914, 8, 375–377.

—— & Mackinnon D L, 'A preliminary statement on the treatment of *E. histolytica* infections by Alcresta Ipecac', *ATMP*, 10, 1916–1917, 397–410.

Stephens J W W, 'A new malaria parasite of man', *ATMP*, 16, 1922, 383–386.

Stephens J W W & Yorke W, 'A case of sleeping sickness (*T. gambiense*) treated with "Bayer 205" ', *ATMP*, 16, 1922, 421–424.

Stephens J W W, 'Studies in the treatment of malaria XXXII: Summary of studies I– XXXI', *ATMP*, 17, 1923, 303–316.

Sweeney A W, 'The malaria frontline, pioneering malaria research by the Australian Army in World War II', *Medical Journal of Australia*, 166, 1997, 316–319.

Tansey E M, 'The Wellcome Physiological Research Laboratories 1894–1904: the Home Office, pharmaceutical firms and animal experiments', *Medical History*, 33, 1989, 1–41.

—— & Milligan R C E, 'The early history of the Wellcome Research Laboratories, 1894–1914', G J Higby & E C Stroud (eds), *Pill peddlers: essays on the history of the pharmaceutical industry*, Madison: American Institute of the History of Pharmacy, 1990, pp. 91–106.

Taplin E, *Liverpool dockers and seamen 1870–1890*, University of Hull: Hull, 1974.

Theakston R D G, 'An ultrastructural study of host-parasite relationships in malaria and related infections', PhD thesis, University of Liverpool, 1969.

Townson H, 'Studies of enzymes in the *Simulium damnosum* complex and *Aedes scutellaris* group', Working paper for WHO species complexes in vectors of disease with special reference on *Simulium damnosum* and malaria vectors, Geneva: 1976. *WHO Cyclostyled Report* VBC/SC/76.21.

—— Meredith S E O & Thomas K, 'Studies of enzymes in the *Aedes scutellaris* group', *TRSTMH*, 71, 1977, 110,

—— 'Enzyme differences between species of the *Simulium damnosum* complex', *TRSTMH*, 71, 1977, 111.

Vaughan M, *Curing their ills: colonial power and African illness*, Cambridge: Polity Press, 1991.

Weatherall M, *In search of a cure*, Oxford: OUP, 1990.

Weindling P (ed), *International health organisations and movements 1918–1939*, Cambridge: CUP, 1995.

Whitehead R G, 'Kwashiorkor in Uganda', E M Widdowson & J A Mathers (eds), *The contribution of nutrition to human and animal health*, Cambridge: CUP, 1992, pp. 303–313.

Widdowson E M, 'Protein-energy malnutrition', F E G Cox (ed), *Illustrated history of tropical diseases*, London: Wellcome Trust, 1996, pp. 370–377.

Wilkinson L & Hardy A, *The London School of Hygiene and Public Health: a twentieth century quest for global public health*, London: Kegan Paul, 1998.

Williamson J, Bertram D S & Lourie E M, 'Acquired resistance to Paludrine in *P. gallinaceum*: effects of Paludrine and other antimalarials', *Nature*, 159, 1947, 885–886.

Wright F J, Letter, *Proceedings of the Royal College of Physicians of Edinburgh*, 25, 1995, 709710.

Worboys M, 'The emergence of tropical medicine: a study in the establishment of a scientific specialty', G Lemaine (ed), *Perspectives on the emergence of scientific disciplines*, The Hague: Moulton, 1976, pp. 76–98.

—— 'Science and British colonial imperialism, 1895–1940', DPhil thesis, University of Sussex, 1979.

—— 'Manson, Ross and colonial medical policy: tropical medicine in London and Liverpool, 1899–1914', R Macleod & M Lewis (eds), *Disease, medicine and empire*, London: Routledge, 1988, pp. 21–37.

—— 'The discovery of colonial malnutrition between the wars', D Arnold (ed), *Imperial medicine and indigenous societies*, Manchester: MUP, 1988, pp. 208–225.

Yorke W, Carter H F, Mackinnon D L, Matthews J R & Malins Smith A, 'Persons who have never been out of Great Britain as carriers of *E. histolytica*', *ATMP*, 11, 1917–1918, 87–90.

Yorke W & Macfie J, 'Observations on malaria made during treatment of general paralysis', *TRSTMH*, 18, 1924, 13–33.

Yorke W, 'Further observations on malaria made during treatment of general paralysis', *TRSTMH*, 19, 1925, 108–122.

Yorke W & Rees Wright W, 'The mosquito infectivity of *P. vivax* after prolonged sojourn in the human host', *ATMP*, 20, 1926, 327–328.

Yorke W, 'Drug resistance', *British Journal of Venereal Diseases*, 9, 1933, 83–97.

Yorke W, Murgatroyd F, Glyn-Hughes F, Lester H M O & Ross A O F, 'A new arsenical for the treatment of syphilis and trypanosomiasis', *BMJ*, i, 1936, 1042–1048.

# INDEX

273

# INDEX

outpatients, attending, 29
public health measures, advocate of, 24
remuneration, complaining at, 21
research, supervision of, 27
resignation and return to School, 21
Sierra Leone expedition, leading, 23, 24
Royal Army Medical Corps
courses for, 192, 193
Royal Microscopical Society, 194
Royal Society
Anti-malaria Commission, 24
Royal Southern Hospital
consulting physicians, appointment as lecturer, 20
friction with LSTM, 20
in-patients, 30–32
military casualties at, 36
new site, transfer of clinical work to, 33, 34
outpatient facilities, 29
roles of, 15
School, end of association with, 34
staff, 15
teaching arrangements, problems with, 32
teaching hospital, as, 32
tropical cases, types of, 31, 32
tropical diseases patients, 28–34
tropical medicine, initiatives in, 17
Runcorn laboratory
directors, 26
drugs, testing, 89
motivation for, 26
parasites and hosts, study of relationship between, 26
work of, 27

Sanitation, 24
Schistomiasis, 165
research, 60, 122
Schools of Tropical Medicine
aims of, 15
Britain, in, 3, 12
different structure of, 4
initial work, analysis of, 14
Liverpool. See Liverpool School of Tropical Medicine

London. See London School of Tropical Medicine
Scientists, correspondence between, 26
SEAMEO Tropical-Medicine project, 146
Seidelin, Dr Harald, 25
Sherrington, Charles, 18, 22
Sierra Leone
Alfred Lewis Jones Research Laboratory. See Alfred Lewis Jones Research Laboratory
British view of inhabitants, 51
establishment of, 51
expeditions to, 24, 28
geography, 51
Government pathology, 57–60
higher education college, 136
main hospital, refitting, 58
Mount Aureol Hospital, 58
pathology service offered to, 57
permanent laboratory, establishing of, 48, 49
research activities, 60–62
role for laboratory, 133
Ross, visits of, 52
staff, relationships with, 50
surveys, 63–66
Slave trade, 11
Sleeping sickness
cure for, 26
treatment of, 90
Smallpox, 219
Smithdown Road Tropical Diseases Centre, 111
Social development, emphasis on, 105
Social epidemiology, 203
Southwell, Dr Thomas, 81
Space Allocation Committee, 234
Spooner, Professor E T C, 149
Stephens, John William Watson, 22, 27, 81, 83, 84, 88
Honorary Pathologist in Tropical Medicine, as, 33
World War I, work in, 34–36
Students
destinations, 206
health care personnel, 206
interchange among, 234
international nature of, 117
number of, 187, 207, 208